Enhancing Legislative Drafting in the Commonwealth

Legislation has traditionally been viewed as a text addressed to and used by lawyers and judges. But with enhanced accessibility via electronic publication of legislation in many Commonwealth jurisdictions, drafters "speak" not only to lawyers and judges, but also to untrained users. This shift of the legislative audience has changed radically the requirements for legislation and its drafting. This is crucially important as the quality of legislation within the Commonwealth remains an essential element of democracy and the rule of law.

The book aims to alert policy officers, legal officers, law reformers, and drafters of the many innovations in the drafting of legislation within the Commonwealth. And ultimately to bring to light the academic foundations of the modern approach to legislative quality, which really boils down to effectiveness of the legislative product.

This book was based on a special issue of *Commonwealth Law Bulletin*.

Helen Xanthaki is Professor of Law and Legislative Drafting at the University of London, and Academic Director of the Sir William Dale Centre for Legislative Studies at the Institute of Advanced Legal Studies of the University of London. She is the Director of the Commonwealth Course in Legislative Drafting, and Co-Director of the LLM in Advanced Legislative Studies via Distance Learning. She teaches legislative drafting at the University of London. She is the editor of the 2014 edition of *Thornton's Legislative Drafting*, author of *Drafting Legislation: Art and Technology of Rules for Regulation*, and numerous articles on legislative drafting, legislative quality, and law reform. Helen is a consultant legislative trainer and drafter, and has worked for the EU, and numerous governments in the Commonwealth and beyond.

Enhancing Legislative Drafting in the Commonwealth
A Wealth of Innovation

Edited by
Helen Xanthaki

LONDON AND NEW YORK

First published 2015 by Routledge

2 Park Square, Milton Park, Abingdon, Oxon, OX14 4RN
605 Third Avenue, New York, NY 10017

Routledge is an imprint of the Taylor & Francis Group, an informa business

First issued in paperback 2020

Copyright © 2015 Commonwealth Secretariat

All rights reserved. No part of this book may be reprinted or reproduced or utilised in any form or by any electronic, mechanical, or other means, now known or hereafter invented, including photocopying and recording, or in any information storage or retrieval system, without permission in writing from the publishers.

Notice:
Product or corporate names may be trademarks or registered trademarks, and are used only for identification and explanation without intent to infringe.

British Library Cataloguing in Publication Data
A catalogue record for this book is available from the British Library

ISBN 13: 978-1-138-79452-8 (hbk)
ISBN 13: 978-0-367-73981-2 (pbk)

Typeset in Times New Roman
by RefineCatch Limited, Bungay, Suffolk

Publisher's Note
The publisher accepts responsibility for any inconsistencies that may have arisen during the conversion of this book from journal articles to book chapters, namely the possible inclusion of journal terminology.

Disclaimer
Every effort has been made to contact copyright holders for their permission to reprint material in this book. The publishers would be grateful to hear from any copyright holder who is not here acknowledged and will undertake to rectify any errors or omissions in future editions of this book.

Contents

Citation Information	vii
1. Quality of Legislation in the Commonwealth Helen Xanthaki	1
2. Is legislative drafting a form of communication? Constantin Stefanou	4
3. Clarity, precision and unambiguity: aspects for effective legislative drafting Esther Majambere	14
4. In pursuit of clarity: how far should the drafter go? Alain Songa Gashabizi	24
5. Plain language: give it a try! Noor Azlina Hashim	32
6. Drafting and plain language Augustin Mico	42
7. Gender-neutral language: an essential language tool to serve precision, clarity and unambiguity Kadija Kabba	50
8. Is gender-neutral drafting an effective tool against gender inequality within the legal system? Venessa McLean	58
9. Legislative drafters: lawyers or not? Norismizan Haji Ismail	70
10. The role of the Rwandan legislative drafter in the legislative process: analysis stage Ruth Ikiriza	77
11. Prioritising legislation in the policy process Odethie Birungi Kamugundu	85
12. Savings clause: get it right Rosmizan Muhamad	93

CONTENTS

13. The effect of transplanting legislation from one jurisdiction to another 101
    Rosaline Baindu Cowan

14. Prerogative legislation as a paradigm of bad law making: the Chagos Islands 108
    Ronan Cormacain

15. Incorporation of international and regional human rights instruments: comparative analysis of methods 130
    Reyneck Matemba

16. Properly drafted arbitration agreement as a safeguard to its adequate interpretation: Rwanda as a case study 140
    Froduard Munyangabe

    Index 149

Citation Information

The following chapters were originally published in the *Commonwealth Law Bulletin*, volume 39, issue 3 (2013) and volume 37, issue 3 (September 2011). When citing this material, please use the original page numbering for each article, as follows:

Chapter 1
Quality of Legislation in the Commonwealth
Helen Xanthaki
Commonwealth Law Bulletin, volume 39, issue 3 (2013) pp. 411–413

Chapter 2
Is legislative drafting a form of communication?
Constantin Stefanou
Commonwealth Law Bulletin, volume 37, issue 3 (September 2011) pp. 407–416

Chapter 3
Clarity, precision and unambiguity: aspects for effective legislative drafting
Esther Majambere
Commonwealth Law Bulletin, volume 37, issue 3 (September 2011) pp. 417–426

Chapter 4
In pursuit of clarity: how far should the drafter go?
Alain Songa Gashabizi
Commonwealth Law Bulletin, volume 39, issue 3 (2013) pp. 415–422

Chapter 5
Plain language: give it a try!
Noor Azlina Hashim
Commonwealth Law Bulletin, volume 39, issue 3 (2013) pp. 423–434

Chapter 6
Drafting and plain language
Augustin Mico
Commonwealth Law Bulletin, volume 39, issue 3 (2013) pp. 435–442

CITATION INFORMATION

Chapter 7
Gender-neutral language: an essential language tool to serve precision, clarity and unambiguity
Kadija Kabba
Commonwealth Law Bulletin, volume 37, issue 3 (September 2011) pp. 427–434

Chapter 8
Is gender-neutral drafting an effective tool against gender inequality within the legal system?
Venessa McLean
Commonwealth Law Bulletin, volume 39, issue 3 (2013) pp. 443–454

Chapter 9
Legislative drafters: lawyers or not?
Norismizan Haji Ismail
Commonwealth Law Bulletin, volume 39, issue 3 (2013) pp. 455–461

Chapter 10
The role of the Rwandan legislative drafter in the legislative process: analysis stage
Ruth Ikiriza
Commonwealth Law Bulletin, volume 39, issue 3 (2013) pp. 463–470

Chapter 11
Prioritising legislation in the policy process
Odethie Birungi Kamugundu
Commonwealth Law Bulletin, volume 39, issue 3 (2013) pp. 471–478

Chapter 12
Savings clause: get it right
Rosmizan Muhamad
Commonwealth Law Bulletin, volume 37, issue 3 (September 2011) pp. 445–452

Chapter 13
The effect of transplanting legislation from one jurisdiction to another
Rosaline Baindu Cowan
Commonwealth Law Bulletin, volume 37, issue 3 (September 2011) pp. 479–485

Chapter 14
Prerogative legislation as a paradigm of bad law making: the Chagos Islands
Ronan Cormacain
Commonwealth Law Bulletin, volume 39, issue 3 (2013) pp. 487–508

Chapter 15
Incorporation of international and regional human rights instruments: comparative analysis of methods
Reyneck Matemba
Commonwealth Law Bulletin, volume 37, issue 3 (September 2011) pp. 435–444

CITATION INFORMATION

Chapter 16
Properly drafted arbitration agreement as a safeguard to its adequate interpretation: Rwanda as a case study
Froduard Munyangabe
Commonwealth Law Bulletin, volume 39, issue 3 (2013) pp. 509–516

Please direct any queries you may have about the citations to
clsuk.permissions@cengage.com

Quality of Legislation in the Commonwealth

Helen Xanthaki

This is the second Special Issue on Legislative Drafting for the *Commonwealth Law Bulletin*, and once again I am truly honoured to introduce the papers in this section.

William Leonard Dale was born in Hull, Yorkshire, on 17 June 1906. From this provincial launching pad, he took off to a career of singular variety and achievement as solicitor, barrister, civil servant, teacher and musician. He combined in a rare degree his father's common sense with a fine intellect, the power of eloquent and simple expression, and a highly developed ability to instruct and impart knowledge. Educated at Hymers College, Hull, he was articled to a Hull Solicitors firm where he studied externally for his LLB from London University. He then read from the Bar at Gray's Inn. A chance reading of an advertisement took him to Palestine to work for the firm of Richardson, Turtledove, solicitors in Jerusalem in 1934. He returned to England in 1935 and took up a job as legal assistant in the Colonial Office. Thereafter, his formidable abilities took him rapidly through the ranks of the civil service. During the war, he served at the Ministry of Supply and afterwards returned to the Colonial Office where he soon found himself on the way to Sarawak to examine Rajah Brooke's offer to cede the country to Britain. From 1951 to 1953, he was legal adviser to Libya, charged with producing a single legal system from many differing codes. The Libyan Government paid tribute to his wisdom and single mindedness and indeed wanted him to stay as a judge of the Supreme Court. Instead, he returned to London to be legal advisor to the Ministry of Education. Between 1961 and 1966, William Dale was legal adviser to the Commonwealth Relations Office and was seconded to act as legal adviser to the Central Africa Office to deal with the break-up of the Central African Federation. In 1965, he was knighted. Back in London, he founded the *Commonwealth Law Bulletin* and became Director of Studies of the Government Legal Advisors Course, an influence over several hundreds of Commonwealth lawyers for a generation. In 1997, he founded the Sir William Dale Centre for Legislative Studies at the Institute of Advanced Legal Studies of the University of London, and appointed me as a researcher.

I took over the Academic Directorship of the Centre in 1999 and I was appointed as the first Professor in Law and Legislative Drafting in the UK in 2011, thus confirming to the university, the academic community and the world that legislative drafting is indeed an academic discipline and an area well worth study and analysis. Within the realm of my centre's mandate to lead and facilitate research in legislative studies, it is an honour and a pleasure to introduce the second issue of the *Law Bulletin* on legislative drafting and in memory of Sir

William Dale. This issue is rich in its pickings: a variety of authors from diverse jurisdictions address general and specific issues from the field.

Alain Songa, a Rwandan drafter, writes persuasively on the pursuit of clarity in drafting legislation, identifies the difficulty in attaining its fruitful pursuit and suggests ways in which this can be done. Noor Hashim, a Malaysian drafter, reasserts the crucial role of plain language for the attainment of effective legislation, and proves rather inventively that drafting enforcement provisions in plain language can be done; in fact, they are more readable and comprehensible. Mico Augustin, a Rwanda drafter, confirms convincingly that, among many other techniques of enhancing clarity in drafting law, the use of plain language is one which can help to improve clarity. Plain language and clarity undoubtedly make the law as simple, clear and precise and this drafting should be the fundamental style in all laws. Venessa McLean, a consultant from the Caribbean, takes the argument further and asserts quite radically that the technique of gender-neutral drafting on its own is not an effective tool in the fight against deep-rooted gender inequality within our legal systems: gender inequality has penetrated deeper into our legal systems than assumed, and it is a fallacy to think that gender-neutral drafting is an effective cure for the disease of patriarchy.

Norismizan Haji Ismail, a drafter from Brunei, argues quite credibly that it is not impossible for a non-lawyer to become a legislative drafter. In applying Kotz's criteria, a non-lawyer can be a good drafter if he/she has the relevant knowledge, language skills and creative and analytical ability, plus training. Ruth Izikira, a Rwanda drafter, makes an eloquent argument for the necessity of the thorough analysis of drafts: this promotes good quality of legislation, in conformity with the constitution, resulting in turn in effective implementation. Birungi Kamugundu Odethie, a Rwandan drafter, argues compellingly that prioritising legislation is a tool that may be used by the drafting office for achieving practicability of legislation: in order to prove her point she uses the Seidman and Seidman criteria of gravity of the social problem being addressed, the legislation's anticipated social impact, do-ability and the drafting programme.

Rosaline Baindu Cowan argues credibly that legal transplant is a haphazard means of legislating, whereby a complex and difficult situation arises if the drafter cannot harmonise the laws being transplanted with that of the recipient country. She focuses on legal transplant through private contracting, citing China as an example, the introduction of the doctrine of equity into colonial West Africa and how the laws of equity were transplanted into African customary laws. The theme of special issues of legislation is carried on by Ronan Cormacain, a consultant drafter, who does a fantastic job in bringing to light the quality of legislation related to the almost unknown Chagos Islands, a British Overseas Territory in the Indian Ocean. He argues that the British Indian Ocean Territory (Constitution) Order 2004 is bad law because it is of low quality and is inaccessible. Finally, Froduard Munyangabe considers whether improper drafting of arbitration agreements can have an impact during its interpretation by the arbitrators: in this case, bad interpretation is likely to cause enforcement problems.

Having read all the articles, I can only express my humble gratitude to each and every one of the authors. They have done a wonderful job in leading the debate in the field of legislative studies. I thank them for trusting me with their work, and I thank the *Bulletin* for remaining at the forefront of legal developments in the Commonwealth and beyond.

Helen Xanthaki
Sir William Dale Centre, IALS, University of London
Charles Clore House, 17
Russell Square, WC1B 5DR, London

Is legislative drafting a form of communication?

Constantin Stefanou

Institute of Advanced Legal Studies, School of Advanced Study, University of London

> Experts on legislative drafting almost take it for granted that drafting is a form of communication. Indeed, the few articles on the topic tend to look at drafting as a form of communication in the context of legal theory and legal philosophy. This article takes a different perspective and attempts to examine legislative drafting as a form of communication using communications theory. The logic is that if drafting is a form of communication then it should conform with basic communication models. The implications of this hypothesis are quite important in establishing a multidisciplinary perspective for future research in legislative drafting.

Introduction

It is almost an axiom among experts that legislative drafting is a form of communication and there is hardly a textbook in legislative drafting that does not mention *en passant* that 'drafting is a form of communication'. However, these references never seem to be further analysed and are usually followed up by a section on 'words and sentences':

> An Act of Parliament expresses legal relationships. It is also a form of communication. It lays down our rights and our obligations, our powers, our privileges and our duties. In this it tells us what to do and what not to do. It is a command to others. There should, therefore, be no *misunderstanding* as to the message it seeks to convey. It is part of the language of a people. It will be understood as language of that jurisdiction is understood. In that respect an Act of Parliament should be drafted in accordance with principles that govern as a means of communication in that particular jurisdiction ... The ability to communicate depends on our ability to think. One is of essence of the other...[1]

Clearly, a normative act should leave no room for misunderstanding and the correct use of language is important. However, as the drafters are policy translators the question is are the drafters communicating or are they simply passing on others' attempts to communicate?

> The great misconception about drafting is that it has very much to do with writing. The truth is, the actual task of writing – choosing the words and putting them into effective form – is only a small piece of the drafter's task. The draft is merely the output, not the essence, of the drafter's work.

---

[1] VCRAC Crabbe, *Legislative Drafting* (Cavendish Publishing Limited, London 1993) 27. See also the section on communication in R Dickerson, *The Fundamentals of Legal Drafting* (Little Brown and Co, Boston 1986) 25–50 (Chapter III).

The process of drafting is, more than anything else, a process of spotting, presenting and resolving issues[2].

In the era of digital communication we all understand that the ability to control aspects of communication, e.g. content, style and flow, is a crucial, if indirect, source of power. Especially in public affairs where sometimes words speak louder than actions, the ability to determine how issues are discussed is an important source of power.

Obviously a law expresses legal relationships. At a very simplistic level law is a form of communication in that it tells us what we can or cannot do. At a more complex level law is a form of communication where legal relations are comprehended and appreciated through a communicative process. Thus, philosophy, sociology, linguistics and psychology together help us understand the communicative nature of law.[3] But does this mean de facto that legislative drafting is a form of communication?

The aim of this article is modest. It attempts to examine legislative drafting as a form of communication using one of the basic models of communication theory. The logic here is that in order to understand the relationship between legislative drafting and communication, if indeed such a relationship exists, it might be useful to utilise more traditional communication theory tools. And if more traditional communication theory tools are relevant, then these should possibly be added to our list of theoretical approaches to legislative drafting.

A basic communications model

Although Aristotle's model of proof is sometimes seen as the first communication model,[4] most communication models are post-World War II, twentieth-century inventions mainly by engineers, mathematicians and communication experts.[5] The earliest and most influential of these twentieth-century models is the *Shannon–Weaver Mathematical Model* (1949), which forms the basis of practically all linear communication models [6]and has been widely adapted in social sciences.

---

[2]TA Dorsey, *Legislative Drafter's Deskbook: A Practical Guide* (The Capitol.NET, Alexandria, VA 2006) 4.
[3]M Van Hoecke. *Law as Communication* (Hart Publishing, Oxford 2002).
[4]AH Monroe, BE Gronbeck and D Ehninger, *Principles of Speech Communication* (Addison-Wesley, New York 1988).
[5]See CD Mortensen, *Communication: The Study of Human Communication* (McGraw-Hill Book Co., New York 1972) Chapter 2. Also see U Nerula, *Handbook of Communication: Models, Perspectives, Strategies* (Atlantic, New Delhi 2006).
[6]CE Shannon and W Weaver, *A Mathematical Model of Communication.* Urbana, II, University of Illinois Press, 1949. Claude Shannon and Warren Weaver were engineers working for Bell Telephone Labs in the US. Their model was intended to assist engineers to send electrical signals from one location to another. Over the years this communication model has become quite influential with claims that it has wider applications to human communication in general. See D Chandler, 'Transmission Model of Communication', University of Aberystwyth, 1994 <http://www.aber.ac.uk/media/Documents/short/trans.html>.

The Shannon and Weaver Model forms the basis of the basic communication model, which is a simple and easy to understand linear and sequential model often referred to as 'the transmission model'. The logic of the model is very straightforward, as can be seen in Figure 2, a *sender* sends a *message* through a *channel* to a *receiver* in order to achieve an *impact* or result. It is the breadth of possible applications of this model to so many different forms of communication that make it so successful. In its simplicity the transmission model has become a powerful tool in the hands of social scientists who wish to apply it to different instances of human communication. Of course, this model is linear and in some respects quite simplistic – for example it does not include 'feedback'.[8] Nevertheless, it allows us to have a ready-made model to be applied in most instances of human communication.

The basic communications model and the law

Rarely used with reference to law, the transmission model has not really been tested enough to ascertain whether it can offer alternatives to traditional legal theory or legal philosophy in examining law as a form of communication.[9] The very simple example in Figure 3, though, indicates that the transmission model is not completely irrelevant to the development of legislation and using law as a means of achieving a specific result. Although the diagram is not very elaborate and perhaps raises more questions than it provides answers, nevertheless, it does present the reader with a reasonable 'who? – what? – how? – why?', which might itself be adequate communication about an event.

---

[8] It is interesting to note here that Shannon later introduced a mechanism which corrected differences in the transmitted and received signal. This mechanism was later added to the model and became the well-known concept of 'feedback' in communication theory.

[9] See however the interesting application of the Shannon-Weaver model in SM Huszagh and FW Huszagh, 'A Model of the Law Communication Process: Formal and Free Law', *Georgia Law Scholarly Works* Paper 99 (1978) <http://digitalcommons.law.uga.edu/fac_artchop/99>.

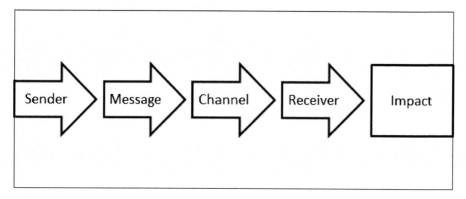

Figure 2. The transmission model.

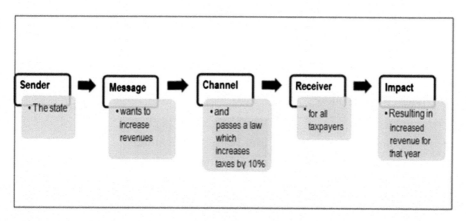

Figure 3. The transmission model – first applied example.

Once again, this simple linear model is perhaps simplistic; for example, by including feedback the communication process would be more accurate and perhaps allow greater scope for discussion. However, from a practical point of view it pretty much covers the main points and, should one decide to proceed with further discussion, each step of the communication sequence described in the model can become the subject of further analysis.

Noise

It is a feature of the basic communication model that the transmission of information from one stage to the next is not always free and clear. In fact, most communication models include *noise* as standard feature in the transmission of information.

So, what exactly is 'noise'? Noise represents all those elements that can and do interfere in the flow of the original message to the receiver (see Figure 4). In the original Shannon and Weaver model, noise referred to elements such as faulty cables or apparatus (e.g. a crackling microphone) that originated from

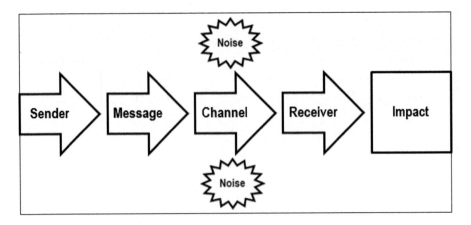

Figure 4. The transmission model – additional elements.

within the system and partially destroyed the transmitted signal. Today we use the term *noise* as a metaphor for semantic or organisational problems related to the effective flow of information from source to receiver, or even psychological interference with decoding.

The basic communication model and legislative drafting

So, let us now return to our original question by looking at legislative drafting through the basic communication model. The implicit assumption here is that the drafting of normative acts is a form of communication – although we are still not sure about what kind of communication it is (i.e. is it a form of political communication or intellectual communication or social communication etc?).

In terms of categories, legislative drafting is certainly written and formal communication. However, when looking at the drafting of normative acts as a form of communication there are two starting points. One is the impersonal 'state' (Figure 5) and the second is the more personal starting point of the drafter him/herself (Figure 6). I have decided to look at both simply because they are both valid starting points and because they both look at the same process albeit from different angles.

Figure 5 shows the state point of view, which is similar to the example given in Figure 3 when looking at law in general as a form of communication using the transmission model. In the example in Figure 5, the drafting office, the drafter and the draft are channels for the state in its attempt to achieve a specific goal.

In the second example, in Figure 6, the starting point is the drafter, but essentially both examples look at the same process; the first example stands back looking at the broader picture while the second example zooms in on the drafter. I think both examples identify different aspects of the same process. What is interesting to note, though, is that the 'draft' is the channel in both examples. In the first example, the channel is the drafting office – which prepares the draft – and so it is in the second example where it is more explicitly identified as the

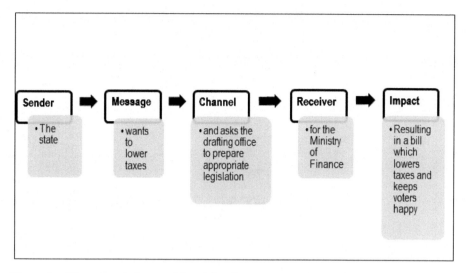

Figure 5. The transmission model and the drafter – example 1.

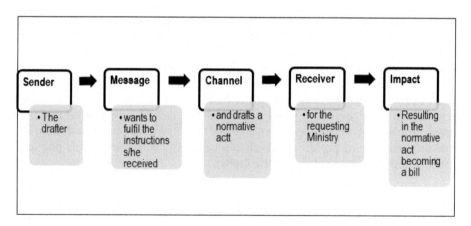

Figure 6. The transmission model and the drafter – example 2.

draft itself simply because the second example zooms in on the drafter. One point to note is that in Figure 6 the 'impact' could be different, for example it could be 'Resulting in the drafter fulfilling the instructions s/he received' or 'Resulting in the Bill being brought to Parliament'. In other words, the 'impact' side of the model seems to be not arbitrary but rather certainly what the observer assumes it to be.

An early assessment of the application of the transmission model to the drafting of normative acts is that it is a reasonably good fit. In both examples the transmission model identified an easily recognisable process, and in both examples the linear sequential steps seems to be a reasonably good description of the process they attempt to communicate. Strictly speaking, that is about all a communication model can do.

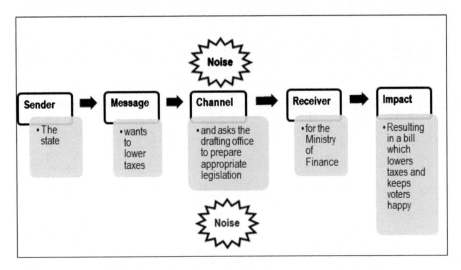

Figure 7. The transmission model and the drafter – with noise – example 1.

Of course, as mentioned earlier, the transmission model does not come without baggage. *Noise* is a standard feature of all communication models and the transmission model is no exception. Figure 7 and Figure 8 show where noise is located in each example and surprisingly – or perhaps not surprisingly – the channel in other words the 'draft' seems to be at the epicentre of 'noise'.

What could constitute 'noise' in drafting a normative act? It is difficult to generalise since each draft has its own life-cycle and its own problems and difficulties but, as Sir George Engle noted, 'bills are made to pass as razors are made to sell',[10] so there are some broad comments that can be made about drafting-related problems or the problems that drafters face.[11] We can distinguish between three different sets of problems, which can certainly constitute 'noise': political, technical and personal qualities of the drafter.

Political

- Bad drafting instructions – vague political targets. This is the most common complaint by drafters, especially in small jurisdictions. Bad or incomplete instructions are a serious problem in preparing a draft bill. Strictly speaking, the drafting office should inform and train ministries on the kind of instructions it requires, but sometimes this is not enough.[12] Bad instructions usually lead to badly drafted legislation which, for the purposes of our model, can be interpreted as 'noise'.

---

[10] G Engle, '"Bills are Made to Pass as Razors are Made to Sell": Practical Constraints in the Preparation of Legislation' (1983) 75 Statute LR.
[11] See GC Thornton, *Legislative Drafting* (4th edn Butterworths, London 1996); A Seidman, RB Seidman and N Abeyesekere, *Legislative Drafting for Democratic Social Change: A Manual for Drafters* (Kluwer Law International, Cambridge, MA 2001).
[12] D Elliott, 'Getting Better Instructions for Legislative Drafting', Just Language Conference, Victoria British Columbia, 21 October 1992.

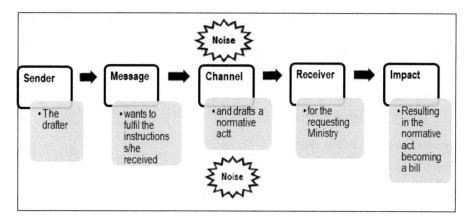

Figure 8. The transmission model and the drafter – with noise – example 2.

- Changes in ministerial policy or changes in government. Unfortunately, when there are changes in government (a cabinet reshuffle or a new government) there are often changes in the priorities of individual ministries and drafting offices have to start with fresh instructions for new bills. Inevitably there are delays and the drafters are rushed to complete new bills in accordance with the new priorities.
- Attempting to circumvent the constitution or the courts. Rare in democracies, but chillingly common in semi-democratic and autocratic regimes, drafters will inevitably be asked to produce bills which attempt to circumvent the constitution or the courts. The result is often not just 'noise' but a loud 'bang'.

Technique

- Clarity, precision, unambiguity. Both semantic and syntactic ambiguity[13] are the enemies of clarity.[14] Despite the fact that some drafting experts believe that 'Drafting too precisely may create unintended loopholes',[15] any draft bill that lacks clarity and precision will inevitably be challenged in court for vagueness. Yet, at the same time, policy-makers occasionally do prefer vagueness in an attempt to cover or defend unpopular laws.
- Complex language. The plain language in law debate has been ongoing for more than 30 years.[16] It is not so much about simplifying the language of

---

[13] R Dickerson, *The Fundamentals of Legal Drafting* (Little-Brown, Boston 1986) 101 and 104.
[14] P Butt and R Castle, *Modern Legal Drafting* (CUP, Cambridge 2001).
[15] Quoted from H Xanthaki, 'On Transferability of Legislative Solutions: The Functionality Test' in: C Stefanou and H Xanthaki (eds), *Drafting Legislation: A Modern Approach* (Ashgate, Aldershot 2008) 10.
[16] JC Redish, 'The Plain English Movement' in: S Greenbaum (ed), *The English Language Today* (Pergamon Press, New York 1985) 125–38; J Barnes, 'The Continuing Debate about "Plain Language" Legislation: A Law Reform Conundrum', (2006) 27 Statute LR 83.

law so that ordinary people can understand it, but about the use of language which is clear and conveys its message without unnecessary complexity. Whether or not it is possible to do so in law, where individual words may carry more than their simple, everyday meaning is a matter personal belief. However, we certainly do not wish to see twenty-first century drafts in nineteenth-century language. Complex language can certainly produce 'noise' especially if it is caught up in political interpretations.

Personal qualities of the drafter

- Ability to do research to gain background knowledge. Producing a good draft is above all an indication that the drafter has understood well the issues/circumstances involved, as well as what is required of him/her according to the instructions s/he has received. Gaining background knowledge is not as easy as it sounds. It requires research skills which, unfortunately, are not always taught at undergraduate level. Unless the drafter is well equipped and has learned how to do research, the resulting draft will probably miss its target.
- Ability to develop a legislative scheme. Perhaps the most vivid description of a legislative scheme is given by Crabbe:

Upon that scheme hangs the balance of the Bill. The legislative scheme represents Counsel's mental picture of how well the Act of Parliament would look in structure and quality, in structure and form ...Without a legislative scheme the resultant Act will look like a patchy, sketchy work ... The legislative scheme is the architectural plan of the building that is called an Act of Parliament.[17]

Without a legislative scheme any proposed draft would not fit in well with the existing corpus of legislation and if this becomes a habit then quickly the corpus of laws becomes a mosaic.

Conclusion

This article has looked at legislative drafting as a form of communication by using tools drawn from communication theory – rather than the traditional legal theory/legal philosophy approach. The aim of the article was not an in-depth new theoretical paradigm, but a modest first look at whether or not the basic communication model makes any sense in the context of legislative drafting.

What this article has shown is that legislative drafting as a form of communication is compatible with the 'transmission model' and that the transmission model is applicable from both the state's and the drafter's point of view. Of course, whether or not the transmission model is better at explaining law as a form of communication compared to traditional legal theory is a matter of speculation. Should we use a multidisciplinary approach to examine legislative drafting? In other words, would we understand and examine drafting as a form of communication better by using a combination of philosophy, sociology, linguistics and psychology? At this stage it is difficult to offer a qualified answer

---

[17]Crabbe (n 1) 16.

simply because more research is needed. It may well be that a combined approach, i.e. one that utilises traditional legal theory and the basic communications model, is the best way forward. At the moment, though, it is clear that the transmission model and, by extension, communications theory offers reasonable proof that drafting is indeed a form of communication.

But what does this mean from a practical point of view; in other words, why is this kind of research useful? I think there are three main points here. First, it means that we can now regard drafting as a form of communication not based on an axiom put forward by experts, but as an academically tested hypothesis. Second, by engaging theoretical tools from a different discipline, we open legislative drafting to interdisciplinary research. Third, in the absence of a general or *macro*-theory of drafting using *micro*-theoretical tools borrowed from other disciplines to examine aspects of legislative drafting appears to be a logical, if not inevitable, alternative – indeed, one that other disciples or sub-disciplines have adopted. In the absence of a general theory of legislative drafting, one of the well-known problems for those conducting academic research in the field has been the lack of a theoretical edifice on which they can build and test hypotheses. The use of *micro*-theoretical paradigms provides interesting and useful testing grounds. Perhaps, with a lot of hard work and a bit of luck, in the future the different *micro*-theoretical perspectives can be united in a general or *macro*-theory of legislative drafting.

A final point/question to be addressed – although this might well be the topic for another article – is: what kind of communication is legislative drafting? If we accept that drafters are policy translators, then obviously drafting is a form of *formal political communication* since drafters turn into normative acts the wishes of their political masters. It is 'formal' because it is related to an established procedure aiming to give a proposed normative act binding effect – unlike informal methods of political communication, e.g. well-timed interviews, leaks to the press etc. which have no official status. It is political because inevitably the wishes of the political masters are part of an overall political strategy aiming to fulfil the package of policies on which the government was elected. But while, I think, there is little doubt that drafting is a 'formal' form of communication, it is reasonable to question whether it is indeed a form of political communication. What are the criteria for identifying a form of communication as 'political'? How do they differ from other forms of communication, e.g. intellectual communication or social communication? Clearly, more work is necessary if we want proof and precision in our identification of legislative drafting as a form of political communication. Perhaps a different point of view can shed more light on this point.

Acknowledgements

This article is based on a presentation given at the 9th Congress of International Association of Legislation, *Quality of Legislation: Principles and Instruments*, Universidade Nova de Lisboa, Lisbon, Portugal, 24–25 June 2010. The full version of the article will be published in 2011 as C Stefanou, 'Legislative Drafting as a Form of Communication' in: M Travares-Almeida (ed), *Quality of Legislation* (Nomos, Baden-Baden 2011).

Notes on contributor

Constantin Stefanou (BA MA MPhil PhD) is LLM Director, Institute of Advanced Legal Studies, School of Advanced Study, University of London.

Clarity, precision and unambiguity: aspects for effective legislative drafting

Esther Majambere

Senior Legal Officer, Uganda Law Reform Commission, Uganda

> When drafting legislation, the drafter's primary duty is to give effect to the policy of the sponsors of the law, but it is important for the drafter to have in mind the category of people who will read and use the legislation. It is also worth noting that when drafting legislation, a drafter should ensure clarity, precision and unambiguity. A drafter bears an obligation to maintain the rule of law. As part of this burden, a drafter must take care that the form of the law lends itself to clarity, precision and consistency. For without clarity, precision and consistency the law has no predictability. The rule of law demands that as much as is possible, people should know in advance what the law demands of them, what the law grants to them and what sorts of behaviour they can expect from officials. It is therefore important that a drafter makes the law as simple and as clear as possible. This can only be achieved by employing the aspects of clarity, precision and unambiguity as tools of effective legislating drafting which is analysed in this article. Also analysed is the use of plain language and gender-neutral drafting as a measure of ensuring clarity, precision and unambiguity when drafting legislation.

1. Introduction

1.1. Background

The English language of today is still recognisably the language of Chaucer and Shakespeare, of Abraham Lincoln and Winston Churchill, of the *Book of Common Prayer* and Authorised Version of *The Bible*.[1] It is also the language of lawyers in many countries: the United Kingdom, the United States, Canada, Australia, New Zealand and India, to name but a few. It is the language in which laws are written and in which cases are argued and judgements are given.

Language is an important aspect in drafting. When drafting legislation, the drafter's primary duty is to give effect to the policy of the sponsors of the law, but it is important for the drafter to have in mind the category of people who will read and use the legislation. It is worth noting that the way in which a drafter drafts a piece of law depends on the principles which will be applied by those reading it. While there are occasional rules of things that may assist, they will do

---

[1] P Butt and R Castle, *Modern Legal Drafting: A Guide to Using Clearer Language* (2nd edn Cambridge University Press, Cambridge 2006) 1.

so only if applied flexibly and with an eye constantly and achieving the most clear, simple and effective result in each context.[2] It is important for a drafter to know the audience to whom the law is being drafted in order for the text to be written in the way that is understandable to current and prospective users. To write understandable documents, the drafter needs to gauge the legal sophistication of the users.

There is little doubt that in the past drafters drafted primarily for judges and lawyers. Today there is a real effort, not just to improve readability for a legal audience, but to make Acts increasingly accessible to administrative and public officials;[3] although it depends on the nature of the subject matter.

It is worth noting that when writing a legislative sentence, drafters should ensure clarity, precision and unambiguity. Drafters bear an obligation to maintain the rule of law. As part of that burden they must take care that the form of their laws lends itself to clarity, precision and consistency. For without clarity, precision and consistency, the law has no predictability. The rule of law demands that, as much as is possible, people know in advance what the law demands of them, what the law grants to them, and what sorts of behaviour they can expect from officials.[4] Almost as important is the duty to make the law as simple and as clear as possible.[5]

It is against the above background that I intend to analyse clarity, precision and unambiguity as aspects of effective legislative drafting.

1.2. Methodology

In this article, I will argue for the hypothesis that clarity, precision and unambiguity promote certainty in the law. I will briefly discuss the definition of the 'rule of law'. I will then make an analysis of clarity, precision and unambiguity in drafting and the drafter's role in ensuring clarity, precision and unambiguity in drafting and finally I will argue for plain language drafting and gender-neutral drafting as tools for promoting clarity, precision and unambiguity.

In a bid to promoting clarity, precision and unambiguity, renowned writers in the area of legislative drafting have come up with books and articles, law reform commissions have made reports and cases have been decided. Available literature on the topic will be considered in this article.

The article will make conclusions in favour clarity, precision and unambiguity as tools of certainty and effective drafting.

1.3. Rule of law

'Rule of law' generally refers to the judiciary's authority to determine the state of the law in a given case, to pass sentence and to review legislation for its compatibility with prevailing norms, including constitutional rights. On the other

---

[2] Ibid.
[3] JF Burrows and RI Carter, *Statute Law in New Zealand* (LexisNexis, Wellington 2009) 83.
[4] A Seidman, RB Seidman and N Abeyesekere, *Legislative Drafting for Democratic Social Change – A Manual for Drafters* (Kluwer Law International, The Hague 2001).
[5] ML Turnbull, 'Legislative Drafting in Plain Language and Statements of General Principle' (1997) Statute L Rev 21.

hand, 'rule of law' refers to the right of a legally authorised government to pass laws according to the formalities and to have them obeyed. The rule of law has been extensively written about and there are several definitions. However for the purposes of this article, I will explore the fact that the rule of law requires certainty in the law. According to Kramer,[6] the rule of law is understood to have the eight principle of legality as set out by Fuller.[7] Kramer continues:

> Although these basic precepts are never perfectly satisfied by any regime of law, the satisfaction of each of them to a substantial degree is essential for the existence of any legal system. The state of affairs constituted by the substantial fulfilment of those precepts is the rule of law.

The internal morality of the law demands that there be rules, that they are made known, and that they be observed in practice by those charged with their administration.[8] She continues that those who are expected to obey the rules must be able to find out what the rules are and the rules must be understandable by those who are expected to obey them. In order for those to whom the rules are addressed to know what they are commanded to do, the commands must be public, congruent and non-contradictory, clear enough to understand and they must not change fast.[9] Suffice to say, therefore, that all the above can be achieved by employing the tools of clarity, precision and unambiguity in drafting.

2. Importance of clarity, precision and unambiguity in drafting

Clarity or clearness is defined by Tullock as 'the state or quality of being easily perceived and understood'.[10] Ambiguity is defined as uncertain or inexact meaning. Ambiguity exists when words can be interpreted in more than one way: e.g. is a 'light truck' light in weight or light in colour?[11] Precision is traditionally viewed as the main aim of common law drafters who make the greatest effort to 'say all'; to define all; to leave nothing to the imagination, never to presume upon the reader's intelligence.[12]

Clarity and precision in drafting require specificity.[13] Ambiguity is a legal drafting's chief curse; its avoidance is the drafter's chief goal.[14] Dickerson calls ambiguity 'perhaps the most serious disease of language.[15] Consider the sign on a highway that states 'speed limit 120km'. It leaves its addressees uncertain

---

[6] HM Kramer, 'On the Moral Status of the Rule of Law', Cambridge LJ (2004) 65.
[7] L Fuller 'The Morality of Law' (rev edn New Haven 1969), Chap 2 cited by Kramer, ibid.
[8] MJ Radin, 'Reconsidering the Rule of Law' (1989) Boston U L Rev 786.
[9] Ibid.
[10] Tullock (1978–80) cited in C Stefanou and H Xanthaki (eds), *Drafting Legislation, A Modern Approach* (Ashgate, Aldershot 2008) 666.
[11] Ibid. 9.
[12] Pigeon (1988), cited in Ibid. 9.
[13] CF PM Bakshi, *An Introduction to Legislative Drafting* (4th edn, 1992) 45.
[14] Butt and Castle (n 1) 22.
[15] R Dickerson, *Fundamentals of Legal Drafting* (Little Brown and Company, Boston 1986) 32.

about some aspect of required behaviour. In that respect, the law remains insufficiently detailed.[16] In essence such a law does not promote certainty.

It is important to keep the goal of ambiguity-free drafting in perspective. Language can be wrenched out of context. Perverse interpretations are almost always possible. Not every word or sentence is ambiguous; nor is every word or sentence a lawyer writes subject to 'every conceivable misinterpretation'.[17] But the lawyers' fear of ambiguity is one of the principal reasons why the language of legal documents has reached its present parlous state.[18]

Legislatures sometimes choose to be vague or general and to let administrative agencies supply the specifics,[19] but legislatures rarely choose to be ambiguous. Thus clarity, in the sense of intelligibility and unambiguity, signifies that a document is not only easy to understand but that it conveys the same message to those who read it.

So far as is possible, a drafter should draft according to the commonly accepted understanding of the words. A drafter should try to make the sentences mean precisely what they intend them to mean so that the readers of the law do not twist the meaning for their own purposes. In effect, the drafter must try to 'box in' the reader so that he or she if faithful to the text must give the words the meaning the drafter intended.[20]

The Law Reform Commission of Victoria made the surprising statement that precision and clarity (i.e. simplicity) are not competing goals. In support of this statement it argued as follows:

> Precision is desirable in order to minimise the risk of uncertainty and consequent disputes. But a document which is precise without being clear is as dangerous in that respect as one which is clear without being precise. In its true sense, precision is incompatible with a lack of clarity.[21]

Thus it is not possible to separate, clarity, precision and ambiguity when drafting.

2.1. *The drafter's role in avoiding ambiguity*

There are two main objects that the draftsman aims at, and they are not easy to reconcile. First and foremost, to get the Bill right. The test is that when it is passed, and a trained lawyer or judge has mastered its intricacies, the meaning is clear (in the sense of unambiguous) and the intention carried out. Subject to this, the subject is to make the Bill as intelligible as possible to Parliament and the general public.[22]

---

[16] Seidman (n 4).
[17] E Gowers, *The Complete Plain Words* (3rd edn HMSO, London 1986) 19.
[18] D Crystal and D Davy, *Investigating English Style* (Longman, London 1969) 193.
[19] Dickerson (n 15) 11; see also Burrows (n 3) 174.
[20] Seidman (n 4).
[21] Report of Law Reform Commission of Victoria (No.9) 'Plain English and the Law' (1987) para 65.
[22] H Kent, *Memoir of the Law Maker* (Macmillan, London 1997) 97.

According to Craise, it is impossible to give an exhaustive account of how legislation should be drafted.[23] Apart from the impossibility of predicting all the difficulties and questions that the draftsman may face in the course of his work, the only drafting matter on which it is wise to be dogmatic is that it is unwise to be dogmatic on any drafting matter. While there are occasional rules of thumb that may assist, they will do so only if applied flexibly and with an eye constantly on achieving the most clear, simple and effective result in each context.

An important preparatory remark is that the way in which a person drafts a law or any other document must depend on the principles which will be applied by those reading it. In the context of United Kingdom legislation, the point is expressed by Lord Bridge of Harwich as follows:

> The courts' traditional approach to construction, giving primacy to the ordinary, grammatical meaning of statutory language, is reflected in the parliamentary draftsman's technique of using language with the at most precision to express the legislative intent of his political masters and it remains the golden rule of constructions that a statute means exactly what it says and does not mean what it does not say.[24]

This eases the job of the drafter considerably and facilitates economy and simplicity in drafting. Reliance on a purposive interpretation is not however an excuse for imprecision. The main cause of imprecision in drafting is not that the draftsman cannot find or does not wish to trouble to find a precise way of expressing the concept in his mind, but rather that the concept in his mind is not sufficiently precise to admit of clear expression. The principal task in drafting is to refine and analyse the policy to the state of clarity in which the words for its expression suggest themselves naturally. When the draftsman struggles to find the words or structure to express a thought, it is generally time to abandon the struggle and return to analysis or refinement of the thought.[25]

All that being so, it is not sufficient to draft imprecisely and hope that courts will supply the draftsman's deficiencies by adopting a purposive construction. If the thought behind the draft is unclear, the courts will not be able to discern its purpose and will not be able to adopt a beneficial construction without trespassing on the legislature's province.[26]

Writing for a less knowledgeable audience means that a drafter must work hard at keeping sentences short and eliminating or defining difficult words. But writing for a knowledgeable audience does not give the drafter an excuse to write long, unwieldy sentences. For sophisticated readers you may be able to be briefer; you can pack information into specialised words. For other readers your material must be less dense.[27]

To this end, Russell had this to say:[28]

---

[23] D Greenberg (ed), *Craise on Legislation* (9th edn Thomas Sweet and Maxwell, London 2008) 336.
[24] *Associated Newspapers Ltd v Wilson* [1995] 2 WLR 354 at 362 HL.
[25] Greenberg (n 23) 336.
[26] Ibid 369.
[27] Dickerson (n 14) 26–31.
[28] AKC Russell, *Legislative Drafting and Forms* (Butterworth, London 1938) 12.

> The simplest English is the best for legislation. Sentences should be short. Do not use one word more than is necessary to make the meaning clear. The draftsman should bear in mind that his Act is supposed to be read and understood by the plain man. In any case, he may be sure that if he finds he can express his meaning in simple words all is going well with his draft. While if he finds himself driven to complicated expressions composed of long words it is a sign that he is getting lost and he should reconsider the form of section of course in Acts of a technical kind, he may find it necessary to use technical expressions: but such Acts will usually only affect readers who are qualified to understand them.

Stephen, J expressed the challenge for the drafter thus:[29]

> It is not enough [for the drafter] to attain a degree of precision which a person reading in good faith can understand, but it is necessary to attain if possible to a degree of precision which a person reading in bad faith cannot misunderstand. It is all better if he cannot pretend to misunderstand it.

3. Plain language as a tool for promoting clarity, precision and unambiguity

Plain language has been viewed by many authoritative writers as a tool for clarity, precision and unambiguity. In many countries, such as Australia, New Zealand and Canada, the plain language movement in law is well established.[30] The terms 'plain language' and 'plain English' are often used interchangeably by the plain language activists, but there is a difference between the two. Plain language is perhaps the broader term, and more suitable for jurisdictions that are bilingual, and it reflects language as any method or means of communicating words.[31] English on the other hand, is a particular type of language and is therefore a narrow term.[32] Plain language or plain English has been defined by many writers as follows:

> Plain English is clear, straightforward expression, using only as many words as are necessary. It is language that avoids obscurity, inflated vocabulary and convoluted sentence structure. It is not baby talk, nor is it a simplified version of the English language.[33]

According to Butt and Castle calls to simplify legal language are hardly new.[34] A number of leading nineteenth-century reformers made scathing attacks on lawyers' language. They quote Jeremy Bentham, who was particularly vitriolic in attacking the argument that 'precision' or 'certainty' demanded a repetitious style:

---

[29] *Re Castioni* [1891] QB 149 at 167.
[30] P Butt, 'Drafting and Property Law' (2005) 7 Eur JL Reform.
[31] Stefanou and Xanthaki (n 10) 13.
[32] Ibid.
[33] RD Eagleson, *Writing in Plain English* (Commonwealth of Australia 1990) 4; See also R Sullivan, 'Implications of Plain Language Drafting' (2001) 22 Statute L Rev 175.
[34] Butt and Castle (n 1).

For this redundancy – for the accumulation of execrementitious matter in all its various shapes, in all its various forms ... for all the pestilential effects that cannot but be produced by this so enormous load of literary garbage, the plea commonly pleaded [is] ... that it is necessary to *precision* – or to use the word which on similar occasions they themselves are in the habit of using, *certainty*.[35]

In New Zealand, the New Zealand Law Commission embarked on a series of initiatives designed to change the language and format of New Zealand legislation and with effect from 1 January 1997, the Parliamentary Counsel Office had already adopted a number of arguably cosmetic changes in its drafting style.[36] Plain language contributes to clarity and therefore serves effectiveness in drafting. It also serves democracy and the rule of law.[37]

3.1. The arguments against plain language

The traditional view of drafters in the English-speaking world has been that their prime responsibility is to draft laws that give precise effect to the intentions of sponsors of those laws. In this sense, the conflict between the need to achieve certainty of the legal effect and the public demand for the need for the use of ordinary language which the man in the street can understand will be minimised. Accordingly, the draftsman should never be compelled to sacrifice certainty for simplicity, since the result may be to frustrate the legislative intention. An unfortunate subject may drive to litigation because the meaning of an Act was obscure which, could by use of a few extra words, have been made plain. The courts may hold a government to be driven to conclude, that the Act which was intended to mean one thing, does not mean that thing, but something else.[38]

This view was supported by the Victorian Supreme Court in Australia. The court was critical of a recent Act of the Victorian Parliament on the grounds that precision had been sacrificed in the interests of the simple language. The court had this to say:

> No doubt such drafting is always prompted by a desire to simplify legislation. Unfortunately, attempts to do so usually leave a number of questions unanswered. They also leave courts without guidance as to how the questions should be answered and when dealing with legislation courts' only task is to interpret and apply the law laid down by the Parliament. The courts cannot be legislators.

One of the major concerns attached to the adoption of a policy of plain language, is that drafting legal documents and particularly legislation in this style may lead to a loss of precision and certainty.[39]

---

[35] Tait (1838–43) cited in Butt and Castle (n 1).
[36] G Tanner, QC, 'Confronting the Process of Statute-Making' in: R Bigwood (ed), *The Statute Making and Meaning* (LexisNexis, Wellington 2004) 67.
[37] Stefanou and Xanthaki (n 10) 13.
[38] IML Turnbull.
[39] ML Turnbull, 'Problems of Legislative Drafting' (1986) Statute LR 67 'clear Legislative Drafting: New Approaches in Australia', II Statute law Review (1990) 164. See also 'Preparation of legislation (Renton Report) Comnd 6053(London 1975).

Gowers expresses this concern as follows:

> Legal drafting must therefore be unambiguous, precise, comprehensive and largely conventional. If it is readily intelligible, so much the better; but it is by far more important that it should yield its meaning accurately than that it should yield it on the first reading, and legal draftsmen cannot afford to give much attention, if any, to euphony or literary elegance. What matters most to them is that no one will succeed in persuading a court of law that their words bear a meaning they did not intend, and, if possible, that no one will think it worthwhile to try.[40]

Plain language becomes less precise if simplicity is overemphasised. According to Thornton,[41] the purposes of legislation are most likely to be achieved by the draftsman who is ardently concerned to be intelligible. The obligation to be intelligible, to convey the intended meaning so that it is comprehensible and easily understood by the affected parties, is best satisfied by writing with simplicity and precision ... 'A law which is drafted in precise but not simple terms may, on account of its incomprehensibility, ... fails to achieve the result intended. The blind pursuit of precision will inevitably lead to complexity; and the complexity is a definite step along the way to obscurity'.

The other concern is that plain language will lower standards of good drafting. This concern stems from the view that plain language consists of monosyllabic words, very short sentences and a complete rejection of complex words or sentence construction. If this were true of plain language, then the criticism would be valid. It would certainly not be useful to draft statutes and legal documents in simplistic monosyllabic words. However, as other commentators have pointed out, this is to misunderstand plain language. As the Law Reform Commission of Victoria notes in its report:

> Plain English involves the use of plain, straightforward language which avoids defects and conveys its meaning as clearly and as simply as possible, without unnecessary pretension or embellishment. It is to be contrasted with convoluted, repetitive and prolix language. The adoption of a plain English style demands simply that a document be written in a style which readily conveys its message to its audience.[42]

The other argument is that plain language might lead to the loss of established meanings of words settled over centuries of judicial interpretation. Plain language advocates accept that there are certain phrases that have in fact attained this status. There is a small area of relative precision in the language of the law, but they point out that the extent of this area of precision can be grossly overestimated. Much of what are considered terms of art are only meaningless jargon.[43]

3.2. *Gender-neutral drafting as a tool for clarity, precision and unambiguity*

Gender-neutral drafting is seen as a tool for promoting clarity, precision and unambiguity. It aims to promote gender specificity in the pronoun used when

---

[40] Gowers (n 17) at 7.
[41] GC Thornton, *Legislative Drafting* (3rd edn Butterworths, London 1987) 47.
[42] Law Reform Commission of Victoria (n 21) paras 61–6, 67–72.
[43] J Kimble, 'A Plain English Primer' (1987) 33 The Practical Lawyer 86.

drafting legislation.[44] Gender-neutral drafting has therefore gained popularity in drafting legislative drafting. In addition to plain language, gender-neutral drafting serves the promotion of precision, clarity and unambiguity.[45] In the United Kingdom, for example, it is a policy of the Office of Parliamentary Counsel for all Government Bills to take a form which achieves gender-neutral drafting so far as is practicable, at more than reasonable cost to brevity or intelligibility.[46] Clarity and certainty are the most important objectives used in legislation. 'There is no technical reason why legislation should not be drafted in a way that avoids gender-specific pronouns ... The only reason why we continue to use these pronouns is that they seem to us to help in achieving simplicity and therefore clarity and certainty (which is an essential element of good legislation)'.[47]

4. Conclusion

As already seen above, clarity, precision and unambiguity are used to achieve goals that are clear, precise and unambiguous, which leads to effective legislation. A drafter has to ensure that policy is achieved; implementation will be as it was intended by policy-makers and there will be less statutory interpretation. Without clarity, precision and consistency the law lacks predictability. In order for the addressees to do what is commanded of them, in response to the commands, the commands must be prospective, not contradictory or non-congruent, and not physically, mentally or circumstantially impossible for human beings addressed to follow.[48]

It is worth noting that there is no hierarchy between clarity, precision and unambiguity. Some laws require more clarity, such as criminal law, whereas others require precision, such as rules of evidence.[49] The bottom line is to achieve effectiveness of the law. The prism under which the choice is to be made rests *in abstracto* and relates to effectiveness. It is therefore important to observe that clarity, precision and unambiguity are tools of effective drafting. Depending on the message that the drafter intends to convey or depending on what the policy-makers want to convey, as long as effectiveness is attained by the drafter, there should be no question as to whether clarity, precision or unambiguity prevail. The three virtues must be viewed as tools of effective drafting at equal footing. If the audience consists of mainly laypersons, then clarity and unambiguity as part of clarity, must be put forward.

As Craise argues,[50] clearly when dealing with a relatively simple concept and imposing rules of relative simplicity, the draftsman ought to draft in a manner

---

[44]'Avoidance of "Sexist" Language in Legislation' 11 (1985) Commonwealth L Bull, 590
[45]S Petersson, 'Gender Neutral Drafting: Recent Commonwealth Developments' 20 (1999) Statute LR 35 at 57.
[46]See Statement by Leader of House of Commons, HC Deb 8 March 2007 c 146 WS.
[47]Greenberg (n 23) 65.
[48]Radin (n 8) 786.
[49]Stefanou and Xanthaki (n 10) 11.
[50]Craise on Legislation (Thomas Sweet and Maxwell 9th edn) 339.

which will be easily penetrable by one class of readers. But when writing about matters of technical complexity, or imposing in relation to simple concepts rules of complexity, the draftsman will be forced to aim for clarity only in so far as he can assume his primary audience to be familiar both with the substantive area concerned and with construction of legislation.

Notes on contributor
Esther Majambere is Senior Legal Officer at the Uganda Law Reform Commission. She has an LLM (Merit) from The Institute of Advanced Legal Studies, University of London, a Post Graduate Diploma in Legal Practice from the Law Development Centre, Kampala, Uganda and an LLB (Hons) from Makerere University, Kampala, Uganda.

In pursuit of clarity: how far should the drafter go?

Alain Songa Gashabizi

Principal State Attorney/Legislative Drafting Service, Ministry of Justice, P.O. Box 6433, Kigali, Rwanda

> Clarity is very important in legislative drafting to allow the drafter to eliminate ambiguity and vagueness in the law, which may affect the rights of citizens. Ambiguity occurs when in the law words can be interpreted in more than one way and vagueness occurs when there is doubt to where the words' boundaries are or when the word has an open textured meaning. It is difficult to attain clarity due to the fact that in legislation ambiguity and vagueness may be caused by insufficient drafting instructions, and it is incumbent on the drafter to seek further clarifications. In pursuing clarity, some tools are needed such as the use of plain language which makes legislation clear and understandable for a lay person, gender-neutral language and the proper structuring or layout of the legislative intent to enhance clarity.

1. Introduction

The importance of clarity in legislative drafting as a means to eliminate ambiguity and vagueness cannot be overstated.[1] A drafter must strive to ensure clarity in drafting legislation because of the importance attached to laws by members of the public and because a drafter is a custodian of the Statute Book. That the drafter is writing laws that affect the rights of citizens and ultimately justice reinforces the need for a drafter to try as much as possible to produce legislative proposals that are clear, simple and precise for the reader and those who are expected to abide by the law.

Having ambiguity in the law may lead to judicial review in its broadest sense and judge-made law which goes against the doctrine of separation of power. Ambiguity in legislation exists when words can be interpreted in more than one way.[2] Vagueness on the other hand occurs when there is doubt as to where the word's boundaries are or when the word has an open textured meaning.[3] Dickerson argues that legislatures sometimes opt to be vague or general so as to give space for the implementers of the law to provide the specifics.[4] But they rarely

---

[1] VCRAC Crabbe, *Legislative Drafting* (Cavendish, London 1993) 43.
[2] C Stefanou and H Xanthaki (eds), *Drafting Legislation: A Modern Approach* (Ashgate-Dartmouth, Aldershot 2008) 9.
[3] GC Christie, 'Vagueness and Language' (1963–64) 48 Minn L Rev 885–912 at 889.
[4] R Dickerson, 'The Diseases of Legislative Drafting' (1964) 1 Harv LJ 5–15 at 11.

choose to be ambiguous.[5] The drafter thus is faced with a challenge of balancing between being accommodative while at the same time cautious of the dangers that lie in so doing. It is therefore argued that vagueness is a necessary tool for clarity and precision.[6] The drafter therefore must always pursue clarity because the writing of the law is different from any other form of writing. The drafter is writing the law which affects the rights of citizens and ultimately justice itself. This paper therefore seeks to examine the importance of clarity in legislation generally while at the same time highlighting the tools that can be used to achieve clarity. However, this paper seeks to illustrate that it is not always possible for a drafter to achieve clarity in legislative proposals because of other reasons beyond the drafter's control, such as subject complexity, for instance, in drafting tax legislation where the pursuit of clarity might lead to the loss of intended meaning. Notwithstanding the above challenge, this paper will seek to prove that the drafter should as much as possible pursue clarity so as to draft laws that are effective and implementable. Often, the cause of ambiguity and vagueness in legislation begins with insufficient drafting instructions, and it is incumbent on the drafter to seek further clarifications. This can be done by asking probing questions to try filling up the missing links, all aimed at achieving clarity.

To prove this hypothesis further, a literature review will also be undertaken to see what other people have written on clarity.

2. Why clarity in drafting legislation?
2.1. *Meaning of clarity and its purpose*

Clarity or clearness is the state or quality of being clear and easily perceived or understood.[7] Without clarity, precision and consistency the law has no predictability.[8] It is, thus, a cardinal principal of the rule of law that citizens should know in advance their rights and obligations under the law. Laws drafted clearly will encourage markets to flourish as entrepreneurs will have the confidence to invest their monies in such an economy. It is important to note that in order to achieve clarity in drafting a drafter needs specificity, that is, to establish who should do what.[9] The devotion of special attention and time by drafters in writing their Bills in clearly stated legislative sentences that use words accurately is of paramount importance in the pursuit of clarity.

As Seidman et al. have correctly observed, drafters should try to make their sentences mean precisely what they intend them to mean, so that even the person reading the law with intent to subvert it cannot successfully twist the meaning to

---

[5]H Xanthaki (n 2) emphasises the fact that where a law is drafted in a wide and general nature, the possibility of it being misconstrued and subjected to litigation is real.
[6]See Christie (n 3) at 912.
[7]See *Compact Oxford English Dictionary of Current English* (Oxford University Press, Oxford 2005).
[8]AW Seidman, RB Seidman and N Abeyeskere, *Legislative Drafting for Democratic Social Change*: A *Manual for Drafters* (Kluwer Law International, London 2001) 255.
[9]Cf. PM Bakshi, *An Introduction to Legislative Drafting* (4th edn, N.M. Tripathi, Mumbai 1992) 45.

another purpose.[10] Indeed, clarity depends on the proper selection of words and on their arrangement and on the construction of sentences.[11] In addition, understanding and transparency in legislation can be enhanced by clarity.[12] Therefore the call by Butt and Castle[13] for legal documents to be written in modern Standard English as currently used and understood is timely as it leads to clearer comprehensible legislation.

3. The role of the drafter in the quest for clarity

3.1. Techniques that a drafter can use to ensure clarity in legislation

The drafter plays an important role in ensuring that legislation means what it says, thus clarity is of paramount importance to a drafter. This is based on the fact that ideally the lay person should be able to look at a piece of legislation and know what it means. The drafters of proposed legislation intended to translate government policies into law will often strive to ensure that it is done in as precise, clear and logical a manner possible. At the back of a drafter's mind, the drafter seeks to write laws that are certain and unambiguous.[14] Therefore a drafter will make sure that the intensions of the policy-makers are exactly met and that in so doing, both the general aims and the particular applications of the new policy are realised. It is important thus that a drafter chooses language that clearly brings out what is intended in the policy.

The drafter of any proposed legislation will, while writing and refining the legislative text, do so in a manner that ensures certainty, consistency, clarity, comprehensiveness and conciseness in the language of the text. Crabbe[15] lists five considerations that a drafter should have in mind in the pursuit of clarity, these are:

(a) that a word has no meaning by itself, for its meaning is derived from the context in which it is used;
(b) that a concept is vague if in a given context it leaves open too wide a range of borderline cases to delimit precision in that context; and
(c) that the subjective intent of the writer or speaker must coincide with the objective meaning of the word or phrase used in its context and be so supported by some external source such as a dictionary, reasonable interpretation or even antecedent experience.

In addition, knowing who your audience will be is very important to the drafter in the pursuit of clarity. Michèle Asprey correctly observes that even the most accurate and elegantly drafted document can turn out to be completely

---

[10]Seidman (n 8) at 261.
[11]Lord H Thring, *Practical Legislation: The composition and Language of Acts of Parliament and Business Documents* (John Murray, London 1902) 61.
[12]See P Wahlgren, 'Legislative Techniques' in LJ Wintgens (ed) *Legislation in Context: Essays in Legisprudence* (Ashgate, Aldershot 2007) 77–94 at 84.
[13]See P Butt and R Castle, *Modern Legal Drafting: A Guide to Using Clearer Language* (Cambridge University Press, New York 2001) at 129.
[14]KW Patchett, *Legislative Drafting Course* (1993 RIPA International Course Notes) at 9.
[15]See n 1.

ineffective if it misses its mark.¹⁶ Therefore in an effort to achieve clarity, precision and consistency, the New South Wales Parliamentary Counsel's office consider the following as it audience for purposes of drafting legislation:

(a) parliament itself;
(b) the public of the section of the public to whom the legislation is directed; and
(c) the courts and the legal system.¹⁷

Each of these three categories has different requirements which are adhered to while drafting its laws. Tailoring legislation to the prevailing circumstance is thus important for the purpose of keeping the audience in mind.

The above considerations notwithstanding, there are tools that a drafter can use to achieve clarity in legislation, for example use of plain language, gender-neutral drafting and the use of the structure of the Bill to ensure clarity, which will be next examined.

3.2. Gender-neutral drafting as a tool to enhance clarity

Some authors are of the view that sexist usage is not strictly a matter of clarity,¹⁸ that any writing habit that builds a barrier between the writer and half of his or her readers must reduce the impact of the message. In most traditional Commonwealth countries, the Interpretation Act has been used to enhance the masculine gender pronouns in legislation.¹⁹ However, the trend over the years in many jurisdictions has been to advocate for the use of gender-neutral language in our laws.²⁰ Gender-neutral language is thus seen as a tool for enhancing clarity, precision and unambiguity in legislation that a drafter can employ. This the drafter can achieve by avoiding words which suggest that maleness is the norm or superior or positive and that femaleness in the non-standard, subordinate or negative.²¹ The reverse is neither desirable in contemporary legislative drafting; hence, there is need to remain neutral in language unless the task is peculiar to a specific gender. Thus, where it is intended in a law to recognise a particular gender, such recognition should be granted because to do otherwise would be tantamount to interfering with the meaning and application of a policy. For instance, where a law seeks to address issues related to pregnancy, the woman should be named as 'woman' and not pregnant person. Therefore, specific terms like 'businessmen', 'firemen', 'poetess', and 'headmaster' can be replaced by less

---

¹⁶See Michèle M Asprey, *Plain Language for Lawyers* (Federation Press, Annandale 2010) at 78, where in he goes on to emphasise the need of the drafter to play to the intended audience.
¹⁷<http://www.pco.nsw.gov.au>.
¹⁸M Cutts, *The Plain English Guide* (Oxford University Press, Oxford 1996) 140.
¹⁹Section 44 Interpretation Act of Botswana; s 3(2) Interpretation Act of Uganda, Cap. 3 Laws of Uganda.
²⁰For the UK case, in 2007 the move gained momentum with Mr Jack Straw's statement in the Commons that the government would strive to encourage its use in the UK legislation (quoted from n 2).
²¹See n 18 at 71.

restrictive words like 'business people' or 'executive', 'firefighters', 'poet' and 'head teacher', respectively. However it is vital to note that some sex-specific terms may survive this trend because, as earlier noted, some tasks are peculiar to one gender.

Notwithstanding the above, a drafter should be careful when introducing gender-neutral language into an existing Act, especially when an amendment is being made so as to avoid introducing ambiguity and inconsistency. The language of the parent Act should not be departed from significantly so as to shock the legal system hence creating ambiguity. Rather, any attempt to introduce gender-neutral drafting should be done subtly. This is achievable in most jurisdictions practising the traditional common law systems where in their Interpretation Acts, the masculine gender 'he' is taken to mean 'she' as well. Thus, introducing gender-neutral laws will not affect or contravene the Interpretation Act. In the UK, it has become the practice for the Parliamentary Counsel to employ gender-neutral drafting so that it is practicable, at a more than reasonable cost to brevity or intelligibility.[22] Some of the techniques used in gender neutral drafting are as follows:[23]

(a) omitting the pronoun;
(b) use of masculine and feminine pronouns;
(c) repeating the noun;
(d) use of the plural;
(e) converting a noun to a verb;
(f) use of a relative clause;
(g) use of standard occupational references; and
(h) avoiding gender-specific words and phrases.

3.3. *Plain languages as a tool to enhance clarity*

Plain language is an approach to organising and writing documents which makes materials clear and understandable to the user while making use of everyday vocabulary yet still remaining legally binding.[24] Simply stated, it is a practice of writing English in a clear and simple style.[25] This comes against the background that most drafting offices, especially in the English speaking countries, had inherited the traditional style of legislative language used in the UK way back in the nineteenth century.[26] The focus for the drafters then, was to draft in a way that left no room for misunderstanding or deliberate distortion of meaning, hence they went to extreme lengths to avoid all sorts of possible ambiguity and ended up

---

[22] See n 2 at 15.
[23] This information was obtained from a presentation on clarity, plain language and gender-neutral drafting by Lydia Clapinska to Masters Students at IAL, 2011.
[24] GS Dykatra, 'Plain Language, Legal Documents and Forms: Background Information' (1988) 2 (2) The Loophole 4–32.
[25] Note 16 at 11.
[26] I Turnbull, 'Plain Language and Drafting in General Principles' The Loophole (July 1995) 25–38.

being too verbose.[27] This defeated the purpose of clarity and affected the accessibility of laws. Greenberg, while emphasising the importance of putting the reader first, observes that the issue of access of laws has always been of great concern to legislative counsel to the extent that older drafting standards revolving around the use of conventional verbose drafting or the slavish use of precedent are not good drafting.[28]

Premised on the above, the use of plain language as a tool to enhance clarity in legislation has found momentum over the years, having begun in New Zealand and Australia. The pursuit for clarity therefore is a worthwhile pursuit and can be achieved by employing plain language as a tool to achieve it. Be that as it may, in an effort to be clear, a drafter should not lose sight of precision.[29] This is because sometimes a drafter tends to over-explain a concept to the detriment of being precise while using plain language. This will occur especially when the drafter wants to demystify some complex or technical concept.

Therefore, the drafter should be more concerned about how to enable the reader to easily understand what is required by the law as clearly as the subject matter allows. To achieve this, the choice of language and the style of writing should be measured against the parameter of intelligibility. The legislative proposal should be written in a straightforward and clear language which as far as possible is used daily in that surrounding. This too goes to illustrate the extent that the drafter should go in order to achieve clarity.

3.4. *Use of the structure of the Bill to enhance clarity*

In order to draft legislation that is unambiguous and precise, the drafter has to ensure consistency, coherence and clarity. This to some extent can be achieved by proper structuring of the Bill, that is, the layout of the Bill can enable the reader to be gently introduced to the legislation. This is premised on the fact that words are the drafter's tool used to create sentences that form the legislative directives contained in the law. Therefore the study of syntax, which is the arrangement in patterns of words in a sentence in such a manner as it shows their relationship is vital to the drafter. Thornton notes that a sentence may be ambiguous because the grouping of words is inappropriate or misplaced.[30] The drafter's job to study the sentence's syntax is to detect and deal with ambiguity.

As noted earlier, the drafter must always bear the reader in mind when writing any piece of legislation.[31] Therefore, as far as coming up with a proper structure of the Bill's concern, the drafter should know that, like any good writing, drafting legislation ought to begin with a plan, and that even before a plan can be con-

---

[27] Ibid.
[28] See D Greenberg, 'Access to Legislation: The Legislative Counsel's Role' (CALC Conference, Hong Kong 2009).
[29] See n 16, where Asprey argues that a plain language document needs not only to be clear and straightforward but also precise and complete (p 14).
[30] See GC Thornton, *Legislative Drafting* (Bloomsbury, London).
[31] R Bigwood, *The Statute: Making and Meaning* (LexisNexis, Wellington), states that for as long as there is statute law, there will always be difficulties for the users in understanding and applying legislation and interpretations for the courts. That it is therefore incumbent on the legislature to make the meaning of a statute as clear as possible so that uncertainty for the users and recourse to the courts is reduced.

ceived, there is the thinking stage.[32] Much as the drafter might be tempted to copy an existing layout for his or her Bill, this should not be encouraged because the circumstances for drafting bills vary. Therefore, the drafter should devise his or her own plan tailored for that particular task based on the drafter's ideas.

Organisation of the Bill will depend on what the document is, but it is important to set out the substantive provisions of the law preferably from the onset or beginning, so that they should not be hidden among administrative and procedural aspects of the law.[33] To organise the draft in the above manner therefore necessitates the drafter looking at things from the reader's perspective. Related materials ought to be put together, for if the readers can see a pattern in the drafter's writing of the law, they can easily comprehend the law. This kind of skill requires the ability to identify and place material in a coherent manner, which does not come naturally.

Hence, with a well thoughtout plan, the drafter can develop the right structure for a particular legislative proposal to achieve clarity. Things such as tables of contents, arrangement clauses and the use of short sentences can thus be used to design a simple and clear layout of the legislative proposal and, in so doing, enhance clarity.

4. When clarity is difficult to attain

Drafters attempt to express propositions in any clear logical manner but how this is achieved will differ depending on the nature of the proposition that needs to be expressed.[34] Asprey rightly observes that plain language can be used to express highly technical or complex concepts far more effectively than drafting using 'legalese' language because it does not ban the use of technical terms completely.[35] However, sometimes the drafter cannot draft a law any more clearly. Some of the instances in which it might be impossible to achieve clarity are when writing the law in a subject that is complex such that any attempt to use plain language might lead to loss of intended meaning. Matters of taxation and highly specialised disciplines such as those in the sciences are but some examples to show that a drafter might not make it any clearer in the law.

The pursuit of clarity by a drafter may be difficult to attain when the policy is being used to cover political disagreements, thus the makers of the policy may decide to utilise ambiguity purposely. In this case the drafter not being a policy-maker can only advise the instructing officials of the implications of the legislative measure. Whether the advice is taken or not is not for the drafter to be blamed. In addition, sometimes when a problem cannot be resolved by departmental legal officers and the drafter, then the available option can be the use of an intransitive Bill, which will give way a ministerial regulation by delegation.

---

[32]See n 16 at 92.
[33]See n 16 at 95, where Asprey notes that in any legislation, the most important thing is what the law is about, the behaviour it seeks to regulate.
[34]H Rogers, 'Drafting Legislation at the Tax Law Rewrite Project' in C Stefanou and H Xanthaki (eds) *Drafting Legislation: A Modern Approach* (Ashgate-Dartmouth, Aldershot 2008) 80.
[35]See n 16 at 14.

5. Conclusion

The pursuit of clarity is a worthwhile pursuit for the drafter because of the onerous task they do; that is, writing law that will affect all facets and aspects of life one way or another. Legislation is increasingly being used to regulate the behaviour of society by those elected to govern and make laws. Therefore, since the citizens are expected to abide by the laws that are being made, it is right that the law itself should be predictable so as to create some form of stability. Clarity in legislation is just one aspect that can be used to make the law predictable, clear and easy to understand.

This paper set out to prove the fact that the pursuit of clarity in drafting legislation much as it is often difficult to attain is a fruitful pursuit. Clarity was defined in simple terms to mean the state of or quality of being clear and easily perceived or understood.[36] The important role that the drafter plays in the quest for clarity in legislation was emphasised, for the drafter uses skills that can make laws clearer to understand. Based on this fact, an examination of tools that can be used to achieve clarity was made, with more focus being placed on the use of plain language, gender-neutral language and the proper structuring or layout of the legislative intent to enhance clarity. Indeed, all this should be done bearing in mind the readers of the law. Craies notes that when dealing with a relatively simple concept and imposing rules of relative simplicity, the draftsman ought to draft in a manner which will be easily penetrable by one class of readers. However, when writing on matters of technical, complex subjects, the pursuit of clarity will be achieved in so far as the target reader is indentified. Therefore, there is no hierarchy between clarity, precision and unambiguity because depending on what the drafter is working on, some laws require one of them more than the other.[37] What matters is for the drafter to achieve effectiveness of the law. Clarity, precision and unambiguity must be observed as tool to achieve effectiveness and should be viewed at an equal footing.[38]

Notes on contributor

Alain Songa Gashabizi is a lawyer who is working with the Ministry of Justice of Rwanda as a principal state attorney in charge of Legislative Drafting. He has a master's degree in Legislative Drafting obtained in 2011 at the University of London, School of Advanced Studies. He studied law at Butare University in Rwanda. In the past, he has worked in different departments of the Ministry of Justice. He started his law career in 2002 as a legal adviser in the European Union projects in the said Ministry, where he was in charge of assessing and reporting on the justice situation in Rwanda. After that, in 2006, he served as a Legal Consultant in Legislative Drafting Services with main duties of drafting bills and coordinating the drafting of national legislation. He published an article in the *European Law Journal* in March 2012 entitled: 'The Challenges of Rwandan drafters in the drafting process for Good Quality Legislation'. Since 2011, he has been among legal experts of the East African Community who are negotiating the EPA EAC-EU agreement with the European Union.

---

[36]Note 7.

[37]H Xanthaki, 'On Transferability of Legislative Solutions: The Functionality Test' in C Stefanou and H Xanthaki (eds), *Drafting Legislation: A Modern Approach* (Ashgate-Dartmouth, Aldershot 2008) at 11.

[38]Joseph Kimble, 'Answering the Critics of Plain Language' <http://www.plainlanguagenetwork.org/kimble/critics.htm>, observes that most of the time clarity and precision are complimentary goals, thus drafters do not have to choose between precision and plain language and that when the drafter aims for both, the drafter will usually improve on both.

Plain language: give it a try!

Noor Azlina Hashim

Attorney General's Chambers, Drafting Division, Level 6, 10 & 12, No. 45, Lot 4G7, Persiaran Perdana, Precinct 4, Federal Government Administrative Centre, Putrajaya 62100, Malaysia

> The importance of plain language is acknowledged in various fields including legislative drafting. In Malaysia, although plain language drafting is not a new idea, it is rarely attempted. Many provisions of legislation still portray verbosity and complexity. This article intends to focus on Malaysian legislation, in particular the enforcement provisions, which are still drafted in a complex and verbose way, and to prove that writing enforcement provisions in plain language is possible and can be done.

1. Introduction

> Even in the super-technological 21st century with its high-speed broadband Internet, global satellite connectivity, and wireless cellular communications, there is still a need for clearer, simpler, and more understandable communication.[1]

Over the years, the importance of plain language has been acknowledged in various fields, including legislative drafting. The issue of using plain language in legislation has become a central point of argument amongst legal practitioners, mainly on its advantages, disadvantages and extent. Various views on the use of plain language in legislation have been voiced, either supporting or condemning it. Nevertheless, many drafting offices in Commonwealth countries have now started experimenting using plain language drafting.[2]

In Malaysia, although plain language drafting is not a new idea, it is rarely attempted. Many provisions of legislation still portray verbosity and complexity. The question is, can plain language drafting be done in Malaysia? It is not the aim of this article to discuss in length the plain language subject. This article intends to focus on Malaysian legislation, in particular the enforcement provisions, which are still drafted in a complex and verbose way. The objective of this article is to prove that writing enforcement provisions in plain language is possible and can be done. In fact, this article will show later that enforcement provisions in legislation will be more effective using plain language.

---

[1]Bernard Bekink and Christo Botha, 'Aspects of Legislative Drafting: Some South African Realities (or Plain Language is Not Always Plain Sailing)' (2007) 1 SLR 34.
[2]Ruth Sullivan, 'Some Implications of Plain Language Drafting' [2001] 22 SLR 145 <http://www.lexisnexis.com> accessed 23 January 2011.

To begin with, this article will briefly discuss the meaning of plain language. Then, it will explain the importance of using plain language in legislation. After that, it will look into the current practice of Malaysian drafters when drafting enforcement provisions. This is done by taking examples from various existing legislation. The enforcement provisions gathered, to a certain extent, will indicate whether drafters follow or deviate from the practice. If the provisions are more or less similar, it means that drafters, for some reason, are still reluctant to change the style and follow the old way when drafting enforcement provisions. Next, this article will attempt to rewrite the provisions in question. This rewriting exercise of the actual provisions can, in fact, be considered as the objective of this article. However, this rewriting is selective and based on a representative case study only so that the aim of this article can be achieved and concluded. To do the rewriting, this article will use one section of enforcement provision and apply certain rules on plain language laid down by plain language scholars and proponents. In the end, this article will show and conclude that drafting enforcement provisions in plain language can be done. In fact, it will make the provisions more readable and comprehensible, and at the same time it will contribute towards the effectiveness of legislation.

2. Definition

> Plain language is language which is direct and straightforward. It is designed to deliver its message to its intended readers clearly, effectively and without fuss.[3]

Before defining what plain language is, it is noteworthy to explain the difference between the term 'plain language' and 'plain English'. Plain language is a broader term compared to plain English.[4] While plain English specifically deals with one particular language, which is English, plain language may encompass any type of language, including design, layout and charts.[5] Taking into consideration that Malaysian legislation is drafted in the English and Malay languages, the term plain language is more appropriate to be used in the Malaysian context. But, for the purpose of this article, plain English is to be considered part of plain language and be used interchangeably.

According to Professor Robert D Eagleson,

> plain English is clear, straightforward expression, using only as many words as are necessary. It is language that avoids obscurity, inflated vocabulary and convoluted sentence construction. It is not baby talk, nor is it a simplified version of the English language. Writers of plain English let their audience concentrate on the

---

[3] *Plain Language and Legislation* (2006) at ch 1. Online publication of the Scottish Government <http://www.scotland.gov.uk/Publications/2006/02/17093804/1> accessed 22 April 2011.
[4] See Helen Xanthaki, 'On Transferability of Legislative Solutions: The Functionality Test' in Constantin Stefanou and Helen Xanthaki (eds), *Drafting Legislation: A Modern Approach* (Ashgate, Aldershot 2008).
[5] Ibid.

message instead of being distracted by complicated language. They make sure that their audience understands the message easily.[6]

Likewise, Bryan Garner claimed that plain English can be achieved by using 'the simplest, most straightforward way of expressing an idea'.[7] Plain English is not an exaggerated and flashy language but should not be a dull and boring language.[8]

So, in simple terms, plain English drafting is legislation drafted using simple, clear, straightforward and uncomplicated language in such a way that readers can easily read and understand it. But, plain language is not only about language. It also extends to design and layout.[9]

One would then wonder about the importance and the significance of the extension of plain language and its connection to drafting. There are several answers to the question, but to the writer the most important reason is 'the rule of law'. As legislation affects the rights and interest of the people, so the people themselves must understand the rules behind the legislation.[10] This is very important because ignorance of the law is not an excuse ('Ignorantia juris non excusat'). It is terrible if the reason for people being ignorant is because of the complexity, difficulty and alien phrases and words used in the laws. For the people to understand the rules, legislation must be written in the most comprehensible way and in a simple and plain language; thereby the rules of law will be maintained. It is also important to note that plain language is a very useful tool for clarity, precision and unambiguity and thus, may contribute to efficiency, effectiveness and efficacy of legislation.[11]

There are some critiques on plain language, especially as to readership, inelegance and so forth, but it is not the scope of this article to discuss further on those points.

3. Current practice in Malaysia

It is a known fact that the traditional style of English laws maintains a high quality of literature which is complex and verbose. As Malaysia was a former colony of Britain, its legislation is very much influenced by these English laws. The drafters have to use this model of legislation as a model and precedent. Eventually, they get used to it, become comfortable and feel good with it.

In the Malaysian context, where drafting legislation is done in two languages, the plain language movement is not as impressive as in English speaking or other Commonwealth countries. Indeed, it is not wrong to claim that no such movement exists in Malaysia. Although plain language should not be confined only to English, for some reason it seems that plain language means plain

---

[6] See Robert D Eagleson, *Writing in Plain English* (Commonwealth of Australia, Australia 1990) 4.
[7] See Bryan Garner, *Legal Writing in Plain English* (University of Chicago Press, Chicago 2001) xiv.
[8] Ibid.
[9] Xanthaki (n 4) 13.
[10] See *Merkur Island Shipping Corp v Laughton* [1983] 2 WLR 45.
[11] Xanthaki (n 4) 12.

English language. However, as for Malaysian legislation, poor awareness and ignorance about the influence and importance of language in legislation might be contributory factors as to why the traditional ways of drafting are still being used and maintained. Or perhaps, it is also due to negative perception or misconception that makes the drafters hesitate from trying plain language in drafting.

In respect of enforcement provisions, from 2007 to 2011, there were 17 Bills passed with enforcement provisions.[12] A study on three common provisions from those Acts which are search with warrant, list of things seized and forfeiture of things seized, shows that 14 Acts (subject to their respective subject matters) provide similar wordings of provisions.

The fact that similar wordings have been used for similar provisions in different Acts shows the practice of 'copy and paste', i.e. copying from precedence and pasting to new laws. It also shows that no attempt has been made to simplify them. These provisions, which have been used frequently if needed, if provided in an Act indicate that the drafters like to play it safe. They just follow whatever provisions have been passed and never been questioned in courts. They think this practice can avoid a wrong impression if the same provisions were drafted in a completely new style which may convey different ideas and meanings from those old provisions.[13]

4. Rewriting and analysis

To begin with, this article has chosen the forfeiture section extracted from the Wildlife Conservation Act 2011[14] (however, not all provisions in the section will be rewritten). As has been said before, this provision has also been used in other Acts – except for the subject matter's dissimilarity. Table 1 shows an analysis of the original provisions and the suggested rewriting.

The original provision shows the typical way of traditional drafting, i.e. definite, detailed and exhaustive. Precision is good but at the same time may create loopholes.[15] In this case, the drafter tried to list all things that have probably been seized, but, at the end of the list, the word 'thing' was included, which in its ordinary meaning would cover all of the things listed before it. Perhaps this is due to the fear that something might be omitted unintentionally and therefore a general word that may cover anything is included.

Another point is the use of the word 'shall'. Great discussion and criticisms have been made about its use. It is a long standing notion that 'shall' is for imperative mood, but this word could cause ambiguity as it could be a future statement as well.[16] In this case, if the Malay translation is applied, it gets worse because the Malay translation for the word 'shall' is 'boleh', which is equivalent to 'may' in English. Thus, it causes more ambiguity when the Malay language is the authoritative text.

---

[12]See Annex 1.
[13]ML Turnbull, 'Clear Legislative Drafting: New Approaches in Australia' (1990) 11 SLR 161, 165.
[14]See Annex 2 for complete section.
[15]See Xanthaki (n 4) 10.
[16]Plain Language and Legislation (n 3) 35.

Table 1. Example of an original provision and the suggested rewriting.

Original provision Forfeiture of wildlife, etc. seized	Rewriting
(1) Any wildlife, part or derivative of any wildlife, snare, trap, bait, poisoned bait, arms, conveyance, book, record, document or *thing seized* in the exercise of any powers under this Act *shall be liable* to forfeiture.	Any thing seized is liable to forfeiture.

To the writer, listing all things seized is absolutely unnecessary. The disadvantage of doing this is that it would cause confusion and definitely embarrassment if in any case the drafter omits something listed in the list unintentionally. For comprehensibility and readability of the provision, removal of unnecessary words is helpful.[17] The new provision proposed is simpler, shorter and easier to read and understand. The way it is drafted is effective and efficient. Table 2 shows other examples of the original provisions and the suggested rewriting.

As can be seen from the tables, the original provisions are obviously long and verbose. Verbosity is the enemy of clarity.[18] And as expected from traditional legal drafting, a long provision has only one full-stop and words are used superfluously and unnecessarily. These 'long slabs of unbroken text' are usually complicated and difficult to understand.[19] It is evident when reading the original provisions. Not only are they difficult to understand, but the way they are presented is not appealing to the eye, thus giving an instant negative impression to the readers. It is also worth mentioning that in practise, when people read a long sentence, they tend to forget the beginning when they reach the end of it. Not to mention when so many alien words are being used! Again, the word 'shall' is being used throughout the provisions.

Another point is 'stuffing' the sentences, which means that there is more than one rule stuffed into each provision. To ensure clarity and avoid ambiguity, a legislative sentence should not contain more than one idea.[20] Stuffing or packing so many rules into a provision would lead to loss of certainty.[21] As can be seen from those provisions, they have more than one rule in each provision. And to make it worse, in some provisions, the rules themselves are not orderly.

Thus, to rewrite the provisions, the writer breaks down the sentences of the provisions into short sentences.[22] This would give an instant signal to the readers

---

[17] Robert J Martineau and Michael B Salerno, *Legal, Legislative, and Rule Drafting in Plain English* (Thomson/West, USA 2005) 53.
[18] Edwin Tanner, 'Clear, Simple and Precise Legislative Drafting: Australian guidelines Explicated Using an EC Directive' (2004) 3 SLR 223, 243.
[19] Ibid. at 226. See also Butt and Castle, *Modern Legal Drafting: A Guide to Using Clearer Language* (Cambridge University Press, Cambridge 2001) at 138.
[20] Ann Seidman, Robert B Seidman and Nalin Abeyesekere, *Legislative Drafting for Democratic Social Change: A Manual for Drafters* (Kluwer Law International, London, The Hague, Boston 2001) 269.
[21] Mary Arden DBE, 'The Impact of Judicial Interpretation on Legislative Drafting' (August 2008) The Loophole.
[22] See Tanner (n 18), see also Butt and Castle (n 19).

Table 2. Examples of the other original provisions and the suggested rewriting.

Original provision Forfeiture of wildlife, etc. seized	Rewriting

(2) An order for the forfeiture of any wildlife, part or derivative of any wildlife, snare, trap, bait, poisoned bait, arms, conveyance, book, record, document or thing seized and liable to forfeiture under this Act shall be made by the court before which the prosecution with regard thereto has been held and an order for the forfeiture of the things seized shall be made if it is proved to the satisfaction of the court that an offence under this Act or any of its subsidiary legislation has been committed and that the wildlife, part or derivative of any wildlife, snare, trap, bait, poisoned bait, arms, conveyance, book, record, document or thing was the subject matter of or was used in the commission of the offence, even though no person has been convicted of such offence.	(a) Only the court before which the prosecution regarding the things seized has been held may make a forfeiture order.
	(b) The court must make the order when the court is satisfied that:
	  (i) an offence is committed;
	  (ii) the things seized were the subject matter of the offence or have been used in the commission of the offence, regardless of no person is convicted.

(3) If there is no prosecution with regard to any wildlife, part or derivative of any wildlife, snare, trap, bait, poisoned bait, arms, conveyance, book, record, document or thing seized under this Act, such wildlife, part or derivative of any wildlife, snare, trap, bait, poisoned bait, arms, conveyance, book, record, document or thing shall be taken and deemed to be forfeited at the expiration of a period of one calendar month from the date of service of a notice to the last-known address of the person from whom the wildlife, part or derivative of any wildlife, snare, trap, bait, poisoned bait, arms, conveyance, book, record, document or thing was seized indicating that there is no prosecution in respect of such wildlife, part or derivative of any wildlife, snare, trap, bait, poisoned bait, arms, conveyance, book, record, document or thing, unless before the expiration of that period a claim to it is made in the manner set out in subsections (4), (5), (6) and (7).	(a) This subsection applies when no prosecution about any thing seized is made. (b) A notice stating about the non-prosecution must be given to the last-known address of the person from whom the thing is seized. (c) Unless a claim under subsection (4) is received, the thing seized will be taken and regarded as forfeited at the end of one month from the date of service of the notice.

(*Continued*)

Table 2. (*Continued*)

Original provision Forfeiture of wildlife, etc. seized	Rewriting
(4) Any person asserting that he is the owner of the wildlife, part or derivative of any wildlife, snare, trap, bait, poisoned bait, arms, conveyance, book, record, document or thing referred to in subsection (3) and that the wildlife, part or derivative of any wildlife, snare, trap, bait, poisoned bait, arms, conveyance, book, record, document or thing is not liable to forfeiture may personally or by his agent authorised in writing, give written notice to the enforcement officer in whose possession such wildlife, part or derivative of any wildlife, snare, trap, bait, poisoned bait, arms, conveyance, book, record, document or thing is held that he claims the wildlife, part or derivative of any wildlife, snare, trap, bait, poisoned bait, arms, conveyance, book, record, document or thing.	(a) This subsection applies to a claim of person who asserts as owner of thing seized and that the thing is not liable to forfeiture. (b) The person or the person's agent authorized in writing may make the claim. (c) To make the claim, a written notice must be given to the enforcement officer who is holding the thing in custody.
(7) If it is proved that an offence under this Act or any of its subsidiary legislation has been committed and that such wildlife, part or derivative of any wildlife, snare, trap, bait, poisoned bait, arms, conveyance, book, record, document or thing referred to in subsection (6) was the subject matter of or was used in the commission of such offence, the Magistrate shall order the wildlife, part or derivative of any wildlife, snare, trap, bait, poisoned bait, arms, conveyance, book, record, document or thing to be forfeited, and shall, in the absence of such proof, order its release.	(a) If an offence is proved and the thing seized was the subject matter of the offence, the Magistrate must order the thing to be forfeited. (b) If no offence proved, the Magistrate must order for its release.

that the provisions are easy to be read and understand.[23] By separating each rule in different sentences and paragraphing the whole provisions, it would make the provisions neater and structured, resulting in comprehensible and efficient provisions.[24] Short sentences and paragraphing are helpful tools of plain language that ensure effectiveness. The writer should also avoid sexist language and use gender neutral language, which would help to enhance accuracy[25] and avoid confusion.

---

[23]Ian McLeod, *Principles of Legislative and Regulatory Drafting* (Hart Publishing, Oxford and Portland, OR 2009) 72.
[24]Martineau (n 17) 60.
[25]See Xanthaki (n 4) 15.

The word 'shall' is substituted with the word 'must'[26] – since the equivalent word in the Malay text is 'hendaklah', which indicates obligation.

5. Conclusion

First and foremost, legislation is communication. The main goal of communication is effectiveness.[27] Communication involves the transfer of a message from the sender to the receiver. The transfer is effective and successful when the reader understands and responds to the message.[28] One of the most serious obstructions to effective communication is language, i.e. when the language of the transmitter cannot be understood by the receiver.[29] The nature of language and how it is presented and used often lead to confusion and misunderstanding. And all of these principles also apply to drafting legislation.

One must be fully aware that legislation must have the intended legal effect. Many thoughts and critiques have been made to plain language drafting. For them, who advocate plain language, it is claimed that plain language drafting promotes effectiveness and efficiency of legislation.[30] On the other hand, plain language opponents have argued that plain language drafting is inelegant, unsophisticated,[31] anti-intellectual and could jeopardise precision.[32]

To the writer, legislative drafting is not a work of literature. Legislation is drafted to achieve a specific goal. How the goal is to be achieved is subject to the intelligence and creativity of the drafter to put the language together in the most effective way. If plain language can be used to achieve that goal, why shouldn't the drafters change to plain language drafting? So long as it serves the purpose and effectiveness of legislation and does not raise ambiguity, the writer is in favour of plain language. Plain language drafting intends to express legislation as simply and clearly as possible, without sacrificing its main goal and objective. That means that legislation is not only written simply and clearly but it also reflects legally effective statements.[33]

From the rewriting exercise, this article has proved that drafting enforcement provisions in plain language can be done and, in fact, they are more readable and comprehensible. All it needs is courage, skill and habit. It is asserted that plain language skills will develop with practice and will improve as long as we continue to write.[34] It is like the old saying goes: 'practice makes perfect'. So, the Malay-

---

[26] The use of 'must' is gaining momentum as substitute for 'shall'. See Plain Language and Legislation (n 3) 35.
[27] Clarice Pennebaker Brantley, and Michele Goulet Miller, *Effective Communication for Colleges* (Thompson, South Western, USA 2007) 4.
[28] Ibid.
[29] Herbert A Simon, Victor A Thompson and Donald W Smithburg, *Public Administration* (4th printing, Transactions Publisher, New Jersy 2010) 229.
[30] See Xanthaki (n 4) 13.
[31] *Plain Language and Legislation* (n 3) 4.
[32] See Briant Hunt, 'Plain Language in Legislative Drafting: Is it Really the Answer' (2002) 23 SLR 24.
[33] Anthony Watson-Brown, 'Defining "Plain English" as an Aid to Legal Drafting' (2009) 2 SLR 85, 86.
[34] Michèle M Asprey, *Plain Language for Lawyers* (3rd edn Federation Press, Sydney 2003) 12–13.

sian drafters have to change their habits of depending on precedence as this would be a great barrier to modern legislation.[35] Language has evolved and is still evolving; the public perception towards legislation has gradually changed. People demand more from the drafters to write legislation comprehensibly for them.[36]

From the exercise, the writer, being a legislative drafter, also found that the enforcement provisions are somehow confusing and complicated and realised that the provisions are not effectively drafted. If a drafter cannot understand the provisions, how can laypersons be expected to do so? So it is about time to change and do not hesitate to give it a try. Plain language drafting is worth trying as long as it does not sacrifice completeness and precision. At the end of the day, the effectiveness of legislation is all that matters.

Notes on Contributor

Noor Azlina Hashim holds an LL.B (Hons) degree from the National University of Malaysia and an LL.M in Advanced Legislative Studies from the School of Advanced Legal Studies, University of London. She is a Senior Assistant Parliamentary Draftsman in the Drafting Division of the Attorney General's Chambers of Malaysia and has served the Division since 2003.

---

[35] *Plain Language and Legislation* (n 3) 10.
[36] Asprey (n 34), 3.

Appendix 1

Section \ Act	Price Control and Anti-Profiteering 2011	Wildlife Conservation Act 2011	Competition Act 2010	Personal Data Protection Act 2010	Credit Reporting Agencies Act 2010	Strategic Act 2010
Search with warrant	29	94	25	113	44	-
List of things seized	34	103	29	117	48	**35**
Forfeiture	35	110	-	125	56	**43**

Section \ Act	Land Public Transport Act 2010	Feed Act 2009	National Kenaf and Tobacco Board Act 2009	International Trade on Endangered Species Act 2008	Malaysian Anti-Corruption Commission Act 2009	Malaysian Biofuel Industry Act 2007
Search with warrant	218	24	58	23	**41**	20
List of things seized	222	29	64	-	-	26
Forfeiture	227	40	70	34	**40/41**	32

Section \ Act	Biosafety Act 2007	Pathology Laboratory Act 2007	Solid Waste and Public Cleansing Management Act 2007	Anti-Trafficking in Person Act 2007	Youth Society and Youth Development Act 2007
Search with warrant	40	54	81	30	**108/109**
List of things seized	43	57	85	33	-
Forfeiture	45	64	90	36	-

Note: Numbers in bold indicate that the provisions are not similar.

Drafting and plain language

Augustin Mico

Rwanda Parliament/Chamber of Deputies, PO Box 352, Kigali, Rwanda

> Producing law which is clear and easily accessible to the reader is a priority for the drafter. Thus, the use of plain language is one key issue which can help to improve clarity in drafting law. It can make the law much easier to understand and can maintain good standards. At the level of structure, plain language drafters try to organise laws in a clear and meaningful way. If everybody decides to use language in any way he or she likes, it would be impossible to meet the requirements of every listener and reader.

Introduction

My hypothesis is as follows: the use of plain language in drafting legislation is essential to achieve clarity. The methodology followed to prove my hypothesis is that the use of plain language in drafting legislation is essential to achieve clarity the in way that it helps to avoid long and complicated sentences, it uses shorter and well-constructed sentences by retaining only that which is essential, it organises legislative and legal documents in logical manner and it uses words and expressions that are familiar to everyone. The preferred approach is to focus more deeply on the use of plain language in improving clarity and how plain language is used and its benefits. In addition, I will use arguments put forward by different legal experts and legal professionals.

Plain language and clarity in drafting

Plain language advocates have never been unanimous on the definition of plain language[1] and clarity.[2] Plain language is defined in different ways, but for the purpose of my work it is a consistency with modern attempts to write legislation clearly.[3] It is just the practice of writing English, or any other language, in a simple and clear style.[4] Clarity can be defined as the 'state or quality of being clear and easily perceived or understood. Clarity depends on the proper selection of

---

[1] Dr Janice Redish, 'Defining Plain English' (January 1997) (38) Clarity 30.
[2] Jack Stark, 'Should the Main Goal of Statutory Drafting Be Accuracy or Clarity?' (1994) 15(3) Stat LR 207.
[3] Anthony Watson Brown, 'Defining Plain English as an Aid to Legal Drafting' (2009) 30 (2) Stat LR 91.
[4] Michèle M Asprey, *Plain Language for Lawyers* (3rd edn The Federation Press, Annandale 2003) 11.

words, on their arrangement and on the construction of sentences. Clarity in the language of the law enhances understanding and transparency of legislation'.[5]

Plain language combines content and format to create documents that can be understood by anybody. It is the language of the law and a bridge between the audience and the legislation. It is an approach which helps readers to understand what they are reading. It is language which is not complicated, but is clear and effective[6]; it has been used with success to transform complex thoughts into a format that is accessible by all.[7] Plain language is intended to be just and precise in comparison with traditional drafting[8] and at the level of syntax it creates sentences that are easy for the average person to understand.[9]

Plain language will avoid legislative sentences which are very long, because readers are not able to understand the meaning from what they have just read. Such sentences contain ideas that readers can understand when they reach the end of the sentence, and relate to the ideas that the sentence contains.[10] Plain language consists of only one syllable words and one clause sentences; it is not simplified or reduced English, it is the opposite of obscure language in that it seeks to have the language and the message understood at the first reading. It is clear, straightforward language for an audience.[11]

Applying plain language to legal writing can create a revolution in the way documents, forms, regulations and even statutes are drafted. This approach to legal writing creates documents that are written in language that is appropriate for the needs of the reader, and the purpose of the document is designed so that information can be easily located, understood at the first reading and is legally binding. Drafting should be a focus: technical knowledge of a special kind that unites many minds to produce a unity of thought ennunciated as a command or communication.[12]

Drafting in plain language does not require the use of a specialised language, but uses the same language as in other kinds of formal writing for the purpose of achieving clarity. Most legislative sentences are addressed directly to particular persons or groups of persons, and this needs to be done in a clear and consistent way.[13] The whole purpose is to take what appears long and complicated and

---

[5]Helen Xanthaki, 'On Transferability of Legislative Solutions: The Functionality Test' in Constantin Stefanou and Helen Xanthaki (eds), *Drafting Legislation: A Modern Approach* (Ashgate, Aldershot 2008) 1.
[6]Peter Butt and Richard Castle, *Modern Legal Drafting: A Guide to Using Clearer Language* (2nd edn Cambridge University Press, Cambridge 2006) 113.
[7]Gail S Dykstra, 'Plain Language, Legal Documents and Forms' (September 1988) 2(2) The Loophole 6.
[8]Ian Turnbull, 'Plain Language and Drafting in General Principles' (July 1995) The Loophole 29.
[9]J Paul Salembier, *Legal and Legislative Drafting* (LexisNexis, Canada 2009) 409.
[10]Duncan Berry, 'Reducing The Complexity of Legislative Sentences' (January 2009) (1) The Loophole 37.
[11]Robert D Eagleson, 'Efficiency in Legal Drafting' (October 1989) 2(5), The Loophole 19.
[12]VCRAC Crabbe, 'The Ethics of Legislative Drafting' (2010) 36(1) CL Bull, Routledge 11.
[13]Roger Rose, 'The Language of the Law: How do we Need to Use Language in Drafting Legislation?' (2011) (3) The Loophole 4.

reduce it to what is concise and clear.[14] Plain language is not rigid; one of its advantages is that it is flexible for all.[15] Modern drafting contract and form design techniques all need the use of plain language, and the readers always take priority in it.[16]

Clarity is one of the requirements for accessibility of laws.[17] It is better to abandon the use of Latin and jargon because the average reader will not understand them and they only have value when used between professionals. Jargon may be acceptable in a document that a lawyer drafts only for another lawyer.[18] Clarity of expression is more likely to produce clarity of thought[19] and is correctly used to transmit the meaning for rapid comprehension.[20] For instance, it is not easy to read and understand a sentence which has 232 words such as Section 3 (1) of the Charitable Trusts Act 1957.[21] For a long sentence like this, the use of the tool of plain language for improving clarity is necessary. There is a need to break this long sentence into a number of paragraphs to make it easy to read and understand.

Plain language is clear and uses straightforward expressions and only that which is necessary. It is language that avoids obscurity, extensive vocabulary and complicated sentences. It is neither baby talk nor a simplified version of language. Plain words are eternally fresh and fit. More than that, they are capable of great power and dignity.[22] The use of plain English will give clear statements[23] in a manner which makes it as easy as possible for people to understand what it is intended.[24]

Principles that govern drafting require that a legislative counsel ensures clarity and avoids ambiguity, archaic language, complex grammatical structures, long sentences and punctuation that make the sentence incomprehensible. Clarity is preferred at all times, even if this may result in long sentences.[25] Plain language is not only for drafters, as it helps people know and appreciate the message of law and attempts to provide access to information on the law through legal aid, public legal education activities, government information services, advocacy services and volunteer efforts.[26]

---

[14] Robert J Martineau and Michael B Salerno, *Legal, Legislative, and Rule Drafting in Plain English* (Thomson/West, 2005) 11.
[15] Ibid., 12.
[16] Dykstra (n 7) 8.
[17] New Zealand Law Commission, *Presentation of New Zealand Statute Law* (Wellington, 2008) 42.
[18] Mark Adler, 'In Support of Plain Law: An Answer to Francis Bennion' (2008) (1) The Loophole 26.
[19] Martineau and Salerno (n 14) 10.
[20] Watson Brown (n 3) 207.
[21] JF Burrows and RI Carter, *Statute Law in New Zealand* (4th edn LexisNexis, 2009) 107.
[22] Adler (n 18) 28.
[23] Watson Brown (n 3) 85.
[24] Daniel Greenberg, 'The Three Myths of Plain English Drafting' (Special Issue, 2011) The Loophole 107.
[25] Fredrick Ruhindi, 'The Need for Simplicity in Legislation and Challenges in its Attainment' (2009) The Loophole 14.
[26] Adler (n 22) 24.

Plain English has brought the general public back into the line of the writer, reminding us again of the ethical dimension of writing. Documents are not fair if they cannot be understood by stakeholders who have to use them.[27] When claiming that your document is in plain language, your intended audience must be able to find that they understand it to fulfil their purpose. When the writer decides to use an uncommon technical word, it is because the reader is familiar with it and there is no substitute for that word, or the word is the shorter version of a complicated one, and if the reader is not a familiar of this word, it will be explained in plain language.[28]

Principles, benefits and critics of plain language
Principles of plain language

Many authors have written about principles, techniques, rules and skills of plain language. 'Mellinkoff lists seven rules; Wydick has eight; Redish recommends six steps; Goldfarb and Raymond describe ten rules to follow'; Robert Dick details 33 rules; the Australian Commonwealth drafting adopts four style strategies.[29] The UK Plain Language Commission lists 15 tips on writing plain English and factors for evaluating plain language,[30] and many other writers have written on plain language. The rules may vary from expert to expert but the principle of using plain language stays the same for many authors.[31] However, according to Anthony Watson Brown, many modern writers perceive plain English or plain language principles as follows: 'clear and simple; appropriate to audience; direct and personal; favours informal language when appropriate; draws on common everyday language; accessible to a wide audience; explains technical words in simple language; attempts to interest readers and hold their attention; relies heavily on simple sentence structures; avoids passive voice; respectful of the reader'.[32]

Some authors have proposed to create a plain language manual and commenting features in Microsoft Word as tools and techniques that are accurate and well organised and written to help in the use of plain language. Some techniques can enhance communication and contribute to the development of a clear, easy and understandable language.[33] Employing plain language features that do not compromise precision will help all classes of reader.[34] Even if all experts had not unanimously agreed on application of plain language principles, many of them agree on the use of plain language. If we consider that there is an observation that plain language can help few citizens, or if only one person can be helped by

---

[27] Dykstra (n 16) 6.
[28] Asprey (n 4) 14.
[29] Turnbull (n 8) 28.
[30] Neil James, 'Setting the Standards: Some Steps Towards a Plain Language Profession' (2008) (59) Clarity 11.
[31] Gail S. Dykstra, 'Plain Language, Legal Documents and Forms' (1988) 2(2) The Loophole 8.
[32] Watson Brown (n 23) 91.
[33] Nad Rosenberg, 'Tools and Techniques for Working with Matter Experts to Create Plain Language Manuals' (2008) (59) Clarity 58.
[34] Salembier (n 9) 491.

its use why shouldn't it be used? Fortunately, results show that plain language is necessary for many users of law: lawyers, judges, political officials and lay persons.

In all countries, there is a principle that law must be accessible to the public, and according to this principle, there is no excuse for ignorance of the law. If the law is not available and accessible to citizens, the principle of accessibility will not be achieved. Governments and states have an interest in the law's accessibility and effectiveness to the entire population, and it cannot happen if the public do not know or do not understand the law. There is a belief that law was reserved only to lawyers and judges but today laws are consulted and used by a large number of people who are not lawyers and have no legal training.[35] It is for that purpose that laws must be clear and easy to read and understand by all users. By using the tool of plain language, law gains clarity, which will help citizens understand the law.

Benefits of plain language

Benefits from plain language are so many: it makes information more accessible, readers are more likely to understand why and how decision are made, there is a huge impact on the quality of working life on all levels and more readers can find out what rights they have.[36] Many plain language promoters have indicated that lawyers also benefit from plain language in that it makes their documents more effective, and in particular saves them time, money and mistakes. The contribution of the plain language movement has been of great significance.[37]

Plain language will contribute to removing existing complaints in different sectors of law namely: legislators, judges, lawyers, teachers and writers of law and it will help to remove complications, darkness and ambiguities in the language style of Acts.[38]

Many organisations such as the Society of Legal Scholars, the Statute Law Society and Clarity are promoting good examples of clear and simple styles of plain language. In the UK, many institutions, in the both the public and the private sectors, instruct experts to draft or redraft codes, regulations and rules in plain language. Courts, tribunals, panels and committees composed totally or mainly of non-lawyers demonstrate the wish and demand for defenders to present their cases simply and clearly in plain language.[39]

The use of plain language will help people in different institutions and companies who refer to legislation in their jobs. Every day lay citizens refer to the law to find responses to challenges that affect them in their personal lives, and internal problems can lead them to consult legislation.[40] There is a tendency to think that the law is a very complicated domain that should be only aimed at for people who have studied law. When an Act is not understood by the majority of

---

[35] Adler (n 18) 22.
[36] Ruth Baldwin, 'Plain Language for Municipalities: Tools and Efforts' (2008) (59) Clarity 48.
[37] Adler (n 18) 19.
[38] Alec Samuels, 'Plain Language in the UK' (2006) (56) Clarity 6.
[39] Ibid.
[40] Adler (n 18) 22.

people it is intended for, the use of plain English will enhance clarity and remove that obscurity.[41]

Critics of plain language

The biggest problem about the utilisation of plain language in legislative drafting is that it works.[42] The truth is that for several reasons, a law can never be written in a way that makes it understandable to a lay-reader and the more it uses plain English the more danger that the lay-reader will be misled into believing that he or she has understood more of it than is actually the case.[43] Many plain language campaigners fail to understand that the goal of a piece of a bill consists in explaining the Act. The fact that legal texts cannot be easily understood by those most affected by them does not necessary lead to a growing ignorance of the law, which can be avoided by ensuring that adequate explanations of the law are available to the public by all means.[44] The plain language movement, through the illusory aim of having law that is directly clear to the lawyer in other words, is fit for everybody.[45]

There is no objective standard of plain language; it has been set by the flow of fashion in the natural use of language outside of the legislative context. It is noticeable that generally the tolerance of readers for sentence length has diminished greatly over the years.[46] It is not that we have discovered a new system of writing in short sentences; it is simply that what amounts to short or long by normal literary standards has changed.[47]

Another mistake made by the plain language movement is that a legal text, even if it has become an Act, is far from being the whole story. Each law is incomplete in itself; it has to be considered in context. This means that no legal text stands alone, it always needs to be read alongside many other laws, and this cannot be achieved by a lay person who does not have a background of law.[48] Even if plain language proponents complain that traditional legal language lacks style, it depends on what they mean by style. One view is that so-called plain language lacks style and learning.[49]

Another problem of plain language campaigners is that they are ignoring the use of legal terms, for example *hereby* and *thereby*, for such terms have an important function in law; more conversational terms should be used in statutes.[50] Plain language causes mistakes in the methodology in the drafting of legal texts and has attracted judicial criticism. The Federal Court of Australia criticised the redrafting in clear English of the Social Security Act 1991 (Cth), which contains

---

[41] Adler (n 18) 25.
[42] Greenberg (n 24) 105.
[43] Ibid.
[44] Francis Bennion, 'Confusion of Plain Language Law' (2010) 19(1) JCLA 61.
[45] Ibid., 62.
[46] Greenberg (n 24) 104.
[47] Ibid.
[48] Francis Bennion, 'Confusion Over Plain Language Law' <http:www.francisbennion.com/topic/plainlanguagelaw.htm> accessed 15 April 2012.
[49] Ibid.
[50] Francis Bennion, 'Confusion of Plain Language Law' (2010) 19(1) JCLA 63.

almost 1400 sections. The court stated that the Act is two or three times longer and is not easier to read. In another Australian case, the appellate court judge criticised the plain language of the Corporation Law as the language of the popular songs. A passage that is plain to the average reader with a wide vocabulary may be opaque to the average reader with a narrow one.[51]

Conclusion

Among many other techniques of enhancing clarity[52] in drafting law, the use of plain language is one which can help to improve clarity in drafting law. Plain language and clarity undoubtedly make the law simple, clear and precise, and this drafting should be the fundamental style in all laws. It can make the law much easier to understand and conduct in a proper manner; it can maintain good standards of clarity and precision.[53] Plain language tries to create a sentence which is very easy to understand for a citizen of medium knowledge. According to specialists, such legal formulation tends to be short, emphasis is on verbs rather than nouns, the active rather than the passive voice, and positive rather than negative sentences to state the intended law.

At the level of structure, plain language drafters try to organise statutes in a clear and meaningful way. There is chronological order, logical order, order of importance or some other principle or combination of principles that is likely to make sense to the reader. The structure of the law is clear through the use of headings and sub-headings, marginal notes, transitions, tables of contents, relevancy and other similar methods.

For the purpose of clarity, if there is no clear line showing how drafters can use plain language which leads to clarity it could lead to chaos if everybody decides to use language in any way he or she likes, and it would be impossible to measure used language to meet the requirements of every listener and reader.[54] For this reason, the use of plain language is strongly needed in drafting legislation. In particular, it is in this line that is advisable for institutions that are dealing most with laws, to take the heavy task of elaborating a manual of plain language that will help people and organisations.

Governments need to adopt guidelines and enact laws that accept and regulate the use of plain language. Even if plain language is broad and many writers have written on it, still it needs to get a clear line of applicability. There is a need for harmonisation of drafting techniques because those that exist are scattered. In order to facilitate drafting, users and communication at all levels to get the intent and the law. Laws that are clear and easy to understand are essential part of an accessible justice system. Clearly written laws can be better understood, respected and implemented.[55]

---

[51] Bennion (n 50) 65.
[52] GC Thornton, *Legislative Drafting* (4th edn Butterworths, 196) 52.
[53] Turnbull (n 8) 35.
[54] Chris Peter, 'A Rant in Favour of Employment and Against Relativism: The Impact of Grammar, Punctuation and Usage on Clarity' (2007) (57) Clarity 18.
[55] Developing Clearer Laws <http:www.ag.gov.au/clearerlaws> accessed 12 April 2012.

Plain language needs to be developed and used even in other official documents.[56] As Daniel Greenberg said, researches on plain language 'should continue the search for ways of presenting law in a manner that makes it as easy as possible for [all users] to understand what it is to mean'. However, research should be conducted in a scientific way so that plain language reaches the level where different experts agree on the use of it.

Notes on contributor
Augustin Mico is legislative drafter and adviser at the Rwanda Parliament/Chamber of Deputies.

---

[56] Anne-Marie Hasselrot, 'What's on in Plain Swedish?' (2006) 55 Clarity 26.

Gender-neutral language: an essential language tool to serve precision, clarity and unambiguity

Kadija Kabba

Legal Officer and Legislative Drafter, Central Bank of Sierra Leone

> This essay is about gender-neutral language as an essential tool that serves precision, clarity and unambiguity, three drafting techniques in achieving effectiveness in regulating society. Scholars and experts, among others, have criticised the use of gender-neutral language in drafting legislations generally, and its unsatisfactory nature for precision, clarity and unambiguity in particular. In light of this, the article focuses on establishing whether the use of gender-neutral language is essential and serves as a tool in achieving precision, clarity and unambiguity. Traditionally, men have been the dominant force and our language has developed in ways that reflect male dominance, sometimes to the total exclusion of women. It is for these reasons that the increase in the use of gender-neutral language has mainly been attributed to the gripe of gender equality in our various societies. However this is not the only reason. This article argues that gender-neutral language is a tool which serves precision, clarity and ambiguity in that it aims to promote gender specificity in the pronoun used when drafting legislation, it reduces and in some cases completely omits redundancies and, in the process, produces shorter sentences which in turn produce clear and unambiguous drafts. It also raises the recognition of the potential for ambiguity and uncertainty in the use of pronouns, especially in sentences with two actors, thus raising doubt over the meaning. Nevertheless, the drafter should never sacrifice clarity, precision or unambiguity for simplicity, elegance or eloquence if clarity, precision and unambiguity achieve effectiveness. And if the tool to achieve them is by the use of gender-neutral language, then by all means they must be used.

1. Introduction

1.1. Aims and objectives

The hypothesis of this article is that gender-neutral language is an essential tool that serves precision, clarity and unambiguity. In order to prove the hypothesis it needs to be established whether gender-neutral language in drafting legislations serves as an essential tool to precision, clarity and unambiguity, three requirements or techniques in achieving effectiveness which is ardently pursued by the drafter in contributing to attain efficacy in regulating society. If this is so, to what extent does it serve as an important tool to precision, clarity and unambiguity? The aim of this article is to prove the above-mentioned hypothesis.

1.2. Methodology and structure

The drafter's job is to transform policy into effective law. Writers, scholars and experts have stated that effectiveness, sought by the drafter, can be achieved through clarity, precision and unambiguity using tools such as plain language and gender-neutral language.[1] The focus of this article is on gender-neutral language and how essential it is as a tool in serving the three techniques of precision, clarity and unambiguity. Other writers, legal professionals and experts, on the other hand, have criticised the use of gender-neutral language in substance and style, and that it lacks specificity and eloquence; hence its unsatisfactory nature to serve precision, clarity and unambiguity in drafting legislation.[2] In light of the above, this research will focus on establishing whether the use of gender-neutral language is essential and serves as a tool in achieving precision, clarity and unambiguity.

In order to prove my hypothesis, I will use arguments put forward by experts, legal professionals and writers in support of the value of gender-neutral language in drafting legislation as against the arguments of critics of the use of gender-neutral language in drafting legislation. The reason for using these arguments to prove my hypothesis is that the recent move towards using gender-neutral language has mainly been attributed to the gripe for gender equality in our various societies. Traditionally, men have been the dominant force and our language has developed in ways which reflect male dominance, sometimes to the total exclusion of women.[3] This may well be the reason for the development and increasing growth in the use of gender-neutral language as a tool in drafting; however some experts and professionals have established how the techniques of gender-neutral drafting serve precision, clarity and unambiguity. In discussing these issues and to establish my hypothesis, I intend to analyse primary and secondary sources in order to draw a valid conclusion.

In section 1, as my introduction, I have stated the aims, objectives, methodology, justification and structure of the article. In section 2, I will briefly define what gender-neutral language is and its purpose in drafting legislation. In this

---

[1] H Thring, *Practical Legislation: The Composition and Language of Acts of Parliament and Business Documents* (John Murray, London 1902); R Dickerson, *The Fundamentals of Legal Drafting* (Little Brown and Company, Boston 1965); R Dickerson (ed), *Materials on Legal Drafting* (St Paul West Publishing Company, St Paul, MN 1981); H Schaffer, *Evaluation and Assessment of Legal Effects Procedures: Towards a more Rational and Responsible Lawmaking Process* (2001) 22 Stat LR 132; D Greenberg, 'The Techniques of Gender-Neutral Drafting' in: C Stefanou and H Xanthaki (eds), *Drafting Legislation: A Modern Approach* (Ashgate, Aldershot) 63–76; P Butt and R Castle, *Modern Legal Language: A Guide to Using Clear Language* (2nd edn CUP, Cambridge 2006); H Xanthaki, *Clarity, Precision and Ambiguity* (Lecture notes Legislative Drafting 2009) <http://studyonline.sas.ac.uk/course/view.php?id=17> accessed 3 March 2010.

[2] WR LaFave and AW Scott, *Criminal Law* (West Publishers Company, St Paul, MN 1986); DT Kobil, 'Do the Paperwork or Die: Clemency, Ohio Style?' (1991) 52 (3) Ohio State LJ 655; KW Graham, Jr and CA Wright, 'Commenting on Gender Neutral Amendments to a Federal Rule of Evidence' (Federal Practice and Procedure, para 5231.1) (Suppl 1998); D Schweikart, 'The Gender Neutral Pronoun Redefined' (1998) 20 (1) Women's Rights Law Report 1.

[3] H Xanthaki, *Gender Neutral Language* (Lecture notes on Legislative Drafting 2009) <http://studyonline.sas.ac.uk/course/view/php?id-17> accessed 2 March 2010.

same section I will further briefly define what precision, clarity and unambiguity are and the relationship between the three concepts in legislation. In section 3, I will put forward the arguments in support of the use of gender-neutral language as an essential tool to serve precision, clarity and unambiguity. Arguments of critics against using gender-neutral language in drafting legislation will be highlighted in this same section. From these viewpoints, in section 4, I will discuss and analyse the importance of gender-neutral language and how it serves as an essential tool to precision, clarity and unambiguity. I will establish my hypothesis with more analyses of the above stated arguments, and conclude with the findings of my hypothesis. I will now go on to define and explain the concept of gender-neutral language in drafting legislation.

2. Definition of concepts

2.1. Description of gender-neutral language

Gender-neutral language refers to language which includes both sexes and treats women and men equally. It is also called non-sexist, non-gender-specific, or inclusive language.[4] Gender-neutral language avoids using male terms to represent women.[5] It is a language that uses a variety of techniques including repetition of the relevant noun, omission of redundant or superfluous phrases, the reorganisation of words or phrases from the active to the passive voice provided it does not create ambiguity,[6] in implementing gender-neutral drafting, the list of techniques being non-exhaustive. The notion of drafting legislation in gender-neutral language is said to have gained momentum due to the recognition by legal professionals, experts and policymakers in various jurisdictions that drafting in 'masculine' language contributes to a large extent to the perpetuation of a society in which men and women see women as lesser beings.[7] The argument against the use of masculine language in drafting is that the general use of masculine nouns and pronouns 'implies that personality is really a male attribute, and that women are a human sub-species'.[8]

The aim of this criticism had been to target the practice of using masculine words to refer to woman. It is in this light that some writers have claimed that gender-neutral language is being adopted to address the criticism that the language of the statute book is chauvinistic. Much as this matter may be the foundation for the development of gender-neutral language in drafting legislation, it is not the only reason. As indicated, gender-neutral language in drafting has for years been the accepted standard in most jurisdictions, for example Australia,

---

[4]Ibid.
[5]S Petersson, 'Gender-neutral Drafting: Recent Commonwealth Developments' (1999) 20 (1) Stat LR 53.
[6]Greenberg (n 1) at 67–75.
[7]Petersson (n 5) at 47.
[8]Articles in Commonwealth Law Bulletin, *Avoidance of Sexiest Language in Legislation* (1985) 11 Commw L Bull 509.

Canada and New Zealand.[9] For the United Kingdom, the Government adopted gender-neutral language drafting in 2007.[10]

2.2. Precision, clarity and unambiguity

Precision is defined as exactness of expression or detail.[11] 'Precision is traditionally viewed as the main aim of common law drafters who make the greatest effort to "say all, to define all": to leave nothing to the imagination: never to presume upon the reader's intelligence.'[12] A word of caution is however given by the Chief Parliamentary counsel in Ireland:

> Precision in drafting is a worthy goal, but can be taken too far. It is frequently unnecessary to name every single thing you are forbidding or requiring. An overzealous attempt at precision may result in redundancy and verbosity. Drafting too precisely may create unintended loopholes.[13]

Clarity is defined as the state or quality of being clear and easily perceived or understood.[14] Clarity is also defined as 'clearness or lucidity as to perception or understanding; freedom from indistinctness or ambiguity.[15] For Thring, clarity or clearness depends on the proper selection of words, on their arrangement and on the construction of sentences.[16] Clarity in the language of the law enhances understanding and transparency of legislation.[17] Butt and Castle recommend that 'legal documents should be written in modern, standard English as currently used and understood'.[18] Domer states that clarity is making draft legislation as easy as possible for your reader to understand what you are saying.[19]

Unambiguity or unambiguous is defined as words or phrases without ambiguity.[20] It simply means the meaning is clear, explicit and unequivocal. Ambiguity, on the other hand, is defined as words having more than one meaning and which can be interpreted in more than one way.[21]

---

[9] Petersson (n 5) at 53.
[10] It was announced in a written ministerial statement made by the leader of the House of Commons at the time (Mr Jack Straw).
[11] C Soanes (ed), *Compact Oxford English Dictionary* (2nd edn OUP, Oxford 2003) 890.
[12] H Xanthaki, 'On Transferability of Legislative Solutions: The Functionality Test' in: C Stefanou and H Xanthaki (eds), *Drafting Legislation: A Modern Approach* (Ashgate, Aldershot 2008) 10.
[13] Ibid 10; Xanthaki (n 1).
[14] Soanes (n 11) at 193.
[15] The Dictionary Reference <http://dictionary.reference.com/browse/clarity> accessed 3 March 2010.
[16] Thring (n 1) at 61.
[17] Xanthaki (n 12) at 9.
[18] Butt and Castle (n 1) at 167.
[19] Lecture by Robin Dormer, Parliamentary Counsel at the Law Commission of the United Kingdom, 6 November 2009, 1.
[20] Soanes (n 11) at 1251.
[21] Dickerson (n 1) at 32–26, 54–7; J Evans, *Statutory Interpretation: Problems of Communication* (OUP, Oxford 1988) 73; Butt and Castle (n 1) at 22; Xanthaki (n 12) at 9; Xanthaki (n 1) at 2; FAR Bennion, *Bennion on Statutory Interpretation: A Code* (5th edn LexisNexis, London 2008) at 444–56.

In juxtaposing the definitions of clarity and unambiguity, one can say that the latter is part of clarity as they share similar characteristics. The relationship between precision, clarity and unambiguity is that they are regarded by many scholars as techniques used for effectiveness, and are requirements for achieving efficacy. As to the question of hierarchy, this depends on the type of legislation that is being drafted, the audience it is drafted for and, more importantly, which of the three techniques serves or achieves effectiveness best.[22] Having described the three concepts and established the relationship between them, one may then ask how does gender-neutral language serve as essential tool?

3. Arguments for the use of gender-neutral language in drafting legislation

3.1. Arguments for the use of gender-neutral language

Gender-neutral language is a tool for accuracy since it aims to promote gender specificity in the pronoun used when drafting legislation.[23] In other words, the use of gender-neutral language in drafting enables the legal language to be more accurate and clear for its readers. Repeating the relevant noun instead of the pronoun 'he' or 'she' avoids ambiguity in sentences especially where there are two actors to whom the pronoun could refer.[24] In using 'he or she' the draft becomes confusing and inelegant, ambiguous and lacking in precision.

The use of gender-neutral language reduces and in some cases completely omits redundancies such as 'if he thinks fit' or 'if he deems it expedient' in legislative drafting and thus promotes precision, clarity and unambiguity.[25] For example, 'If the general thinks fit to do so, having regard to such matters as he thinks appropriate, he may dismiss a corporal'. By using gender-neutral language, this phrase simply becomes 'the general may dismiss a corporal', which is clearer and more precise.

Reorganisation into shorter sentences and the use of the passive voice (in so far as it does not create ambiguity) produces, in most cases, clear and unambiguous drafts.[26] Moreover, the use of gender-neutral language not only alleviates criticism of the legal language being sexist but also eliminates the incomprehensible and verbose language that plagued much legislation in various jurisdictions.[27] Proponents argue that although critics say that gender-neutral drafting does not achieve simplicity and elegance, however, it is said that achieving certainty in terms of precision, clarity and unambiguity must never be sacrificed for simplicity,[28] as achieving effectiveness is the goal of the drafter to regulate society.

---

[22] Xanthaki (n 12) at 11–12.
[23] Ibid. 15.
[24] Thring (n 1) at 82; A Russell, *Legislative Drafting and Forms* (4th edn Butterworth & Co Publishers Ltd, London 1938); WP Statsky, *Legislative Analysis and Drafting* (2nd edn West Publishing Company, St Paul, MN 1984) at 183; Articles in Commonwealth Law Bulletin (n 8) at 591; Petersson (n 5) at 55.
[25] Greenberg (n 1) at 68–9.
[26] Ibid. at 70–71; Statsky (n 24) at 191.
[27] Petersson (n 5) at 57.
[28] A statement made in the 'Renton Report' *The Preparation of Legislation* (Cmnd 6053, 1975) 62.

3.2. Arguments against the use of gender-neutral language

Writers, legal professionals and experts have criticised the use of gender-neutral language from various angles. A substantive complaint is that gender-neutral language creates uncertainty in the law.[29] It is said that gender-neutral drafting distracts readers from its content,[30] and that the use of such language in drafting is not direct.[31] Further criticisms are that gender-neutral language lacks specificity and does not achieve the eloquence sought by drafters; hence it does not serve precision, clarity and unambiguity in drafting legislation.[32] Added to these criticisms, it is argued that the use of gender-neutral language increases the length of the legislation, preventing brevity. It is further highlighted that the increased length of the legislation results in an increase in the cost of legislation.[33] It is in this light that critics of gender-neutral language are advocating for alternative methods of drafting.

4. Gender-neutral language serves as an essential tool to precision, clarity and unambiguity

4.1. The importance of gender-neutral drafting as a tool to achieve precision, clarity and unambiguity

From the arguments raised above, one can deduce that the technique of repeating the relevant noun in place of the pronoun has been in practice for quite some time due to the recognition of the potential for ambiguity and uncertainty in the use of pronouns, especially in sentences with two actors, thus lacking clarity and precision and raising doubt over the meaning. It is in recognition of this fact that Russell stated that:

> If any conceivable ambiguity is caused by the use of a pronoun, 'he', 'him' or 'his', the noun to which it refers should be repeated. A draftsman should never be afraid to repeating a word as often as may be necessary in order to avoid ambiguity.[34]

This counters the argument of critics that the use of gender-neutral drafting creates uncertainty in the law; it is one of the reason that gender-neutral language has gained momentum and is used to alleviate the uncertainty and ambiguity that arise when the pronouns 'he or she' is used.

The repetition of the noun rather than the use of the pronouns is said to increase the length and cost of legislation, and make the text inelegant to read. As reiterated above, the task of the drafter is to achieve effectiveness using the drafting techniques of precision, clarity and unambiguity. Therefore, sacrificing these techniques for simplicity is not the goal of the drafter as such interpretations might lead to litigation, when the use of few extra words might alleviate such litigation and

---

[29] Schweikart (n 2) at 7.
[30] Kobil (n 2) at 664–5.
[31] WR LaFave and AW Scott, *Criminal Law* (West Publishing Company, St Paul, MN 1986) preface; GC Thornton, *Legislative Drafting* (4th edn Tottel Publishing Ltd, London) 60.
[32] Schweikart (n 2) at 7–8.
[33] Greenberg (n 1) at 66–7.
[34] Russell (n 24) at 103.

make the meaning clear. It is in this light that Thring stated that 'nouns should be used in preference to pronouns, even though the noun has to be repeated. Repetition of the same word is never a fault in business composition, if an ambiguity is thereby avoided'.[35] Besides this, the gender-neutral language technique of omitting words and phrases that have become redundant in legislation may in fact reduce the length of the statutes and in the process increase the ease with which the audience may absorb the legislation. Nevertheless, certainty in the law is always preferred to elegance and brevity.

The argument that gender-neutral language lacks specificity is rather vague in that the proper degree of specificity varies from subject area to subject area.[36] For instance, most statues in the penal code are general while most tax statutes are very specific. This is due to the varying nature of both types of statutes, and therefore one can say that no particular level of specificity is clearly appropriate for all statutes. Because of the existence of these variations, the use of gender-neutral language in drafting such legislation is used in so as far as it serves precision, clarity and unambiguity. It is important to state that if it does not achieve these three elements then it must not be used. From the above analysis it can be said that gender-neutral language is an essential tool that serves precision, clarity and unambiguity.

5. Conclusion

What this article attempted to prove is that gender-neutral language is an essential tool to serve precision, clarity and unambiguity. From research done it appears that there are various techniques available to implement gender-neutral language in drafting legislation. However, as with all legislative drafting techniques, there exist certain influential factors that may limit the drafter's application of these techniques. Nevertheless, as has been highlighted above, the guiding principle for the drafter is never to sacrifice clarity, precision or unambiguity for simplicity, elegance or eloquence. More importantly, if the tool to achieve them is by the use of gender-neutral language, then by all means it must be used. It is better to be inelegant than uncertain.[37]

It has been established that the use of gender-neutral language serves not only to eliminate the demeaning nature of gender-specificity in drafting legislation but also to achieve precision, clarity and unambiguity, using the best techniques of the language for the job on each occasion. It is established for instance that the repetition of the noun is better than the slightest chance of ambiguity. It has also been established that clarity takes precedence over elegance and that the drafters' aim is to make their work intelligible, as precise as it can be depending on the law being drafted and as understandable and clear to the audience for whom it is drafted.

In proving the hypothesis, this article has also established the fact that precision, clarity and unambiguity are drafting techniques used by drafters to achieve

---

[35] Thring (n 1) at 82.
[36] Schweikart (n 2) at 7–8.
[37] JK Aitken, *Piesse, The Elements of Drafting* (9th edn The Law Book Company Limited, Sydney 1995) 57.

effectiveness which is the drafter's contribution to efficacy in legislation.[38] It is from these perspectives that one can conclude that gender-neutral language is an essential tool that serves precision, clarity and unambiguity.

Notes on contributor
Kadija Kabba is a Legal Officer and Legislative Drafter at the Central Bank of Sierra Leone. She holds a Masters in Law (LLM) from the University of London, a Masters of Philosophy (MPhil) from the University of Tromsoe, Norway, a Bachelor of Law (LLB) and a Bachelor of Arts (BA) Degree from the University of Sierra Leone. She is also a qualified Barrister and Solicitor of the High Court of Sierra Leone.

---

[38]Xanthaki (n 12) at 17.

Is gender-neutral drafting an effective tool against gender inequality within the legal system?

Venessa Mclean

Office of the Chief Parliamentary Counsel, 2 Oxford Road, Kingston 5, Jamaica

> This article seeks to explore the history of gender-neutral drafting and its purported impact upon deep-rooted gender inequality within the legal system to date. The article draws upon examples that highlight the fact that gender inequality has penetrated deeper into our legal system–deeper than assumed– and contends that it is a fallacy to think that gender-neutral drafting is an effective cure for the disease of patriarchy. The article analyses various pieces of legislation within the context of gender-neutral drafting.

Introduction

Aims and objectives

The hypothesis of this article is that the technique of gender-neutral drafting on its own is not an effective tool in the fight against deep-rooted gender inequality within our legal system. This article seeks to prove that gender inequality has penetrated deeper into our legal system than assumed and that it is a fallacy to think that gender-neutral drafting is an effective cure for the disease of patriarchy.

Methodology and structure

In order to prove my hypothesis, I will use primary and secondary methods to analyse arguments put forward by renowned feminists, experts and writers. The structure I will follow in order to prove my hypothesis is as follows. I will briefly explore the historical background of gender-neutral drafting as a technique. I will then explore the concept of equality in relation to the technique of gender-neutral drafting. I will further analyse the use of the technique of gender-neutral drafting in order to analyse whether or not the use of the technique has penetrated the legal system, thereby creating the perceived gender equality in different areas of law, such as employment, criminal legislation specifically in relation to rape, domestic violence and homicide. I will then draw my conclusion.

Historical background of gender-neutral drafting and the prevailing technique

During the late twentieth century, the question of drafting legislation in the masculine came to light. The context in which the question came to light was that drafting in the masculine promoted social and economic discrimination against women. Sexist language was based on the age-old norms that women are non-persons. Historically, women were exempted from certain duties and, obligations; they were given a special status, which was accorded, due to the belief that they were incapacitated. Francis Power Cobbe[1] wrote that women were no different from criminals, idiots and minors. Therefore, 'men being mentally and morally superior should in justice receive the right to deal with legal matters. This has led to 150 years of sexist language within English language legislative text, whereby he was presumed she. This policy was called the 'Masculine Rule' and emerged in 1827. This policy aborted the use of terms in legislation which made reference to women. By the 1970s, the male dominated language rule met opposition. This led to the adoption of a policy to promote the use of a unisex grammar couched in the terminology of gender-neutral drafting. Thornton makes the following suggestions to get rid of the male pronouns. 'Repeat the noun in place of a pronoun, use his or her in place of his, recast the sentence using the plural, omit the pronoun, replace a nominalisation with a verb form, recast the sentence using a relative clause, and recast the sentence using a participle.' He also suggested that the avoidance of masculine language could be achieved by avoiding demeaning and patronising language.[2]

Has the technique of gender-neutral drafting penetrated the legal system thereby creating the perceived gender equality in different areas of law?

The concept of gender inequality is entrenched in the foundation of every society. It is often said that the family is the foundation of every society and from it flows all other structures including the structure which our legal system follows. From the beginning of the human race, which resulted in the first family, the female specie, Eve, has been blamed for eating the forbidden fruit, tempting the male specie, Adam, and since time immemorial she has been paying for it. In fact, most forms of olden laws which come from religious texts such as the Bible have perpetrated the Masculine Rule in every sense. For example, in the book of Genesis 3:16, the writers of the Bible quoted God as saying that 'the male specie shall rule over the female specie'. This was in my opinion the beginning of the Masculine Rule. The patriarchy in legal drafting started there. The Masculine Rule has been justified by all religions and cultures. As a result, our legal system is based on a male-dominated foundation and has created a caste system, which has resulted in the denial of equality for women, and despite the cosmetic application of gender-neutral legislation, the Masculine Rule is very much alive and well in our legal system.

Has gender-neutral drafting changed the legal definition of equality?

The Oxford Dictionary defines equality as meaning the property of having the same value. When translated in the legislative sense, it is often interpreted as according the same amount of rights to both male and females, which on the

---

[1] (1868).
[2] GC Thornton, *Legislative Drafting* (4th edn Bloomsbury Publishing 1996) 75–7.

face of it seems to solve the problem. The problem with this is that it does not take into consideration the situation that, in order to create equality, it is necessary to give more rights to some persons than others. In the case of women, it may mean creating legislation that pays women more per hour than men, on the basis that they work fewer hours due to child rearing and other socially constructed duties that they are bound to perform. Currently, legislative policy has not been geared towards giving women more because of their status; for example, in the case of personal injury when calculating quantum, women of child bearing age are paid less than men when they have an accident.[3]

Treatment of women as workers

There has been a rise in the twentieth century towards a policy of equality in legislation. This has led to the passing of the Sex Discrimination Act 1975 and the Equal Pay Act 1970. When the UK joined the EEC in 1972, the Equal Pay Act 1970 was already on the statute book. The act enabled workers to claim equal pay to a colleague of the opposite gender if their work was the same or broadly similar. Alongside the Equal Pay Act is the Sex Discrimination Act 1975. The problem with this whole area of law is that it upholds the male norm as women are expected to find the hypothetical man to compare her with in the strife for equality. In fact, the Equal Opportunities Commission has described the Equal Pay Act as a 'paradise for lawyers and hell for women'.[4] Also, both pieces of legislation do not challenge stereotypical, patriarchal assumptions upon which employment law is founded; therefore, they are ill equipped to diagnose the symptoms of sex-based discrimination, in order to provide a cure.

The drawback with both of these pieces of legislation is that they have not been drafted in a gender-specific manner: they are aimed towards men and women. As a result of this, they have failed to effectively deal with women's issues. For example, paternalism is still very much entrenched in our legal system. Paternalism in legislation is a denominator that neutralises women's rights in accordance with what society views as not being good for them. This has the effect of taking away women's freedom of choice and promotes the stereotypical view that women are vulnerable and in need of protection. Surely this view does not accord with the concept of effectiveness; in order to create equality, laws should be applied in a manner to enable both sexes equal choices. For example, in the case of *Page v Freight Hire (Tank Haulage) Ltd*,[5] a divorcee who expressed the fact that she did not want children was stopped from driving a tanker containing DMF which was said to be harmful to her reproductive systems. The substance was also known to be harmful to men. The employers refused to employ her and gave the job to a male employee who also stood the risk of other harm being done to him.

Here, it can be seen that so-called protective laws may have a discriminatory impact because it can be seen that the male employee was given a choice to retain autonomy over his body when the female employee was denied. This

---

[3] Kemp and Kemp, *Quantum of Damages* (Sweet and Maxwell 2010).
[4] See Equal Opportunities Commision, *Equal Pay for Men and Women: Strengthening the Acts* 1990.
[5] [1981] ICR 299.

example also highlights that, despite harmony in legislative drafting techniques, legislative drafting does not in practice harmonise with common practice and the interpretation given to legislation by judges and as such it has failed to be effective in the sense of combating the old age problems of gender equality. These sorts of laws are still inherent in our legal system today despite the perceived cure of gender neutrality.

Another problem that arises in employment legislation is using women as a comparator to a man. The damage that this may cause can be seen from the case of *Hayes v Malleable Men's Working Club and Institute*.[6] The Sex Discrimination Act 1975 made it unlawful to treat a woman less favourably than a man on ground of her sex. This has the impact of connoting a like for like comparison. What does this translate to? It translates to the fact that a man can never be pregnant. Therefore, he does not have the same issues as a pregnant woman. In this particular case, the woman in question was dismissed on the grounds of her pregnancy. The judge held that because of the male comparison requirement in the legislation, she was not treated less favourably because a man could never be pregnant.

Similarly, in the case of *Webb v EMO Air Cargo*,[7] a woman was employed as a maternity cover, but shortly after found that she was pregnant and needed to take time off as the same woman she was covering. As a result her employers dismissed her. The court held that she was not dismissed on the grounds of her sex because a sick man would have been dismissed in the same circumstances. She was not able to work on the days she was contracted for. This is an example of the masculine rule at work here as the legislation is being interpreted from a male perspective, coupled with the connotation of construing pregnancy as an illness. Here, the concept of equality has been used to take rights away from pregnant women. Is this achieving true equality in the sense of effectiveness in drafting legislation? What this indicates is that despite drafting so-called gender-neutral legislation, which should translate to gender equal legislation, the quest for equality was not achieved. As such the legislation in question lacks effectiveness.[8]

Harassment in employment

Legislative drafting as a technique has not cured the courts' attitude towards the questioning of women in sexual harassment cases. The masculine rule is still being indirectly used in the sense that women are still being questioned about their attitude towards sexual harassment, their dress and behaviour. This has the impact of shifting the focus to the victim.[9] In addition, feminists have advocated for years that harassment in employment cases should be a criminal offence. This would create a real sense of equality as it would result in legislation becoming a deterrent because the real perpetrators would pay for their actions instead of companies who are not real persons in the sense of being a human being.[10]

---

[6] [1985] ICR 703.
[7] (UK) [1992] 2 All ER (CA); A All ER 929 (HL).
[8] Anne E Morris and Susan M Nott, 'Working Women and Law, Equality and Discrimination' In *Theory and Practice* (Routledge/sweet and Maxwell, New York, 1991).
[9] *British Telecommunications plc v Williams* [1997] IRLR 668.
[10] Haralambos and Holborn, *Sociology Themes and Perspectives* (Collins, 2004) 135.

Domestic violence

It is surprising to note that we are in the twenty-first century and the word 'domestic' is still being used as a description for the area of law concerning violence towards women. For example, the Domestic Violence, Crime and Victims Act 2004 still uses the word domestic. First, legislation has failed to adequately label this area of law. What this confirms is that violence towards women is a private matter. This confirms the ancient position of the public–private divide, in which the man is head of his house and can do as he pleases within the home, including inflicting violence on a woman, still stands. In addition, legislation does not differentiate between domestic violence and any other kind of violence. Domestic violence comes under the Offences Against the Persons Act 1861, and depending on the severity of the injury may amount to common assault, assault occasioning actual bodily harm or grievous bodily harm. Here, the title of the legislation could be used to send a message. For example, an effective way of naming domestic violence legislation would be to name the act in question, 'Violence Against Women Act'. This would in my opinion send a strong message that violence against women is a matter which the public takes seriously.[11]

Another important issue to consider is that domestic violence legislation has been drafted in a manner that makes it applicable to both men and women. What this method of drafting coupled with gender neutralisation has done is in essence diminished the fact that domestic violence is a gender-specific crime and hides the fact that in reality this type of crime is committed mainly by men against women. This method of drafting has not been fruitful in creating a successful deterrent to violence against women. A suggested approach would be to couple the above-mentioned legislation with features aggravating sentences in cases of domestic violence where the victim is a woman.

In addition, our laws still require a prosecutor to consider whether prosecution is in the public interest; public interest grounds require consideration of issues such as whether or not the sentence would be nominal amongst other criteria. This approach is clearly putting forward the idea that the family comes before the woman in concern, and has the impact of upholding the Masculine Rule by closing the door to prosecution, as it has the effect of sending a signal that it is acceptable to inflict small amounts of violence on a woman as one may not be prosecuted on the grounds that the sentence would be nominal.

Another problem that gender-neutral drafting has not been effective at correcting within the area of domestic violence is that there is the possibility for husbands to evade prosecution though the rules of evidence, for example, in the case of *Hoskyn v Commissioner of Police for Metropolis*,[12] the Court of Appeal convicted Hoskyn, confirming that his wife was a compellable witness to give evidence against him with regard to the violence he committed against her. The House of Lords, ignoring the wife's right, ruled that she was not a compellable witness. In fact, Lord Wilberforce asserted the Masculine Rule once again by stating that to allow the wife to give evidence would give rise to 'discord and Perjury and would be to ordinary people repugnant'. I will place emphasis on the use of the words 'ordinary people' here. This statement connotes that the

---

[11] Judith Bourne and Caroline Derry, *Women and Law* (Old Bailey Press, 2005) 98.
[12] [1979] AC 474.

ordinary persons in question would be men, thereby upholding the Masculine Rule, which in effect is a statement that women are non-existent. It should be noted that they had regard to the principle of 'one flesh', which could be interpreted as 'all references to he means she', which means 'she' is non-existent.

Rape

The Sexual Offences Act 2003 has been drafted using the gender-neutral technique. Once again this has taken the focus off the real victims of rape. Rape has been known to be a gender-specific crime perpetrated by men against women.[13] Here, we have taken one step forward and two steps backwards. This has the impact of trivialising rape, which is a very serious crime. Within this area of law there are various stereotypes that still exist. For example, rape is still seen as a violent act committed by a stranger upon a ladylike woman which she reports immediately afterwards. I will analyse each aspect of this mythical definition in turn to prove that the judiciary and various state actors apply these myths to the peril of women.

Violence

The mythical definition of rape has shaped the legal system attitude towards rape. As such it is often perceived that a woman has not really been raped unless she has cuts and bruises to show. The problem with this is that a mythical legal definition of rape does not require force. Instead, it requires for their to be a lack of consent. This has created a clash between the social definition and the legal definition of rape and often the social definition is upheld by the courts, the prosecutors, the police and society in general. In the case of *R v Olugboja*[14], it was confirmed that there is no need to show that any violence was used. What was required is consent. However, despite this clarification, the myth of violence is still being used in trials; it is being used as a weapon to uphold the common theme of patriarchy that women cannot be trusted to tell the truth. In the case of *R v Goodman*,[15] Lord Lane remarked that 'as everybody knows rape is an easy allegation to make and may be very difficult to refute. In addition, Under s 33 of the Criminal Justice and Public order Act 1984. Judges have a discretion to give a warning that the jury should be wary of convicting on the evidence given by the woman alone. This has upheld the myth that women lie about rape. The danger of this is that this has become an unwritten code of interpretation used by judges and members of the jury, which can be devastating to victims as it is very hard to challenge unwritten assumptions used as guidelines in rape cases. In addition, when Lord Lane refers to 'everybody' he is asserting the male norm, which does not take into consideration the view shared by women in rape cases. Again, the 'she' is deleted, replacing her opinion, with his opinion, which has

---

[13] Liz Kelly, Jennifer Temkin and Sue Griffiths, 'Home Office: An Evaluation of New Legislation Limiting Sexual History Evidence in Rape Trials', p 70 <http://rds.homeoffice.gov.uk/rds/pdfs06/rdsolr2006> accessed 14 January 2011.
[14] [1981] 3 All ER 1382.
[15] (1989) 11 Cr App R (S) 194.

created yet another imbalance. Lastly on this point, the use of force has been sexualised. In the name of sexual liberalisation, comments made by the court have indicted that what was previously considered as violence and force is now considered to be part of the normal sexual act.[16]

Stranger

The myth that the rapist is always a stranger has led to the courts giving less severe sentences where the victim is known to the rapist. In the case of *R v Billam*,[17] this was a factor that the judge took into consideration as a mitigating factor. This in my opinion should be an aggravating factor, because it means that the fact that a woman knows a man means that she should trust him more. The above example demonstrates that despite the best efforts of policy-makers to create equality through written legislation and policy guidelines, in reality the Masculine Rule often raises its ugly head through the concept of common mythology and male perception, which continues to be a feature within our legal system. This is saying that deeply entrenched patriarchal views take precedence over written laws despite the techniques used.

On the street

How often have you heard the saying that if a woman goes inside a house she wanted a man to have sex with her. This myth is still a common feature of judicial interpretation. This male interpretation of events means that situations can be twisted to suggest that there was in fact no rape by virtue of the existence of the fact that the woman invited the man inside her home or she went to his home, when in fact the woman might have gone to the perpetrator's home for a totally different reason.[18] This has upheld the Masculine Rule that once a man enters a woman's home or she goes to his home it is outside the public domain, and the man is given the exclusive right to do as he pleases with a woman behind the closed doors.

Ladylike

Francis Olsen observed that:

> By refusing to grant women autonomy and by protecting them in ways that men are not protected, Men are treated differently. Their bodies are regarded as part of them, subject to their free control.

Because of society's perception that men are free to do as they please sexually, the courts do not in the case where the victim is a man consider a man's sexual history. On the other hand, no amount of equality legislation or gender-neutral drafting has been able to tackle the entrenched mythology that

---

[16] Susan Edwards, *Sex and Gender in the Legal Process* (Blackstones Press 1996) 351.
[17] [1986] 1 All ER 985.
[18] Judith Bourne and Caroline Derry, *Women and Law* (Old Bailey Press 2005).

has enabled the court to use a woman's sexual history to suggest that she has not been raped. The myth of 'real rape' requires the victim to be a chaste woman: she should be either a virgin or a married woman whose only sexual relationship is with her husband. If a woman does not conform to this male construction of a 'ladylike woman', the courts are most times inclined to deem her a promiscuous woman who cannot ever be a victim of rape.[19] For example, example, in the case of *R v Brown*[20] the court took into consideration the fact that the complainant had sex with her boyfriend and had a child with another man. They described the above mentioned acts as being near the borderline of 'relevant promiscuity'.

Evidence of this male form of mythical stereotype was illustrated in research conducted by Zhusanna Adlers, 'The Relevance of Sexual History Evidence in Rape Problems of Subjective Interpretation' [1995] Crim LR 769. She found that in trials where a complainant fit into the male construction of 'chaste and virginal', the conviction rate was 98%, in contrast to 48% when the complainant's sexual reputation was discredited.[21] Therefore, from the above-mentioned analysis, it can be seen that male mythology has the impact of putting off victims from using the criminal justice system. In fact, Home Office reports confirm the link between falling numbers of women reporting rape out of the fear that the mythology of sexual evidence may be used against them. The report quoted women stating the following:

> That they thought seriously about the potential of their sexual history and reputation being 'up for grabs', but chose to report despite these concerns. Sexual history was, therefore, a factor for over a third of the sample when considering whether to make an official complaint, and half of the women volunteered comments that the issue of sexual history acted as a deterrent to reporting'. Oh, I think a lot [of victims] wouldn't go [to the police] in the first place ... I was worried about that. (C13: ex-partner, conviction). For instance it may be inferred that having had a large number of sexual partners, I am in some way immoral and that this has a bearing on whether or not I was a victim of rape ... [When I reported to the police] I knew that I might be asked questions about my previous sexual history. I think I had probably picked this up from other cases that have been in the press. Although I went ahead it did make me think twice about it. My biggest fear was not being believed and being made to feel somehow dirty. (C14: acquaintance x 2, did not proceed, reason not known)[22]

What this report is saying is that despite the best efforts of policy-makers and adopted methods of drafting techniques, we are far from achieving gender equality.

---

[19] A conflict theorist argues that social structures serve the interest of the powerful, being men in this instance. Thus, it should noted that such structures are used to keep other groups in their place, being women in this instance. Tonflict theorist uses the analysis that when there is a dysfunction or disadvantage due to conflict of interest in solving such a problem, the question that should be asked is, who is benefiting from the disadvantage? The answer would be men in this instance.
[20] (1999) 89 Cr App R 97.
[21] Liz Kelly, Jennifer Temkin and Sue Griffiths, 'Home Office: An Evaluation of New Legislation Limiting Sexual History Evidence in Rape Trials' <http://rds.homeoffice.gov.uk/rds/pdfs06/rdsolr 2006> accessed 14 January 2011.
[22] Ibid.

Immediate report of attack

There is a common assumption that in order to be truthful in cases concerning rape, a complaint should be made at the first opportunity, and if not the complaint is deemed not to be truthful. This mythology ignores that fact that as a result of trauma a victim may delay in going to the police or telling anyone. This mythology has created inequality in the law in that, usually, evidence of a previous consistent statement would not be admissible. In other words, a witness cannot give evidence of having given some version of events in the past. However, in the case of rape, the rules are different. If a rape victim tells somebody at the first opportunity that she is raped then this is admissible as true and in accordance with male mythology, it is called a recent complaint. The effect of this rule in practice is that if there is no such complaint, the victim is deemed to be telling a lie. Here, it can be seen again that the existing body of legislation reeks of imbalance as despite the so-called equality that legislative drafting technique and policy purports to give, disharmony between judicial attitudes and the other existing corpus of laws is fuelling disharmony by giving with one hand and taking back with the other. Lastly, I will discuss Homicide.

Homicide

The law on homicide has a number of defences in the case of persons who have killed. I will discuss each in turn. On the face of the legislation, it appears to be gender neutral. However, on a closer observation, the rules do not impact equally on women and men. For example, in s 56 of the Coroners and Justice Act 2009, the common law defence of provocation is abolished and replaced by ss 54 and 55 of the Act, which create the new defence of loss of control.

The defence of loss of control

Under s 54 of the Coroners and Justice Act, the defendant will not be convicted of murder and will have their charge reduced to murder if the following elements can be proven: that the defendant's acts or omissions in doing or being a party to the killing resulted from the defendants loss of self-control; that the defendant's loss of self-control had a qualifying trigger; that a person of the defendants sex and age, with a normal degree of tolerance and self-restraint and in the circumstances of the defendant, might have reacted in the same or in a similar way to the defendant. First and foremost, the effort to use gender neutrality has not created equality.

Loss of self-control

A loss of self-control defence will only apply to an act happening on the spur of the moment; where there has been a cause, which for some reason the defendant has been unable to tolerate, which has caused her to take the required action. The Act specifies certain situations which would not fall within the definition of a loss of self-control, for example, if the defendant acted in a considered manner for revenge. What this has done is to ignore the manner in which violence is perpetrated against women. Often the violence is ongoing for a number of years. This connotes that to be availed the defence, a female victim of, for example, domestic violence who kills would have to have acted on the spur of the moment in a one off incident. The reality of this is that women are often battered for years before they retaliate. Furthermore, psychiatrists also argue that generally people will only vent their anger by losing their self-control with another person when when they 'can afford to do so'.

This reinforces the gender imbalance perpetuated by the old defence of provocation defence, as it is unlikely that a victim of domestic violence would feel as though she could lose self-control without placing herself in a significantly more vulnerable position. This invention of loss of self-control is a legal construction which fails to take into consideration psychological behavioural patterns of women, in that women are slow to anger due to the fact that they are biologically weaker than men. This makes it an inadequate defence for women who retaliate in the face of violence. In addition, the danger of legal construction is that the judiciary is predominantly male, and this will be interpreted from their point of view, which does not reflect the reality of the situation. Thus, we are still stuck with the old adage of *R v Ahluwalia*, [23] a case which upheld the fact that the longer the delay in retaliating the stronger the evidence of deliberation. Therefore, the purported gender neutrality has once again failed to create gender equality.

Qualifying trigger

What is meant by a qualifying trigger? According to s 55 of the Coroners and Justice Act, a loss of self-control is said to have a qualifying trigger if any of the following two events, or a combination of both, occur:

1. The defendant's loss of self-control was attributable to the defendant's fear of serious violence against him or another party.
2. The defendant's loss of self-control was attributable to things done or said which:

    (a) constituted circumstances of an extremely grave character;
    (b) caused the defendant to have a justifiable sense of feeling wronged.

According to the Act, when establishing whether there was a qualifying trigger, the court's attitude is that the defendant's fear of serious violence must be disregarded if it was caused by an event which the defendant incited and is simply being used as an excuse for the act. Similarly, a sense of being seriously wronged by a thing done or said will not be justifiable if the defendant incited the thing to be done or said and is simply using it as an excuse to use violence. Here, we are back to where we left off, with the old legislation: a delay in violence does not mean that it is not imminent. Often abusers take a break from their actions. This does not mean that it is not imminent that they will act in the future. Therefore, it would be wrong to deny a victim of the defence because she

---

[23] [1992] 4 All ER 889.

was not being attacked specifically at the time she retaliated in respect of the past actions of her abuser. In addition, the law is back to accusing women as being provokers in the face of violence by stating that the defence will not be available if the defendant incited the act in question. Therefore, the baggage of provocation is in practice still with us, upholding the male norm that women provoke men to perpetuate gender-based violence against them

It is also the policy that things done or said constitute sexual infidelity. This will not be considered in establishing a qualifying trigger for the violence. This again is a reiteration of the previous entrenched position that women are men's exclusive property and this gives men the right to use violence to deny women autonomy.[24]

Self-defence

Self-defence comes under s 63 of the Criminal Law Act 1967. It has proved very difficult for women to successfully use self-defence due to the fact that the response has to be proportionate and the threat has to be imminent. First, women face difficulty in showing that it was reasonable to use a weapon against an unarmed man and, secondly, it does not find favour with in the behavioural patterns of most women who would wait for their attacker to be in a subdued state before taking action. The court's reasoning is that the woman should run to safety. This does not take into consideration the social sanctions that tie women to abusive relationships.

Diminished responsibility

Despite the gender-neutral drafting of s 2 of the Homicide Act 1957, giving rise to a defence where the accused suffers from an abnormality of the mind and impaired mental responsibility, this area of law is a last recourse for women as it supports the male notion that women are irrational and mad.

Conclusion

In conclusion, it is necessary to say that even though the legal system has showed some progress in the diagnosis of gender-based discrimination and has tried to tackle inequality through legislation, gender-neutral drafting as a technique on its own will never be able to tackle gender inequality, as the courts have been very restrictive in their approach. In order for true progress to be made, it is necessary for the actors in the legal system to change the way in which women are portrayed by, for example, using policy and laws to aggressively discourage the stereotypes and myths that have contributed to how women are viewed. In order to correctly diagnose and cure such attitudes, it is important for the legal system to recognise that the time has come for the legal system to include more women judges and advocates as policy-makers.

---

[24]Anna Carline, 'Reforming Provocation: Perspectives from the Law Commission and the Government' <http://webjcli.ncl.ac.uk/2009/issue2/carline2.html> accessesed 1 January 2011.

Policy-makers and legislative drafters will also need to come to the realisation that drafting in the gender neutral on its own will fail in the quest for equality, as drafting in the gender neutral should be differentiated from drafting in a gender-aware manner. Gender-neutral drafting on its own is a cosmetic change, which will lack effectiveness if it is not coupled with post-legislation and pre-legislation impact assessment mechanisms, which will promote checks and balances with regard to whether or not the legislation is question is achieving effectiveness by promoting equality from a female gender-specific point of view. These provisions would, in effect, tangibly demonstrate a wave of change in society, that women have a right to take their place equally within society. Secondly, justice should be dispensed by women as well as for women. This will promote challenge and start the process of curing the scar of gender stereotype, which currently remains in our legal system today as a result of the legacy of the Masculine Rule.

Notes on contributor
Venessa Mclean holds an LLM in Advanced Legislative Studies, University of London (Institute of Advanced Legal Studies). She currently works at the Office of the Chief Parliamentary Counsel in Jamaica as a legislative officer. She is a visiting lecturer for the Special Narcotic Investigation Course at the Caribbean Regional Drug Law Enforcement Centre, Jamaica, and also for the University of London External Degree Programme. She works as a consultant on legislative matters.

Legislative drafters: lawyers or not?

Norismizan Haji Ismail

Deputy Senior Counsel, Attorney General's Chambers, Brunei Darussalam

> The aim of legislative drafting is to express the instructing client's meaning. Legislative drafters are often lawyers with a significant impact on the interpretation and the implementation of the law. This article takes a different perspective and attempts to prove that legislative drafters do not necessarily have to be lawyers. The arguments of this hypothesis are important in establishing that legislative drafting is a specialised skill with general principles and conventions that can be acquired by training and practice. The conclusion would be to prove the hypothesis that legislative drafting could also be undertaken by non-lawyers.

Introduction

The importance of legislation can hardly be over-emphasised as legislation controls virtually every aspect of modern-day life. Legislative drafters are important to the administration of the system of justice and, in particular, to the efficient working of the legislative process through the drafting of well-crafted, cohesive statutes and regulations.[1] Every jurisdiction needs a drafting capacity as the government of any jurisdiction needs legislation to cover a multiplicity of social, economic and political issues. Legislative drafters are often lawyers with a significant impact on the interpretation and the implementation of the law. Having said that, there has been very little written on the subject of whether legislative drafters have to be lawyers or if it is acceptable for non-lawyers to be legislative drafters.

The hypothesis of this article is that legislative drafters do not have to be lawyers. In other words, it is not a necessary requirement that an individual has to be a lawyer in order to be a legislative drafter. In order to prove this hypothesis, I will analyse the criteria put forward by Geoffrey Kolts[2] on what makes a good legislative drafter. I will also identify the functions and responsibilities of a legislative drafter and the attributes needed to perform these functions and responsibilities. This will allow me to analyse the nature of the tasks involved in the drafting of legislation undertaken by the legislative drafter.

---

[1] D MacNair, 'Legislative Drafters: A Discussion of Ethical Standards from a Canadian Perspective' (2003) 24 SLR 125.

[2] G Kolts, 'Observations on the Proposed New Approach to Legislative Drafting in Common Law Countries' (1980) SLR 144 <http://heinonline.org> accessed 3 March 2012.

In addition, by proving that legislative drafting is a specialised skill with general principles and conventions that can be acquired by training and practice, I hope to conclude that I have proven my hypothesis in that legislative drafting could also be undertaken by non-lawyers.

Legislative drafting, legislative drafters and lawyers

The aim of drafting is to express the client's meaning.[3] This would involve ascertaining what the client wishes to do and to ascertain the risks which are legal and 'real world', that is to say, what law applies and what other parties to the documents and third parties might do.[4] The task of writing legislation requires a peculiar combination of skills and is best performed in a slightly peculiar way.[5] The first and most important thing that the legislative drafter is doing is making the law, and the second thing is communicating the law that the legislative drafter is making.[6] It is very easy to forget that these are two distinct processes, but an understanding of each of them is essential for the making of effective law.[7] Geoffrey Kolts identified that what makes a good legislative draftsman is a good basic legal knowledge, a feeling for the proper use of the English language, a critical ability, lots of imagination and plenty of practice.[8] In other words, a legislative drafter requires intellectual ability, creativity, a basic knowledge of the law, critical appraisal and judgment, including sufficient training in the drafting of legislation. Experience has shown that general legal ability by itself is not sufficient and that a competent lawyer without practical experience in legislative draftsmanship cannot perform the craft satisfactorily.[9]

Basic legal knowledge

It is obvious that professionals such as lawyers or doctors claim to have command of specialised, expert knowledge, but the difficulty lies in deciding exactly what kind of knowledge it is.[10] Lawyers usually claim that their skills and qualifications enable them to identify legal problems and to give legal advice and solve problems by the application of objective, legal knowledge. It is essential that a legislative drafter knows the general law that relates to the legislative drafting assignment. This knowledge should include more than the substantive and procedural aspects of the particular area of law, and the drafter should also be familiar with judicial decisions interpreting the law.[11] At the outset, a lawyer

---

[3] R Ramage, 'Effective Draftsmanship – Part 4' (2005) 155 NLJ 166.
[4] Ibid.
[5] D Greenberg, *Laying Down the Law: A Discussion of the People, Processes and Problems that Shape Acts of Parliament* (1st edn Sweet and Maxwell, London 2011).
[6] Ibid.
[7] Ibid.
[8] Kolts (n 2).
[9] Ibid. See also L Dushimimana, 'Aspects of Legislative Drafting: Some African Realities' (April 2012) The Loophole 45 <http://www.opc.gov.au/calcs/docs/Loophole/Loophole_Apr12.pdf> accessed 7 May 2012.
[10] P Harris, *An Introduction to Law* (7th edn Cambridge University Press, New York 2007).
[11] RJ Martineau and MB Salerno, *Legal, Legislative, and Rule Drafting in Plain English* (Thomson/West, USA 2005).

would have no problems in this matter when compared to a non-lawyer. On the other hand, a non-lawyer may find it challenging as he or she is not familiar with any aspect of the law. However, it is also possible that a non-lawyer will make an effort in doing extensive research in order to gain an insight of the particular area of the law. Similar situations often happen in other circumstances such as when an individual tries to find out more about a particular illness to have at least a basic knowledge of what the illness is about, the probable cause and symptoms and any possible cure or treatment.

A drafter does not need an encyclopaedic knowledge of all law.[12] A sound understanding of the constitutional law is necessary, and a good general knowledge of legal issues is also essential.[13] If the drafter does not have at least a basic knowledge of the area of law governing a legal document, it must be acquired because, without this knowledge, it is difficult, if not impossible, to produce a legal document that meets minimum professional standards.[14] Even a lawyer who possesses a detailed knowledge of the particular area of law may find himself or herself doing additional research if necessary. In Canada, for example, jurilinguists, whose background is purely in translation without any legal background, are required, among other things, to formulate, draft, develop, construe, translate and compare legal texts.[15] Legislative drafters are experts in drafting legislation, but this does not necessarily mean that they are also experts in all areas of the law, nor can they be expected to be such experts. Therefore, research skills are one of the key elements to being a legislative drafter in order to have a better sense of whether the requested outcome of the legislation is feasible based on a general knowledge of the law. A non-lawyer may do extensive legal research to ascertain the scope in a particular area of the law or to determine how other jurisdictions have addressed similar issues. In addition, he or she may utilise his or her research skills in interpreting and applying legal provisions which are applicable to the jurisdiction.

Feeling for proper use of English language

It is very important to note that not all jurisdictions draft their legislation in the English language, although most jurisdictions do in the form of bilingual or multilingual legislation. Moreover, there is no stated universal rule or obligation that legislation must be in the English language. The use of language in legislation very much depends on the constitutional provisions and the legal systems of each jurisdiction. Dushimimana[16] rephrased it as requiring a

---

[12] Martineau and Salerno (n 11).
[13] P Quiggin, *Training and Development of Legislative Drafters* (July 2007) The Loophole 14 <http://www.opc.gov.au/calcs/docs/Loophole/Loophole_Jul07.pdf> accessed 23 April 2012.
[14] Martineau and Salerno (n 11).
[15] On the other hand, there are also many jurilinguists in Canada that have training in law. Over the years, hiring jurilinguists solely on the basis of their legal background was less successful than hiring people with more experience on the linguistic side of things, see L Poirier, 'Whose Law Is It? A Jurilinguistic View From the Trenches' (January 2010) The Loophole 50 <http://www.opc.gov.au/calcs/docs/Loophole/Loophole_Jan10.pdf> accessed 23 April 2012.
[16] Dushimimana (n 9).

legislative drafter to have a feeling for the proper use of the language in which the legislation is drafted. To elaborate further on this matter, proper use of the language is a language that is clear and straightforward to the point which effectively delivers its message concisely to its audience.

All professions have their own language, and legalese is a specialised language for lawyers. In using the English language or any other languages, lawyers often appear to find it difficult to explain clearly and simply what they actually want and, more importantly, why they actually want it. More often than not, lawyers are criticised for many reasons. One of the criticisms most prevalent, and at the same time most justified, concerns lawyers' writing skills.[17] Many critics have amplified that lawyers do not know basic grammar and syntax and cannot say anything simply, as well as having no judgment and not knowing what to include or what to leave out.[18] In other words, lawyers have often been criticised for not being able to write well but think that they do write well.

Contrary to what many of them seem to think, there is generally no need in legislative drafting for the use of special language or structure of language.[19] What is important to identify is that a legislative drafter needs an appreciation of the language, in addition to the knowledge of the technical requirements of legislative norms. The drafter's expertise is the ability to deploy the English language to write effective legal rules with clarity and force.[20] A drafter must be able to express complex ideas in a way that is readily understood by appropriate reader groups.[21] A drafter must also know how to explain complex materials in discussions with instructing officers and others.[22] The fact that the legislative drafter may not be a lawyer should enhance the need and requirements to express ideas in a way which is easily understood by relevant readers. It could well be that language experts such as linguists may best serve to fulfil the requirement in the preparation of legislation due to their expertise in language issues. Due to the fact that they are less involved in using legalese language, as lawyers do, linguists are better able to draft legislation in a language that will be understood by the readers, as opposed to lawyers who tend to use legal jargons. Basically, a legislative drafter is not required to use a specialised language, but should use the same language consistently and concisely throughout the legislation. In addition, the ability to inform those affected by the legislation, including those who are to administer or enforce the legislation, what exactly they must do or must not do or how far their power or discretion is given is a requirement that is recommended in a legislative drafter.

---

[17] Martineau and Salerno (n 11).
[18] Ibid.
[19] R Rose, 'The Language of the Law: How Do We Need to Use Language in Drafting Legislation?' (August 2011) The Loophole 4 <http://www.opc.gov.au/calcs/docs/Loophole/Loophole_Aug.pdf> accessed 30 April 2012.
[20] N Horn, 'Shaping Policy Into Law: A Strategy for Developing Common Standards' (February 2011) The Loophole 40 <http://www.opc.gov.au/calcs/docs/Loophole/Loophole_Feb11.pdf> accessed 23 April 2012.
[21] Quiggin (n 13).
[22] Ibid.

Critical ability and imagination

On the other hand, there is also an argument which places the blame for poor drafting on the inability of the lawyers to think clearly rather than their inability to write clearly. Legislative drafting is not a precise science that can be performed by robots or other machines, but a form of technical art that is best performed by people actuated by artistic creativity, and constrained and informed by technical knowledge and an understanding of the purpose of law and the manner of its application.[23] Greenberg added that if the artist in the good legislative drafter is destroyed or over-disciplined, it will remove the ability to function effectively.[24] If drafting is an art or a craft, then creativity and innovation lie at the core of the task.[25] If a drafter wishes to imagine a reader for his draft, the best bet is a judge.[26] There is always a chance that one's statute will be litigated and even if it is not, a draft will profit from such an imagining, particularly if one imagines the judge-reader to be result orientated.[27] It is useful for a drafter to imagine a dialogue between himself or herself and such a judge so that the drafter could think that he or she is playing defence against the judge.[28]

One of the most difficult aspects of the role of the legislative drafter is the need of the drafter to wear different hats.[29] This requires numerous skills that are not normally part of law school training, and it is a role that evolves over time and demands speed, accuracy, clarity and operational knowledge of the substantive subject area of the law.[30] 'What-if' scenarios that all good legislative counsel run through to ensure that the legislation they are working on is comprehensive and workable.[31] Salembier identified that what distinguishes a top legislative counsel from a less skilled legislative counsel is not so much knowledge of the rules of grammar but rather the ability to determine whether a provision gets across the message clearly and effectively.[32] In other words, the creativity should not be confined to issues of the choice of words. The modern legislative counsel's creative imagination is engaged well beyond the four corners of the drafting table.[33] A drafter's analytical ability allows him or her to break a problem into its constituent parts, to explore the relationship between those parts and then build a system for grouping those parts.[34] The drafter needs 'practical' common sense to be able to

---

[23] Greenberg (n 5).
[24] Ibid.
[25] H Xanthaki, 'Duncan Berry: A Visionary of Training in Legislative Drafting' (February 2011) The Loophole 18 <http://www.opc.gov.au/calcs/docs/Loophole/Loophole_Feb11.pdf> accessed 4 April 2012.
[26] J Stark, 'Tools for Statutory Drafters' (April 2012) The Loophole 51 <http://www.opc.gov.au/calcs/docs/Loophole/Loophole_Apr12.pdf> accessed 7 May 2012.
[27] Ibid.
[28] Ibid.
[29] MacNair (n 1).
[30] Ibid.
[31] Salembier, 'Testing Client Policy: The Emperor's Clothes' (August 2011) The Loophole 44 <http://www.opc.gov.au/calcs/docs/Loophole/Loophole_Aug11.pdf> accessed 26 April 2012.
[32] Ibid.
[33] SC Markman, 'Legislative Drafting: Art, Science or Discipline?' (November 2011) The Loophole 5 <http://www.opc.gov.au/calcs/docs/Loophole/Loophole_Nov11.pdf> accessed 4 April 2012.
[34] Quiggin (n 13).

focus on issues that really do need to be resolved and to develop proposed solutions that are viable.[35] To analyse it simply, a non-lawyer should be capable of being a legislative drafter as long as he or she is able to think 'outside the box', and this includes being able to do a reality check to ensure that the legislation will work in practice. In short, creativity and innovation are essential requirements of the drafting job and need to be encouraged and fostered. For this reason, it can be established that the legislative drafter may not necessarily have to be a lawyer.

Practice makes perfect

The major challenge facing the drafting profession is the effort to build sufficient drafting capacity to meet the rapidly increasing demand for legislative counsel.[36] Governments around the world struggle to recruit new legislative counsel who have a genuine aptitude for the work; train these new recruits and integrate them into their drafting offices; evaluate the performance of their legislative counsel, both recruits and veterans; and improve the quality of the legislation produced.[37]

The leading Canadian drafter, Elmer Driedger, believed that it takes about 10 years to train a competent drafter.[38] Legislative drafters must be skilled in drafting and have enough experience to ensure that what they write is clear, precise and unambiguous. This requires training in legislative drafting as well as in research skills. If drafting is a science, there is plenty of scope for formal training, and unless trained, one should expect lawyers and non-lawyers to be bad at drafting.[39] Drafting skills can be studied and learned very successfully in a formal academic setting and much of what a legislative counsel needs to know about the work of the profession is indeed best addressed in that environment.[40] It is certainly true that no profession is ever fully functional without some period of hands-on experience in the field.[41] However, a sound formal training programme can give a new legislative counsel a solid professional foundation that allows those first months and years of on-the-job training to be put to use in honing skills and developing mature professional judgment, rather than in acquiring basic competencies and understanding.[42] As a result, it can be considered that only by training and continuous practice will an individual, although he or she may not be a lawyer, be competent in legislative drafting and, in time, become an experienced legislative drafter. Quiggin[43] analogised learning to draft as rather like learning to play an instrument. It involves talent, theory and practice.

Conclusion

Literally, a legislative drafter writes laws for everyone. The framework of society depends largely on the communication of legislation, and much that is dear to the heart is frequently affected – liberty, life, property, marriage, taxes, indeed all

---

[35] Ibid.
[36] Markman (n 33).
[37] Ibid.
[38] As cited by Dushimimana (n 9).
[39] Xanthaki (n 25).
[40] Markman (n 33).
[41] Ibid.
[42] Ibid.
[43] Quiggin (n 13).

aspects of human conduct within society.[44] In short, it can be rightly identified that laws belong to the citizens. There is a general agreement that drafting is a skill acquired at the expense of great pains and diligence and of long practice.[45] In general, it can be said that all lawyers can be legislative drafters, provided they have the abilities and the skills to be one. Having said that, a legislative drafter does not necessarily have to be a lawyer, and this article has proven so. In the European Union legislative process, the first drafts are generally prepared by civil servants of the Commission who are technical specialists in the sector concerned.[46] In most cases, they are not lawyers and have had little training in drafting.[47] This article does not aim to determine that a non-lawyer may be a better legislative drafter than a lawyer. It only aims to establish an answer to the question of whether a non-lawyer can be a legislative drafter that can draft adequately. A lawyer who is trained and skilled in legislative drafting is very rare. As a result, there has always been a shortage of legislative drafters in most, if not all, jurisdictions. Experience in legal practice is desirable.[48] So is an interest in drafting, a mastery of the use of the relevant language, a systematic mind and orderliness in the formation of thoughts, the ability to pay meticulous attention to detail and to work with accuracy under pressure.[49] What this article has established is that it is not impossible for a non-lawyer to become a legislative drafter if he or she is provided with adequate training and with lots of practice in order to gain experience in the field of legislative drafting. In addition, it would definitely prove beneficial if he or she has the ability to apply solutions to a range of problems of possible scenarios. In other words, a non-lawyer who might be a perfect match in all respects to the criteria, that is with the relevant knowledge, language skills and creative and analytical ability, might acquire the skills of legislative drafting through training and eventually be able to be a legislative drafter. As an analogy, learning the rules of driving do not make a person able to drive; the person has to get into the car. Hence, an individual, albeit a lawyer or not, needs to practice the art of legislative drafting on training. Ultimately, even though the ability to draft legislation improves with experience, an aptitude for the work is essential and necessary.

Notes on contributor
Norismizan Haji Ismail is a deputy senior counsel and the Deputy Head of the Legislative Drafting Division at the Attorney General's Chambers of Brunei Darussalam. She has been working as a legislative drafter in the Division since August 1998. She did her LLB (Hons) – Law Degree at the University of Central England in Birmingham, UK, and was called as a barrister at the Lincoln's Inn. She holds an LLM (Merit) in Advanced Legislative Studies at the Institute of Advanced Legal Studies, School of Advanced Study, University of London, for the academic year 2011–2012.

---

[44]Dushimimana (n 9).
[45]JAS Clarence, 'Legislative Drafting: English and Continental' (1980) SLR 14 <http://heinonline.org> accessed 9 March 2012.
[46]W Robinson, 'Accessibility of European Union Legislation' (February 2011) The Loophole 79 <http://www.opc.gov.au/calcs/docs/Loophole/Loophole_Feb11.pdf> accessed 4 April 2012.
[47]Ibid.
[48]VCRAC Crabbe, 'The Ethics of Legislative Drafting' (2010) 36 CLB 11.
[49]Ibid.

The role of the Rwandan legislative drafter in the legislative process: analysis stage

Ruth Ikiriza

Ministry of Justice, P.O. Box 160, Rwanda

> The topic of my article was chosen so that it could help to evaluate the current practice in legislative drafting in Rwanda and suggest ways for improvement in order to carry out the legislative role effectively. The article discusses the background study made and the next step of analysing whether the legislation complies with the Constitution. It proceeds to the special responsibility area that deals with putting the policy into legislative shape. Ultimately, thoroughly analysed good quality legislation that is in conformity with the Constitution will be effectively implemented.

1. Introduction

Although there are five stages of legislative drafting as rightly put by Thornton,[1] this article focuses on the analysis stage of the drafting process and examines how this stage influences the quality of legislation. This article examines the analysis stage by focusing on three proposals that are subjected to careful analysis in relation to existing law, special responsibility areas, as well as practicality.[2] Ultimately, the objective of this article is to learn how analysis is done, evaluate the current practice in legislative drafting in Rwanda and suggest ways for improvement in order to carry out the legislative role effectively.

This article, therefore, is an important tool to the Rwandan drafting office because it points out the flaw in the tradition of carrying out proper analysis of draft legislation. By applying the existing drafting techniques of analysis as put by Thornton, drafters can improve their capacity and ultimately improve the quality of legislation.

The role of the drafter at the analysis stage is crucial, especially in Rwanda where there is no control of anti-constitutionality before a law is passed by parliament. However, for the case of Rwandan jurisdiction, the Supreme Court has the competence to hear petitions on the constitutionality of the organic laws, laws, decree-laws and international treaties and agreements.[3] For that matter, a drafter who is familiar with the system is needed at this stage to ensure the analysis of the existing law and, hence, needs to study more rigorously the

---

[1] GC Thornton, *Legislative Drafting* (4th edn Butterworth, London 1996) 128.
[2] Ibid., 133.
[3] Art 145, 3, Constitution of the Republic of Rwanda of 4 June 2003, Official Gazette No Special of 04/06/2003, 119.

practical aspects of the legislation and ensure that the scheme will work and the legislation will be capable of enforcement.[4]

This article looks at the importance of the analysis stage when drafting legislation, as this is crucial for the Rwandan legislative process because it concerns analysis of the existing law and its practicality. In the analysis, the current practice in Rwanda will be the yardstick whereby the drafter does not participate in the making of the first draft; rather the first draft is made by consultants.

This article will examine the role of the drafter at the analysis stage of the drafting process and proves that analysis done by the drafter at this stage ensures the quality of legislation, so that it is in conformity with the Constitution and that the legislation will be effectively implemented.

This article examines the drafter's role at the second stage of Thornton's legislative process, which is the analysis stage. The article is divided into five parts. The first is the Introduction, which deals with the background of the topic and the methodology. The second part looks at the existing laws which deal with analysing whether legislation complies with the Constitution and other laws within the Rwandan jurisdiction. The third part looks at the special responsibility area, which deals with putting the policy into legislative shape. The fourth part looks at the legislative proposals and practicality of the legislation which checks for the capacity of the proposed legislation. Finally, the fifth part presents the conclusion. The article looks at Rwandan current practice of legislative drafting. The article focuses on relevant available literature on the subject. The article places considerable reliance on background papers and academic articles. Various internet sources will be consulted for relevant information.

2. Existing laws

In his analysis, Dickerson compared a drafter with a competent architect, who would not dream of remodelling a house without first taking a close look at it. Similarly, the drafter of a legal instrument should closely examine all relevant existing instruments, if any, to see what to amend, what to repeal and what to supplement. Failure to do this results in implied repeals, overlaps and inconsistent terminology in a word-confusion.[5]

The drafter must relate the document under preparation to other existing or proposed documents. This, of course, is to avoid repetition or overlap.[6] Normally, when a drafter receives the drafting instructions, he or she needs to see it in a wider context in order to understand it fully[7] and be able to know whether the written laws in force at a particular time comply with that particular legislation.[8] This is important because the government body concerned will usually know where possible points of conflict with other legislation are to be found

---

[4]Thornton (n 1) 133.
[5]Reed Dickerson, *The Fundamentals of Legal Drafting* (Little Brown and Company, Boston 1965) 40.
[6]Robert C Dirk, QC, *Legal Drafting* (2nd edn Carswell, Toronto 1985) 34.
[7]Thornton (n 1) 124.
[8]Ibid., 133.

but may not realise that the legislation may also by implication have an amending effect on other laws.[9] Furthermore, such analysis helps the drafter to avoid such things as violating freedoms of the citizens by making illegal what was legal and restricting former freedom of action.[10] To address such issues, the drafter should be equipped with information regarding the legislation by taking cognisance of the cultural, economic, political and social conditions within which it is intended to operate.[11] One of the ways which a Rwandan drafter can achieve proper analysis is through research, which enables him to have some basic knowledge of almost every subject matter and understanding of the issues that had created the problem, the solution to which they attempt to find through the process of legislation.[12]

Although the Rwandan drafter does not participate in the making of the first draft, he or she strives to achieve good quality of legislation by focusing on the drafter's main and most valuable function, which is to subject policy ideas to a rigorous intellectual analysis.[13] At this point, the drafter is in a position to judge whether the analysis means that the ideas collapse, hence, sending the client away to think again or even conclude that the particular project should be abandoned.[14] This is very important because the client will come back with refined ideas, thus helping the drafter to achieve his main objective of producing good quality legislation.

Due to the fact that the Rwandan drafter has limited resources and most times finds him or herself in a position where he or she has no expertise required to draft a bill or order, in such a situation he or she makes the analysis by gathering all the ideas to include in the bill and expresses them clearly in the legislation,[15] resulting in good quality legislation.

As the power to initiate laws in the Rwandan jurisdiction is vested in each Member of Parliament[16] and the executive acting through the cabinet, the role of the Rwandan drafter at this point is crucial since it is upon that particular scheme that hangs the quality of the bill.[17] Even the government expects the bill to be in harmony with all existing legislation as well as with the common law or customary law.[18] Therefore, when preparing an amendment to an existing instrument, for example, a drafter must apply the technique of meshing the new with the old.[19]

---

[9] NJC Van den Bergh, 'Legislative Drafting and Drafting Techniques', (Proceedings of a Seminar held on 1–3 September 1983 at the University of Zululand) 40.
[10] Thornton (n 1) 133.
[11] VCRAC Crabbe, *Legislative Drafting* (Cavendish Publishing, London 1993) 12.
[12] Ibid., 13.
[13] Richard Kelly, *Drafting Legislation and the Parliamentary Counsel Office* (22 September 2005) 3.
[14] Ibid.
[15] Art 4 (2) of Instructions of the Minister of Justice no 01/11 of 20 May 2005 on the procedure to be followed when drafting bills and orders in the *Official Gazette No 12 of 15 June 2005*.
[16] Constitution (n 4) Art. 90.
[17] Crabbe (n 11) 16.
[18] Ibid., 21.
[19] Dickerson (n 5) 112.

What is more, the drafter's role at the analysis stage involves asking questions relating to the scheme, such as the source of the enabling power to make such instruments, whether the procedure prescribed by such powers was observed, whether the instrument is not repugnant to the existing law, whether the instrument is consistent with the provisions of the Act under which it is made, and whether the legislation is certain, not vague and reasonable.[20] When legislation is accompanied by information such as that described in this paragraph, a legislative body is in a much better position to understand the issues involved and to focus its own review with a greater speed and accuracy.[21]

3. Special responsibility areas

Good drafting is useless without good analysis from a good drafter, who should take the responsibility to add value to the proposed legislative scheme and to produce legislation of high quality. The initial task of the drafter is to take into account the entire span of the subject matter of the draft and discuss every detail with the concerned ministries and acquire knowledge of the subject matter.[22] This will enable the drafter to bring his thoughts together and prepare a viable legislative scheme.[23]

Furthermore, the drafter's responsibilities are to put policy into legislative shape, and his or her professional duty is to approach each task with objectivity.[24] Although the drafter is not really concerned with policy, he or she is not in a position to wash his or her hands of it,[25] but rather the drafter should ensure that the Attorney General is consulted regarding areas of his responsibility, for example, maintenance of the rule of law, conferring on or removing jurisdiction from a court, evidentiary provisions or penal sanctions.[26]

The drafter's responsibility, therefore, is that which enables him or her to see the legislative proposals against the background of the whole structure of the law[27] and particularly to be aware of certain areas of potential danger.[28] The other responsibility of the drafter is to look at the process and know who lobbied for the legislation, who demanded what and who gave up what.[29] Generally speaking, a bill should deal first with basic objectives and main principles of the legislation so that it becomes effective, implementable, and is the best way for the drafter to achieve good quality legislation.[30]

The drafter has to check that the proposal does not conflict with the Constitution or any other law. If the proposal will conflict with Constitution or

---

[20] 'The National Democratic Institute for International Affairs, Researching and analyzing legislation' p 31. <http://www.elevenpub.com/Eleven/SearchResults.aspx> accessed on 8th April 2011.
[21] Ibid., 32.
[22] BR Atre, *Legislative Drafting* (2nd edn Universal Law Publishing, 2006) 98.
[23] Ibid., 189.
[24] Thornton (n 1) 134.
[25] Ibid.
[26] GC Thornton, *Legislative Drafting* (3rd edn Butterworths, London 1987) 120.
[27] Thornton (n 1) 134.
[28] Ibid.
[29] William D Popkin, *Materials on Legislation*, 105.
[30] Atre (n 22) 99.

any other law, then the drafter has to fully discuss it with the policy-makers and advise on the best way forward.[31] If the drafter fails to meet the above requirement, then he or she is bound to involve the client in very expensive actions with unknown amounts of worry and stress.[32] Furthermore, as regards to the question as to whether the proposed legislation is likely to be in contravention of the Constitution, it is most desirable that the drafter has adequate background knowledge as to the ramifications that could arise if the provisions of the Constitution are not properly taken into account when drafting.[33] However, the drafter can prevent such incidences from happening by drafting safe and foolproof documents which are not open to two or more meanings, as most drafting errors result from a complete lack of due care or attention or both.[34]

In drafting, in case of extraterritoriality, the onus on the drafter increases to advise on the competence of the lawmakers to do so.[35] On this note, Thornton suggests that '[i]f legislative proposals are patently unreasonable or shock the drafter's sense of justice, the drafter must advise the sponsors of the proposal of his or her opinion and draw attention to the inequity or breach of fundamental principle involved'.[36] Furthermore, the regulation and control of society is in the drafter's field to toil and frame the communication of policy decisions having legal consequences to members of society.[37] Thus, this requires the drafter to work hard and be able to iron out such issues as there is no moral judgment as to right or wrong of the principle but drafters should tread very cautiously to highlight all problem areas, which has been dubbed potential danger zones in drafting.[38]

It is the drafter's responsibility to carry out analysis on the legislative proposal to provide for predictability which makes way for the practical implications of the legislation and the reason for a preference for specific solution, which should be included in the drafting instructions.[39] The analysis may bring out many alternative routes to solution of the proposal and point out the most cost effective method for a legislative solution, which is referred to as the cost–benefit analysis of the proposal.[40] So, the drafter should be careful and cautious to bring up pertinent, valid and logical conclusions and to avoid unnecessary and unwarranted repeals of the legislation in the future.[41] However, for the drafter to ensure that the law does not give rise to unnecessary repeals, it must not conflict with any other norm of the same or higher hierarchical level

---

[31] Joseph G Kobba, 'Criticisms of the Legislative Drafting Process and Suggested Reform in Sierra Leone' (2008) 10 Eur JL Reform 234.
[32] John Sinclair, *Legislative Drafting in Scotland* (W Green/Sweet & Maxwell, Edinburg 2001) 1.
[33] Kobba (n 31) 3.
[34] Ibid., 2.
[35] Ibid., 234.
[36] Ibid.
[37] Ann Seidman, Robert B Seidman and Nalin Abeyesekere, *Legislative Drafting for Democratic Social Change: A Manual for Drafters* (Kluwer Law International, London 2001) 25.
[38] Kobba (n 31) 234.
[39] Ibid.
[40] ibid., 235.
[41] Ibid.

and it should have no deficiencies.[42] Since Commonwealth constitutions are too diverse for treatment, it is essential that the drafter bears in mind at all times the competence of the legislature to which the draft will be submitted, so the drafter must be thoroughly familiar with restrictions and limitations affecting his or her work.[43] Apart from that, the drafter is expected to ensure that the bill complies with parliamentary rules governing public bill procedure, and these rules specify the conditions which must be met before a bill can be presented and debated.[44]

What is more, the drafter is expected to look at the nature of the legislation at hand and examined it to find out whether it is retrospective, whether it is in conflict with international law, whether it is *ultra vires* the Constitution in general, whether it has the unnecessary bureaucracies, whether it is affecting other government departments or public bodies, and whether it contains proposals affecting prerogative powers.[45] Thus, in order to achieve this, drafters need a legislative theory and methodology likely to guide them in writing bills that when enacted actually resolve the social problem at which they aim.[46]

4. Legislative proposals and practicality

It is crucial for the drafter to put much emphasis on the practicability, implementation, comments studied and amendments made on a given proposal. At this stage, the skeleton of the draft is looked at, thus a suitable set of concepts that embody the basic ideas with which the bill is concerned and legislative structure of the bill make up the skeleton of the draft.[47] As Peter asserts: 'a pastry cook does not first think about how to make an apple pie, and then make it; a pastry cook does apple-pies', likewise, a drafter does not first conceive legislation and then put it into words, a drafter does bills.[48]

By far, the most time-consuming part of the drafter's work is the analysis of the legislative proposal as well as trying to liaise with the department responsible to advise about the readiness and any procedural or handling matters of particular interest.[49] It is worthwhile still to analyse the legal policy and establish whether the policy affects legislation. Under this analysis, comments on policy as

---

[42]Delnoy, 'The Role of Legislative Drafters in Determining the Content of Norms' <http://www.justice.gc.ca/eng/pi/icg-gci/norm/index.html> accessed 16 April 2011, see also Brian Hunt, 'The Origins of the Office of the Parliamentary Draftsman in Ireland' (2005) 26 Stat LR 171–188, 181, where the author narrated about Arthur Matheson, who was complimented by Senator Brown for his work because, out of a number of laws he had drafted, there was only one case in which the meaning of a section had to be interpreted by the court.
[43]Thornton (n 1) 137.
[44]David R Miers and Alan C Page, *Legislation* (Sweet and Maxwell, London 1982) 79.
[45]Ibid., 135.
[46]Seidman and Abeyesekere (n 37) 39.
[47]Daniel Greenberg, *Craies on Legislation* (Sweet and Maxwell, London 2004) 506–7.
[48]Seidman and Abeyesekere (n 37) 26.
[49]Greenberg (n 47) 506–7.

affecting the legislative proposal, efficacy,[50] effectiveness[51] and legal compatibility are prior elements to be looked at if a law is to be made functional, hence achieving good quality of legislation. Thornton in his analysis gave an example of a sanction that, without some means of enforcement, in other words of exaction of the penalty, is vacuous. This truth indicates that when a legislative proposal lacks some of the ingredients of a criminal proposal, then it is bound to fail. Indeed, as 'penal provisions never stand alone', it also points to 'the wider criminal law', tacitly invoking its general principles.[52]

In making a legislative proposal, drafters prefer to use documents that have been tested in operation.[53] This helps the drafter and policy-makers to reduce pressure and time for creating a new legislative proposal and, hence, good quality legislation. The structure of an Act is another essential element when composing a legislative proposal since it can act as a road map for users of the legislation who want to find the relevant provisions. A well-conceived structure leads the user to the place of interest and, therefore, is important for the overall accessibility of an Act,[54] which amounts to more than just the readability and comprehensibility of the legislative text. The overall accessibility of legislation is also determined by the way it is formally and informally communicated (promulgation, publication, public relations, press releases, etc.) and the manner in which the legislative text may be accessed. Accessibility is vital to the credibility of legal and political systems that operate on the presumption that everybody is supposed to know the law. Credibility in turn creates stability, trust, and confidence and may thus enhance economic performance,[55] thus, achieving good quality legislation.

Drafters are required to analyse the legislative proposal in the most suitable and effective approach. In fact, it requires serious attention to avoid the risk of the proposal being incomplete or unclear, hence failing to achieve the objective of good quality legislation. Whatever the technique used at the analysis stage, the drafter must improvise a means of translating a particular policy into legislation and ensure that all matters affected by the policy are well addressed. This will enable the drafter to proceed to the following stage, which is the design.[56]

5. Conclusion

In the final analysis, study on the importance of the analysis stage in the Rwandan legislative process proves to be vital, especially after examining the

---

[50]Constantin Stefanou and Helen Xanthanki, *Drafting Legislation* (Ashgate Publishing Ltd., 2008) 5.
[51]L Malder, 'Evaluating the Effect: A Contribution to the quality of Legislation' (2001) 22 Stat LR 119–31.
[52]Robin M White, '"It's Not a Criminal Offence" – or Is It? Thornton's Analysis of "Penal Provisions" and the Drafting of "Civil Penalties"' (2011) 32(1) Stat LR, 17–37, 26.
[53]Peter But and Richard Castle, *Modern Legal Drafting* (2nd edn Cambridge University Press, 2006) 7.
[54]Wim Voermans, 'Styles of Legislation and their Effects' (Oxford University Press, 2011) 32(1), Stat LR 38–53, 47.
[55]Ibid., 50.
[56]Thornton (n 1) 138.

three proposals relating to existing laws, special responsibility areas as well as legislative proposals and practicality. A legislative process that is driven by Thornton's five stages of analysis requires reaching solutions to broad political problems that various people of different concerns and different interests can accept and live with. It is not a method of achieving a perfect piece of writing.[57]

Thus, these and similar examples as cited from various sources confirm the hypothesis that the role of the drafter at the analysis stage of the drafting process, which is done by the drafter, ensures good legislation which is in conformity with the Constitution and ensures that legislation will be effectively implemented. In any case, the responsibility to produce good quality legislation must be fulfilled by drafters within the time they have or within the time they may not have.[58] As seen earlier in this article, the responsibility of the drafter at the analysis stage involves asking questions; therefore, it is important to check for clarity issues within legislation, which helps to eliminate ambiguity and vagueness.[59]

In the final remarks, I think Rwandan legislative drafters can achieve good quality legislation which has been thoroughly analysed by developing a close and positive liaison between the drafter and the instructing officer. This is an important necessity if the inadequacies and ambiguities of both the drafting instructions are to be detected and remedied.[60]

Notes on contributor
Ruth Ikiriza, a Principal State Attorney at the Ministry of Justice, Rwanda, has vast experience in the field of law, particularly in legislative drafting, and has gained most of it from the ministry in which she currently works. Some of her responsibilities include: drafting laws; translation of drafted laws into three official languages; and harmonisation of translated laws into accepted legal terminologies.

---

[57]Reed Dickerson, *Professionalising Legislative Drafting, The Federal Experience* (American Bar Association, 1973) 40.
[58]'Pressure of time is common difficulty for the drafter'. See NK Chakrabarti, *Principles of Legislation & Legislative Drafting* (2nd edn R Cambray, Calcutta 2007) 424. See also Michael Zander, *The Law-Making Process* (6th edn Cambridge University Press, UK 2004) 98.
[59]Crabbe (n 11) 43.
[60]Thornton (n 1) 144.

Prioritising legislation in the policy process

Odethie Birungi Kamugundu

Ministry of Justice, P.O Box 160, Kigali, Rwanda

> Drafting a piece of legislation is not an end in itself but its major value lies in its practicability. For some time, jurisprudence has not maintained a distinction between policy formulation and policy implementation. Law without compliance and an enforcement effect is like story telling. It may be a very well-written project but have very little to do with the practical world. Prioritisation as a mechanism towards drafting practicable legislation is also an item for the transparency of the legislative plan and process. Between policy formulation and policy implementation, prioritisation is a key player.

1. Introduction

Legislation comes into being after a long process of interaction and cooperation of the stakeholders who take part in the policy process. For legislation to be effective, there is great need for organisation and devotion of the players involved in the process. In every jurisdiction, government plans the annual legislative activity where a presentation of laws to be passed in a year is introduced.[1]

If the legislative plan intended to be passed by the government is to be effective, it is important that the concept of prioritising legislation be put into practice. The activity of prioritising legislation varies from country to country. In some jurisdictions, prioritising legislation is done by the cabinet, in others it is undertaken by the parliamentary counsel, in others it may be done by the drafting office, while it is non-existent in other jurisdictions.[2]

In most countries, the capacity for drafting legislation is minimal. In addition to that, lawmakers are time constrained and this forces players involved to prioritise drafting projects.[3] Due to lack of proper guidelines on prioritising, haphazard priority drafting projects characterise almost all jurisdictions, which at the end of the day affects the efficiency of laws.[4] The aspect of prioritising legislation aims at ensuring that policies do contribute to sustainable development by assessing the economic, environmental and social impacts of policy proposals.

---

[1] Alfred Kellermann, 'Quality of EU Legislation' (2008) 200 Eur JL Reform 186.
[2] Richard Nzerem, 'Prioritizing Legislative Proposals in the Legislative Process' (2010) (36) 1 CL Bull 73.
[3] Ann Siedman, Robert B Siedman and Nalin Abeyesekere, *Legislative Drafting for Democratic Social Change. A Manual for Drafters* (Kluwer Law International, 2001) 51.
[4] Ibid., 52.

When prioritising legislation, the drafting office should not only consider proposals that tackle the problem they intend to solve but also take into account side effects on other policy areas.[5] In the prioritisation process, the drafting office should screen the drafting projects, considering the merits of each proposal in order to be able to identify policy areas where the draft project is a good candidate for efficiency.[6]

In reviewing the priority drafting project, the drafter should be able to establish the likely consequences the law will impose on different affected interests, the reaction of the people it affects and what will be its cost for both the public and private interests.[7] In the process of prioritising legislation, the drafter should always have in mind the three criteria of the quality of the law: effectiveness, efficacy and efficiency. Although these criteria do not exhaustively exclude the complex social realities, the drafting office must always aim at them.[8] At most, the drafting office is required to be knowledgeable on the social upheavals, the resources and the material needed and what and who is available for drafting a piece of legislation.

This paper intends to prove that prioritising legislation is a tool that may be used by the drafting office for achieving practicability of legislation. I have chosen to use the drafting office as one of the institutions that may be vested with the duty of prioritising legislation. To prove the hypothesis, the article will analyse the criteria of prioritising legislation as set by Siedman and Siedman: the gravity of the social problem being addressed, the legislation's anticipated social impact, do-ability and the drafting programme.[9]

2. The gravity of the social problem being addressed

Many countries, especially those that are less developed, face many social problems, including poverty, crime, drugs, unemployment, delinquency and others. The appropriate priority of the legislative plan should reflect the social challenges.[10] The drafting office must take a keen look at social problems and identify issues being addressed. The drafting office should identify the problem in a narrow context, ranging from nation and sector to specific issues, which may include poverty, equity, social diversity, gender, social capital, social exclusion and others.[11]

Seidman illustrates how it becomes irrelevant to draft laws without considering the social problem. These illustrations include prioritising a project to govern the use of cheques in a country where there are no branches of banks outside the city, protection of intellectual property in a country with no industries

---

[5]Kellermann (n 1) 187.
[6]Ibid., 191.
[7]Ibid., 193.
[8]Kellermann (n 1) 197.
[9]Siedman (n 3) 57–77.
[10]Ibid., 52.
[11]Jonathan Brown, Ayse Kudat and Kristen McGeeney, 'Improving Legislation Through Social Analysis. A Case Study in Methodology from the Water Sector in Uzbekistan' (2005) 5 SDLP 49.

or prioritising a draft that punishes piracy in a landlocked country.[12] These illustrations clearly indicate that where prioritising is properly conducted, such idle laws would not pass only to saturate the statute book.

Prioritising legislation is an unknown concept, especially in developing countries; but even in developed democracies, citizens generally have problems that need to be addressed. There are the reasons as to why it is imperative to prioritise legislation in the order of proposals that seek to address the welfare of the people. The magnitude of the problem and how the legislation will impact on those problems must be the core value when prioritising legislation.[13]

It is most probable that transforming developing economies from a state of economic dependency would require the taking of bold root-and-branch measures by the government determined to address the problems facing the country. The measures that will effectively address the problems will require that problems be given a high priority in the legislative programme.[14] Legal order can help to alleviate the majority's poverty and powerlessness by changing the behaviour patterns that comprise those institutions. This can be addressed when prioritising legislation.[15] The drafting office must always in the prioritising process acknowledge that for any legislation to be effective, it must be attuned to the problems posed, and to the technical and local conditions.[16]

Legislation should be prioritised based on substantive issues associated with social problems and the drafting office should be able to explore its legislative structure and assumptions of the legislative goals. If the drafting office can ascertain that the legislation is designed to develop creative solutions to the social issues by putting into context the concurrent challenges that it is attempting to address, it will have made a step towards drafting practicable law.

3. The legislation's anticipated social impact

The drafting office should prioritise draft legislation with due regard to the ministry's policy for ameliorating the existing social problem.[17] It is probable that the basic theoretical and empirical knowledge on the social impact may not be readily available to develop a legislative priority. However, to attain practicability of legislation, the drafting office may have to make broad estimates in prioritising the legislative proposals, even when the data required for estimating the task are not ample.[18]

The varied aspects of the relationship between legislation and social change pose some challenging problems of great significance for understanding the role of legislation in modern societies. These aspects include new modes for changing

---

[12] Seidman (n 3) 52.
[13] Nzerem (n 2) 74.
[14] Ibid., 75.
[15] Seidman (n 3) 57.
[16] Kellermann (n 1) 190.
[17] Siedman (n 3) 68.
[18] Keith Boyum and Samuel Krislov 'Judicial Impacts, What is Needed, What is Possible' (1982) 66 (3) Judicature 139.

the legislation, lag in the development of law behind social change, the use of legislation as a device to induce social change and others.[19]

The drafting office should prioritise legislation based on social assessment. The legislation's impact should be assessed on factors bearing on legislation as a tool to uncover social causes and impacts associated with development. The drafter may have to visualise drafting projects as a mechanism through which social cohesion can be built and accountability and transparency can be promoted; a proposal where the poor and other vulnerable or marginalised groups can be empowered.[20]

The purpose of the legislation on the one hand may be to address prevalent social problems. On the other hand, the problem may be facing one group of people while another group faces another problem. Therefore, the effects of a given legislation may apply only to some people, which means that it benefits some and not others. In this instance, it becomes apparent that the drafting office will have to realise that there is no same size that fits all. In the wake of such a dilemma, the drafting office will have to exhaust all means in order to find a suitable solution on which to base in prioritising the legislation. The best option would therefore be to prioritise in favour of good laws relating to improving the living conditions and quality of life of the poor majority through, for instance, increased industrialisation and consequently the creation of jobs.[21]

It is not easy for the drafting office to foresee exactly how the use of legislation will impact on society, but it should always attempt to achieve social goals. In any case, it must attempt to ensure and anticipate that the capacity of the drafting project to ease social problems prevails over any other legislative proposals.[22] The drafters should be able to assess the social impacts of legislation because limits of legal directives will always affect human behaviour and thought. They must anticipate that the effects of a regulation will impose symbolic impact on behaviour, moral values and attitudes. The drafting office should be able to appreciate that the proposal impacts on human interrelationships or decisions it makes in this respect.

4. Do-ability

Do-ability is a very crucial part in prioritising legislation. Many goals may be set out by the decision-makers but it is at the implementation stage that those goals are achieved or displaced.[23] The implementation of laws, like that of policy programmes, brings about unanticipated consequences, goal displacements and change in original conceptions. The difference between legally defined programmes and other types of policy is that law does not always lend itself to evaluation by standards of goal fulfilment; rather, it might be evaluated by standards of compliance to specific norms. Both sets of standards are interrelated:

---

[19]Yehezkel Drort, 'Law and Social Change (1958–1959)' 787 Tul LR 787.
[20]Kudat Brown, and McGeeney (n 10) 50.
[21]Nzerem (n 2) 75.
[22]Don W Brown and Donald W Crowley, 'The Societal Impact of Law: An Assessment of Research' (1979) 1 Law & Policy 255
[23]Erhard Blankenburg, 'The Waning of Legality in the Concept of Policy Implementation' (1985) 7 Law & Policy 481.

policy-makers use legislation, among other means, to achieve their ends, and lawmakers have policy goals in mind when they devise regulations, for which they expect some compliance; this thus creates the compelling need to prioritise drafting projects.[24]

For any legislation to be effective, means to implement it must be readily available. There is no need for prioritising legislation to implement a project for which apparently the state has no capacity both in terms of financial and human resources to carry out the task.[25] The drafting office should think of prioritising legislation which they know beforehand will be effective. It is wise to anticipate problems of implementation of the legislation. They should think and analyse in order to be able to foresee likely shifts and problems in the process.[26]

It is possible to pass legislation where there are no institutions to implement it. When prioritising legislation, it is one of the areas that the drafting office should put under consideration. Before deciding on the legislative programme, the drafting must anticipate the capacities of implementation agencies. It would not make any sense to pass a law when there are no agencies to efficiently implement it.[27] Thus, the effectiveness of law depends on availability and infrastructure of institutions that are ready to organise access to legal means.[28] An example in juvenile justice is, if there is need to establish youth justice outside the court system, there should be institutions to deal with youth secure custody. Such arrangements also require other parallel programmes based on the seriousness of the offences and ages of the youth. This means that when prioritising, the drafting office should possess information on existence of such institutions.[29]

The cost for implementation of legislation is one other area among others where the drafting office must consult when prioritising the legislation. There are different types of costs of implementing legislation. One direct cost is the cost to the public sector. There may be other costs, for example if the legislation provides for grants for housing or small businesses. The drafting office should be able to gauge all these costs to ascertain whether legislation can be effectively implemented.[30] For every drafting project, the budgetary consequences of legislation must be put under consideration in the prioritising process in order to achieve practicability of the law.[31]

In his article, Ross Carter refers to a period in time when legislation could not be implemented. This is when, in the UK, mandatory rehabilitation for very short-term prisoners by coupling time spent in custody with a release period under licence had to be put on hold because the resources needed to implement the scheme did not exist. This implies that if the cost of legislation had been

---

[24] Ibid., 482.
[25] Seidman (n 3) 76.
[26] Blankenburg (n 22) 482.
[27] Ibid., 483.
[28] Blankenburg (n 22) 485.
[29] Legislation for juvenile justice (1976) 69 Brit J Criminol 9.
[30] Kellermann (n 1) 200.
[31] Robert P Davis and P Nejelski, 'Justice Impact Statements – Determining how New Laws will affect the Courts.' (1978) 62 (June–July) Judicature 21.

considered in prioritising, the very proposal would not have made its way onto the legislative schedule.[32]

It suffices to note that it would make no sense to give high priority to a Bill intended to implement a project for which the government does not have sufficient funds or the trained human capacity. It would be imperative to bear in mind that there are lurking in the legislative process a range of forces, some favourable, some unfavourable. Having one eye on the parliamentary timetable to get a feel for the nature and volume of the business before a parliament would help to assess the chances of a draft bill being included in the business for a particular session of parliament. It would therefore be wise to make the best use of the resources that are known to be available.[33] The rise in the decreased effectiveness of the law can be highly accountable to the depressingly limited economic resources that would be made available for law enforcement. It is therefore important to prioritise legislation in close examination of the availability of funds to enforce the legislation.[34]

Another important issue in prioritising legislation is delegated legislation. The drafting office must be able to understand the scope of the delegated legislation required to complete a legislative scheme. Effective implementation of primary legislation goes hand in hand with the availability of the secondary legislation and the drafting office has to be aware that delegated legislation needs priority in the legislative scheme for the practicability of the primary legislation that is already published.[35]

Passing the legislation is only one step. The biggest challenge lies in enforcing that legislation. The challenges encompass not only one element but a number of them, all of which have to be considered in prioritising legislation for effective enforcement. Passing legislation which will languish in the statute book without being implemented clutters the statute book and as such it is essential that, when prioritising, the drafter ought to ensure that all measures are in place.[36]

5. The drafting programme

In his view, Harry argues that 'sound legislation is more than a matter of good intentions and enlightened policy choices. Hard technical work has to be done before even the best law-making idea can be made into a clear and enforceable statute'.[37] This is to say that when all other criteria have been met, it would be

---

[32] Ross Carter, '"High-quality" Legislation – (How) Can Legislative Counsel Facilitate It?' (2011) The Loophole 44.
[33] Nzerem (n 2) 67.
[34] H-J Albrecht, 'Countries in Transition: Effects of Political, Social and Economic Change On Crime and Crime Justice – Sanctions and their Implementation' (1999) 479 Eur J Crime, Crim L & Crim Just 448.
[35] Sandra Markman, 'It's Just Your Imagination – Some Thoughts on the Role of Parliamentary Counsel in Ensuring Practicability of Legislative Instruments' (2011) The Loophole 110.
[36] Meixian Li, 'Environmental Laws in China' (2004) 18 Temple Int Comp LJ 156.
[37] Harry W Jones, 'Bill-Drafting in Congress and the State Legislatures' (1952) 65(3) Havard LR 441.

important to take into account that the drafting establishment on which rests the burden of drafting the legislation has limited endurance capacity.[38]

Considering the apparent scarcity of draftspersons, it is important that the drafting office looks at the nature and history of the drafting institution and how it would deal with the formation and development of the legislative policy.[39] The time frame available for drafting the given proposals should be considered when prioritising. The drafting office should be able to prioritise legislation balancing the legislative schedule of the parliament and the number of bills that would be able to be produced by the drafters. The prioritising institution must take note of the drafting capacity because if the drafters work under pressure, it will affect the quality of their output, the legislation. 'By the time instructions are received, there may be not much room for the draftsman to take decisions which will make for simplicity and clarity'.[40] This matter qualifies for attention to avoid pressing the drafting office into producing poor quality proposals.

The available drafting resources and the strains a particular drafting needs, the time needed, the number of the projects and the number of the available drafters should be balanced when prioritising the drafting proposals.[41] Harry denotes that a draftsperson is not a policy-maker, but legislative research and drafting work that is thoroughly done and technically sound contributes notably to the wise legislative decision. These are the reasons why the capacity of the drafting office should be one of the visited areas in prioritising legislation.[42]

Even when the drafting office may be constrained by time, the small number of drafters or lack of specific knowledge on a particular proposal, it is diligent that the drafting office considers the drafting capabilities of the private practice in the country but has to ensure that prioritising legislation goes hand in hand with the availability and capacity of the drafting office.

6. Conclusion

Prioritising legislation should be aligned with the real needs of the people and focused on how the existing problems can be solved. It should weigh options according to cost or benefits and how it will work. Decisions should be more fact based than theoretical and priority be given to certain target groups such as the poor, vulnerable, elderly and women.[43]

To help the drafting office to lay proper drafting projects, certain information needs to be provided. This includes among others the likely social impacts, especially those related to the poor, majority employment opportunities and equality

---

[38]Nzerem (n 2) 76.
[39]Review article. 'On Teaching Legislative Drafting' (1983) 4 SLR 179.
[40]Report of the Renton Committee. 'The Preparation of Legislation' (1975) 43HL.
[41]Seidman (n 3) 77.
[42]Jones (n 36) 442.
[43]Kudat Brown and McGeeney (n 10) 56.

of life. This would enable the drafting office to justify with informed experience the order of the drafting projects.[44]

All issues that affect finance, organisation, personnel and environment must be examined on a separate basis. Evaluating the impacts legislation would impose on different modes of society is a necessary step to prioritising a bill that will be effective.[45]

The drafting office should during the prioritisation in the policy process be able to ascertain whether the legislation both during preparation and implementation takes into account the attitudes and behaviour of the stakeholders. They should consider to what extent the legislative intent will be achieved, and the costs and benefits of the legislation.[46]

The drafter's office should draw up the order of the legislation after identifying the reasons for compliance of the legislation in terms of the goals, values, preferences and expectations of the people involved.[47] Although drafters do not have the primary responsibility for ensuring efficiency and efficacy of the laws they draft, they have to always be conscious of the practicability of legislation. This begins with prioritising.[48]

For legislation to be effective in producing the results desired by its authors and proponents, prioritising in the order as discussed in the preceding paragraphs is a necessary tool. Downplaying prioritising of legislation is one major reason among others that leads to producing many unanticipated and often undesirable effects that the primary proponents did not forecast.[49]

The drafting office has a duty to make an informed consideration of all aspects of the legislative proposals so as to achieve effectiveness of legislation. Without forgetting each country's unique circumstances, if the drafting offices were to assess the legislative proposals from the line ministries and prioritise them according to the above given criteria, no doubt it would greatly improve the quality of the legislation and hence its practicability.

Notes on contributor

Odethie Birungi Kamugundu has been a principal state attorney in the Ministry of Justice of Rwanda since 2010 in the Legislative Drafting Department which drafts, coordinates and oversees the drafting of laws in Rwanda. Prior to that, the author worked in National Public Prosecution as a prosecutor from 2002 to 2010. The author attended the National University of Rwanda and graduated in Law (LLB) in 1999, and studied Legislative Drafting (LLM) in 2011–2012 at the Institute of Advanced Legal Studies, the University of London.

---

[44]Siedman (n 3) 79.
[45]Jyrki Tala, Juhani Korhonen and Kaijus Ervasti, 'Improving The Quality Of Law Drafting In Finland' (1998) 4 Colum J Eur L 629.
[46]Kudat Brown and Mc Geeney (n 10) 49.
[47]Crowle (n 21) 257.
[48]Markman (n 35) 109.
[49]Crowle (n 21) 264.

Savings clause: get it right

Rosmizan Muhamad

The general rule is that a savings clause should not be included automatically in legislation, and it should be specific and used only when necessary. However this rule is devoid of value unless it answers a vital question: when is it necessary to provide a specific savings clause in legislation? This article attempts to show that a specific savings clause is needed when legislation introduces changes in procedure.

A. Introduction

Every law being in the nature either of a command or a prohibition is a displacement of existing civil relations, in which society, as well as individuals, has acquired rights.[1] There is no such thing as a law that does not extinguish rights, powers, privileges or immunities acquired under previously existing laws. The nature of law being as such, at any certain time individuals affected by a law, whether new or amending law, there may be found in different postures. Thus, the savings clause is a device to preserve the designated expectancies, rights or obligations from immediate destruction or interference and to make the transition between one set of laws to another less painful and disrupting.[2]

Savings clause plays an important part to ensure the effective operation of new rules within the existing system. However, savings provision is the most neglected area in statute law.[3] The savings clause is neglected by the instructing officer, because they are preoccupied with the grandeur of the plan for the future and forget the mundane and practical problem of the present.[4] Thus the competence of a drafter is essential to elicit questions and to get the right instruction to ensure the savings clause they draft is right and complete.[5]

---

[1] HR Millard, 'The Savings Clause: Some Problems in Construction and Drafting' (1954–1955) 33 Tex L Rev 285, 285.
[2] Ibid.
[3] FAR Bennion, *Understanding Common Law Legislation: Drafting and Interpretation* (OUP, Oxford 2001) 70.
[4] GC Thornton, *Legislative Drafting* (3rd edn Butterworths, London 1987) 320.
[5] D Berry, 'The Importance of Getting Savings and Transitional Right: Two Contrasting Cases' <http://www.opc.gov.au/calc/docs/Article_Berry_savingstransitional_2001.rtf> accessed 23 March 2010.

Nevertheless, a drafter is always in a dilemma whether to rely on the general savings clause[6] or to provide a specific savings clause. It is not uncommon for a drafter to dither, and often a savings clause is included out of a superfluity rather than an abundance of caution, which leads to unnecessary words in a statute.[7]

The general rule is that a savings clause should not be included automatically in legislation, and it should be specific and used only when necessary.[8] However, this rule is devoid of value unless it answers a vital question, when is it necessary to provide a specific savings clause? Thus, this article seeks to show that a specific savings clause is necessary to supplement the general savings clause when legislation introduces changes in procedure. To prove this hypothesis, this article examines cases relating to legislation that introduce changes in procedure, analyses why reliance on general savings statute is inadequate and how a specific savings clause can complement the general savings clause to fill the gaps. This essay also suggests what a drafter should generally do to determine the necessity to provide a specific savings clause in legislation.

B. General savings clause versus specific savings clause

A universal rule of construction is that statutes will not be applied retrospectively unless it is clear from the language that it is to be applied to both the past and future transaction. The rule is founded upon the ground that justice demands that a citizen be informed of the law before it is applied to his conduct and that retroactive law offends natural justice.[9] This rule is also embodied in Article 7 of the Malaysian Federal Constitution which prohibits criminal law to operate retrospectively. Furthermore, section 30(1) of the Malaysia Interpretation Act 1948 and 1967 (similar to section 16 of the UK Interpretation Act 1978) saves certain matters such as rights, privileges, obligation or liability acquired, accrued or incurred under the repealed law from the changes brought by the operation of new legislation. This constitutional and interpretation provision is the general savings clause in legislation. Based on the general savings provisions, courts have found an implied legislative intention to save even though there is no express savings clause.[10]

A specific savings clause is a provision either to supplement or to supplant the general savings clause.[11] Thus, a specific savings clause should be clear as to

---

[6] 'General savings clause' refers to the general savings provisions provided in the constitution and interpretation act which save certain rights and obligation from the operation of repealing law and prohibit retrospective operation of law. See Millard (n 1).
[7] Thornton (n 4).
[8] Drafting Style Manual <http://lrs.state.al.us/style_manual/style_manual.html#anchor514840> accessed 24 March 2010.
[9] EE Smead, 'Rule Against Retroactive Legislation: A Basic Principle of Jurisprudence' (1936) 20 Minn L Rev 775–9.
[10] Millard (n 1) at 290.
[11] Ibid. at 298.

its purpose to avoid doubt which may have resulted in unnecessary litigation. The next section attempts to illustrate the necessity to provide a specific savings clause to supplement the general savings clause, particularly when legislation introduces changes to a statutory procedure.

C. Specific savings clause when legislation introduces changes in procedure

When legislation introduced changes[12] to a statutory procedure, the general savings clause automatically implied that the existing proceedings will continue under the old law, because the new law does not operate retrospectively and does not impair rights and liabilities already acquired or incurred. The common questions as to when the new procedure begins and whether the new procedure applies only to proceedings commenced after the effective date are easily answered by a commencement and application provisions.[13] A similar principle applies to legislation introduced changes to the nature of conduct that will allow a person to pursue a claim, whether through a judicial or administrative proceedings.[14]

However, possible ambiguity is inevitable if a drafter relies on the general savings statute or uses the broad statements of a general savings clause as to the effect of the law, such as 'this Act does not affect any duty or right accruing, accrued or acquired, or liability incurred, before the effective date of this Act'. This type of savings clause is so general in nature that it is difficult to determine what it does. Litigation could easily result from efforts to determine what is and what is not a 'duty or right accruing, accrued or acquired' before the effective date of the Act.[15] Thus, when changes are made to a statutory procedure, a specific savings clause should be provided to avoid ambiguity as to the application of the new procedure to the various existing situations and to make clear the rights and duties to be saved.

In *Aitken v South Hams District Council*,[16] the issue was whether a notice served under section 58(1) of the Control of Pollution Act 1974 remained effective and a person who breached the notice could be validly prosecuted under the 1974 Act, although the Act has been repealed by the Environmental Protection Act 1990 (the new law which introduced a new procedure in statutory nuisance). The general savings statute only saves the obligation and liability incurred under the repealed law, but does not answer specific question as to whether a person who has been served with a notice has incurred liability under the old law and can be prosecuted under the old law, although the breach was committed after the old law has been repealed. Therefore, a specific savings clause to save the

---

[12] Changes may happen if legislation amends, repeals and replaces, legislation, or being itself a new legislation.
[13] State of Oregon Bill Drafting Manual makes no distinction between application and savings clause. See State of Oregon Bill Drafting Manual Chapter 10 <http://www.lc.state.or.us/drfatingmanual.htm> accessed 19 April 2010.
[14] Ibid.
[15] State of Oregon (n 13).
[16] [1995] 1 AC 262.

life of the notice served under the old procedure is helpful to clear the ambiguity and when the liability is incurred could easily be determined, thus the question retroactive or retrospective may not arise.[17]

In *B v B*,[18] the issue was whether an order made under the Guardianship of Minors Act 1971 that the appellant pay maintenance for his children was not affected by the repealed of the Act by the Children Act 1989. A specific savings clause expressly stated that any pending applications under the Guardianship of Minors Act 1971 would proceed to a hearing and be dealt with under it and not the new law. However, ambiguity arises when an order is issued, but there is no pending application because the application to modify or vary the order has not been made under the old law. A general savings clause does not provide an answer as to the life of an order made under the old law thus should be supplemented by a specific savings clause to save the order and the procedure to be adopted to vary and modify the order issued under the old law when there is no pending application.[19]

In *Chief Adjudication Officer and another v Maguire*,[20] it was held that a right could be acquired under an enactment before its repeal, even though that right was contingent upon an event which occurred only after repeal. Thus, where a person is entitled to money or other benefit at the time of repeal, the requirement that he must take further steps to prove the existence or the extent of that entitlement does not preclude that person's right to claim the benefit. In this case, the right of the respondent to claim special hardship allowance that occurred before the repeal of the statute is not extinguished since he made the claim within the specified limited time, although at the time the claim was made the new law has come into force. The judge suggested that the distinction between what rights are to survive and what rights do not should be made clear so that the costs of endless debate as to whether a particular alleged right has been acquired or not can be avoided. Such suggestion by the judge may be addressed through a specific and clear savings clause.

This case was strongly distinguished in *Odelola v Secretary of State for the Home Department*,[21] when the court held that an appellant who had applied to remain in the UK as a postgraduate doctor after completing her clinical attachment had no accrued right when the immigration rule was changed before her application was decided by the Home Office. The change in the immigration rule resulted in the appellant not being entitled to remain in the UK. It was held that the appellant's pending application did not necessarily give the appellant rights to stay in the UK. Thus, the general savings clause is not applicable since no right was acquired by the appellant under the old rule. On the contrary, *Maguire* has acquired the rights to claim the allowance once he suffered the prescribed

---

[17] See also *Whipple v Howser* <http://www.publications.ojd.state.or.us/A101202.htm> accessed 28 April 2010.
[18] [1995] 1 FLR 459.
[19] It is also possible to allow the courts to decide, on a case to case basis with appropriate guidelines, whether to apply a new procedural rule to pending proceedings. See TLC Drafting Manual <http.tlc.state.tx.us/legal/dm/sec312.thm> accessed 19 April 2010.
[20] [1999] 2 All ER 859.
[21] [2009] 3 All ER 1061.

injury. These cases illustrate that in matters concerning rights to allowance or money, the court will be more inclined to decide in favour of the subject, but not in immigration matters where the government has absolute prerogative. Thus, when the legislature intends to deprive certain existing or accrued rights, it is prudent to make a clear provision about it, otherwise such rights are saved by the general savings statute.

In 1994, the Malaysian Parliament passed the Courts of Judicature (Amendment) Act to create a Court of Appeal (a new tier in the appeal process). The amendment made no savings provision; thus general savings clause are applicable with the effect that appeal against the decisions delivered before the creation of the Court of Appeal can be made to the Supreme Court (as provided under the old law) and not to the newly established Court of Appeal.

In 1995 another amendment was made to rename the Supreme Court as the Federal Court and the amendment was to operate retrospectively to 24 June 1994. A savings provision provided that any pending proceedings before the Supreme Court on 23 June 1994 must be heard by the newly named Federal Court. This specific savings clause was construed to displace the general principle and have the effect that any appeal filed after 23 June 1994 is not within the competence of the Federal Court, although the appeal was against the decision made by the High Court before 23 June 1994. A practical problem arises because the parties who had filed their appeals to the Supreme Court after 23 June 1994, because of the specific savings clause in the 1995 amendment, are now facing jurisdictional challenge on the competence of the Federal Court to hear their appeal and the possibility of the decision made by the Federal Court in many appeals within that time be nullified.[22] Thus, in providing a specific savings clause to supplement the general savings clause, careful thought is necessary to avoid practical problems and inconvenience to litigants. A complete analysis of the effect of the specific savings clause is a must to avoid unintended inconsistency with the general savings clause.

From the above cases, it is clear that the necessity to provide a specific savings clause to supplement the general savings clause depends to a large extent on the facts of each case.[23] It involves practical questions of what is to be saved in any particular situation, what happens to a particular case when the law changes and when exactly the right or obligation accrued or incurred.[24] Given the wide terms used in the general savings statute, the drafter needs to consider whether a specific savings clause is needed to add to the effect of the general savings clause and effectively avoid any ambiguity in the application of the new law to the existing facts and circumstances or particularly identify what constitute rights and obligation under the old law. Obviously, non-existent or

---

[22] *Lim Phin Khian v Kho Su Ming* [1996] The Malayan LJ 1.
[23] See LE Filson and SL Strokof, *The Legislative Drafter's Desk Reference* (2nd edn CQ Press, Washington, DC 2009) 178, where the authors opined that in drafting savings clause, every case is different and there is no standard form for it.
[24] State of Oregon (n 13).

inadequate savings provisions can result in litigation, considerable difficulty and judges sometimes criticise their drafting in their judgments.[25]

Therefore, to decide whether a change in statutory procedure requires a specific savings clause to supplement the general savings clause or otherwise, the drafter must be clear on the application of the new law to the existing facts and circumstances. Take, for example, a new law to establish a tribunal to hear claims on housing matters.[26] The new law changes the procedure for the claim of late delivery penalty from courts to a tribunal. Thus, the important questions are what happened to the cases already filed in court? Should the court continue to hear such claims or the cases be should transferred to the tribunal? Is the new procedure less favourable to the litigant? If so, how will the rights of the litigant be affected and how can the issue of retrospective law be tackled? Because of the fact that the cause of action to claim late delivery penalty originated from a contract, another important question to be addressed is whether the claim can be filed to the tribunal if the contract was entered before the new law comes into force. In other words, a change in procedure usually entails a few common issues about pending proceedings, retrospectives application, what constitutes rights and obligation and when such rights and obligation incurred or accrued.[27] Thus the necessity to provide a specific savings clause should always be considered. Moreover, in a special situation it may be desirable to preserve rights or duties that have not matured, or proceedings that have not begun.[28]

If all the practical questions are brought to the attention of the instructing officers, their answers will be the helpful guides to the drafter to make an informed choice in providing a specific savings clause to deal with specific, intricate and peculiar issues in the implementation of new procedure. In many cases, doubt arises on the application of a new law to a particular case or circumstances occurred under the old law, because often when a law is introduced, it will govern activities that are already taking place.[29] Thus it is also essential for the drafter to identify how the operation of old law could be construed as giving right or incurring liabilities before the drafter can formulate a specific savings clause. In a nutshell, it involves a thorough policy analysis.[30]

---

[25] Legislation Advisory Committee Guidelines, 153 <http://www.justice.govt.nz/lac/index.html> accessed 27 April 2010.
[26] *PuncakDana Sdn Bhd v Tribunal Tuntutan Pembeli Rumah* [2003] 7 CLJ 350, *Tribunal Tuntutan Pembeli Rumah v West Court Corporation Sdn Bhd and Other Appeals* [2004] 2 CLJ 617, *West Court Corporation Sdn Bhd v Tuntutan Pembeli Rumah* [2004] 4 CLJ 203.
[27] In certain cases, such as change in court fees, law of limitation and right of appeal, it may not be purely procedural as those affect substantive rights. See NK Chakrabarti, *Principles of Legislation and Legislative Drafting* (2nd edn R Cambray & Co, Calcutta 2002) 195. See also MA Burnham, 'Savings Constitutional Rights from Judicial Scrutiny: The Savings Clause in the Law of the Commonwealth Carribbean' (2004–2005) 36 U Miami Inter-Am LR 249.
[28] F Reed Dickerson, *The Fundamental of Legal Drafting* (2nd edn Little Brown, Boston 1986) 297.
[29] BH Simamba *The Legislative Process: A Handbook for Public Officials* (Author House, Indiana 2009) 126.
[30] The steps to be taken in analysing policy to determine the necessity to provide a savings clause is elaborated in the LAC Guidelines (n 25) at 154–6.

D. Conclusion

In drafting a savings provision, it is particularly important that drafters are able to identify the gaps in their instructions which the instructing department would have plugged if it had appreciated the need to do so and then ask appropriate questions.[31] It has been claimed that it takes at least seven to eight years for drafters to acquire these skills. Such length of time is needed to gain experience and wisdom to make sound judgement in producing a legislative text,[32] and this is particularly true in drafting a specific savings clause.

Thornton suggested that drafters must have the confidence to rely on the effect of general savings statute where it is adequate, but it is common for drafters to hesitate[33] because of fear of being unclear and ambiguous. Drafters would normally choose not to leave their work to be construed and presumed, thus detailed specific savings clauses are drafted to avoid doubt. Nevertheless, they might fall into the danger of being over-elaborate,[34] over-precise and 'overdrafting'.[35] The more they try to be exhaustive, the more vulnerable the legislation will be to omissions, potential challenge and 'false accuracy'.[36] Thus the great challenge in drafting a savings clause is to achieve clarity[37] by taking the middle path between the need to be clear and the danger of an overzealous attempt to be precise.

The general savings clause is readily implied to take effect in legislation in the absence of contrary intention. The judgement to rely on general savings clause should be made with cautious mind, after the drafters are satisfied that the general savings clause is adequate to preserve what the policy-makers want to preserve. However, it is impossible to encompass all the variety of activities under vastly differing repealed statutes within the general savings statute, thus a specific savings clause in individual legislation are often the best answer.[38] Moreover, if the new legislation has the effect of altering the existing statutory procedure, an abundance of caution is essential to consider providing a specific savings clause to avoid unnecessary litigation because changes to a statutory procedure almost always raise questions on application and retroactivity.[39]

---

[31] I McLeod, *Principles of Legislative and Regulatory Drafting* (Hart, Portland, OR 2009) 98.
[32] S Laws, 'Drawing the Line' in: Co Stefanou and H Xanthaki (eds), *Drafting Legislation: A Modern Approach* (Ashgate, Aldershot 2008) 19–34.
[33] Thornton (n 4) at 321.
[34] M Zander, *The Law-Making Process* (6th edn CUP, Cambridge 2004) 26.
[35] Brian Hunt quoted *Legislative Drafting Manual* (Dublin, 2001). See Brian Hunt, 'Plain Language in Legislative Drafting: An Achievable Objective or a Laudable Ideal?',7 <http://www.plainlanguagenetwork.org/conferences/2002/legdraft/legdraft.pdf> accessed 5 May 2010.
[36] D Greenberg, *Craies on Legislation* (8th edn Sweet & Maxwell, London 2004) 319.
[37] A Fluckiger, 'The Ambiguous Principle of the Clarity of Law' in: A Wagner and S Cacciguidi-Fahy (eds), *Obscurity and Clarity in the Law* (Ashgate, Aldershot 2008) 9–24. The author opined that perfect clarity in legislation is an ideal and cannot be achieved. See also J Stark, 'Should the Main Goal of Statutory Drafting be Accuracy or Clarity' (1994) 15 Stat LR 207; Reed Dickerson, 'The Diseases of Legislative Language' (1964) Mich LJ 5.
[38] J Burrows, 'The Interpretation Act 1999' in: R Bigwood (ed), *The Statute: Making and Meaning* (Lexis Nexis, Wellington 2004) 224.
[39] State of Oregon (n 13).

When legislation introduces changes to procedure, it is the drafter's responsibility to attempt to foresee any problems that might arise and to ensure that they are dealt with appropriately. Foreseeing these problems requires a combination of legal and practical analysis, imagination and common sense. The ultimate aim is to get the savings clause right. An appropriate savings clause makes it possible for a new procedure to take effect with minimum disruption of existing expectations and liabilities. Hence, great care must be exercised in drafting a savings clause.

The effect of transplanting legislation from one jurisdiction to another

Rosaline Baindu Cowan

Law Officers Department, Lamina Sankoh Street, Freetown, Sierra Leone, West Africa

> The hypothesis of the article is that legal transplants are a haphazard means of legislating, whereby a complex and difficult situation arises if the drafter cannot harmonise the laws being transplanted with that of the recipient country.

Methodology

In order to prove the hypothesis of the article, I will be looking at the history of legal transplantation. I shall also look at various institutions and jurisdictions where legislation has been transplanted and the effect it had there. I will look at legal transplantation through private contracting, citing China as an example, the introduction of the doctrine of equity into colonial West Africa and how the laws of equity were transplanted into African customary laws. In so doing, I shall also look into the interpretation of multilingual treaties, issues with constitutional transplanting, legal transplants through private contractors and jurisdictions where sections of an Act have been transplanted, using Sierra Leone as an example.

Introduction

Many scholars and writers have dealt with the issue of transplanting Legislation from one jurisdiction to another and the effect it normally has on the recipient country. Transplanting means moving something from one place to another in order for it to function as it did in the host. The history of a system of law is largely a history of borrowing legal materials from another system and incorporating it into your own country's situation as best as you could. The history of legal transplantation can be traced back thousands of years.[1] Alan Watson describes legal transplantation as 'the moving of a rule or a system of law from one country to another or from one people to another'. It depends on the way the transplantation of a law is done, meaning that whether it is the whole law that is transplanted or just parts will determine the outcome in the recipient country.

Legal borrowing can be traced way back to colonialism. This is so because many of the countries especially in Africa that were colonised by either the

---

[1] Alan Watson, *Legal Transplants: An Approach to Comparative Law* (University of Georgia Press, 1993) 21.

English or the French used their systems, and even when they gained independence they borrowed the structure of the laws that had been used in the colony.

When a legislative drafter is faced with a new policy from the clients, it is up to him or her to determine what the client is looking for. It is during this process that the drafter has to use his or her skills and intellect to make sure that the client receives a draft that is in compliance with the policy. Because in the art of drafting all bills differ, it is not so easy for a drafter to work with precedents, while in the same breath we can say that it is at this point that borrowing becomes inevitable. This is so because if the drafter has been given instructions to work on a topic that is not very familiar, the first thing would be to turn to another jurisdiction that has done work in that area and try to borrow the pattern to use in the recipient country. Regarding legal transplants, discussion has always continued between legal scholars, the most representative being the one between two English scholars since the 1970s. O Kahn-Freund in his article, Uses and Misuses of Comparative Law,[2] quotes some words from Montesquieu, who was the first comparative lawyer to give his opinion. In Montesquieu's view, it was only in the most exceptional cases that the institutions of one country could serve those of another.[3] He is saying that an institution could only be designed to suit one country, and it is very difficult to use it to suit another. For him, legal transplantation is impossible. O Kahn-Freund goes on to explain that there are two main factors that hinder law transplanting. He names them as environmental factors, which could include geographical, sociological and economic, and cultural elements, and the so-called political elements.[4] In 1974, Alan Watson refuted O Kahn-Freund's opinion in his article, Legal Transplants and Law Reform.[5] He argued that history did not prove that legal transplantation is impossible. He gave some examples in his article, such as the French law serving as the model for the Japanese penal code and the code of criminal procedure that were enacted in 1882.

Analysis of transplanting

Having got the views of some writers and scholars with regards legal transplanting I am now going further by looking into various areas of the transplanting process and the effect. First, if we look at the issue of transplanting through private contracts, this area generally focuses on legal transplants through governmental channels (e.g. legislative and judicial processes). In recent times, global economic integration has become a powerful engine pushing the wave of legal transplantation to its apex. International governmental, semi-governmental and non-governmental organisations (NGOs) are the major contributors to legal standardisation and harmonisation today. Most of their projects embarked upon are to reduce the transaction costs for international market participants as well as the hope to improve the constitutional environments of the receiving countries. The transplanted laws under the standardisation or harmonisation movement are usually products of

---

[2] O Kahn-Fruend, 'On Uses and Misuses of Comparative Law' (1974) 37 MLR 20.
[3] Esprit des Lois, Book 1, Ch 3 (des Lois positives)
[4] Id.
[5] A Watson, 'Legal Transplant and Law Reform' (1976) 92 LQR 79.

international negotiations and conciliation, rather than wholesale adoptions of any particular legal system. States generally play a key role in this transplantation process because the standardised rules are made by the states at the international level, and the laws usually need to be incorporated into a legal system through legislative processes at the national level. When it comes to the issue of the transplant aspect, it is a bit more striking for developing countries because they usually have a weak voice in the international law-making process and relatively limited development of their legal institutions. Third world countries are typical of this since they are of the opinion that should they try to speak up as to the content of what is transplanted and how it is done; for example, the NGOs might refuse to cooperate with whatever aids they had intended to help the state in question if they do not incorporate laws that they have brought along with them to either insert into existing legislation or create new legislation. Although the state (the governmental organs, particularly the legislative branch) is the major conveyor of foreign law, holding the power over whether and how to transplant, the transplant motivation is normally associated with political or governmental functions such as regulating a new national problem. In Sierra Leone, for example, there was an issue with legislating for road traffic issues for commercial bike riders. There was already a provision in the road Traffic Act of 2007 but ideas that were borrowed from neighbouring states were not practicable, so it had to be abandoned at a very late stage of the amendments. Law can also be transplanted by non-state actors. For example, the International Accounting Standards Board, a non profit, private sector organisation, develops international standards for financial reporting. These non-state actors usually still follow the typical transplant method, which involves government legislation/regulation processes at national level. With regards contracts also, we have borrowing or transplanting through private actors. Here, laws are borrowed through private contracting. Through the channel of contracting, private transactors have been transplanting regulatory law across borders for quite a while. International commercial arbitration may be put in this category. Arbitration as a dispute resolution mechanism is increasingly popular with international commercial actors.

Secondly, if we look at multilingual treaties, with these the growing trend towards providing authentic texts[6] of treaties (particularly multilateral treaties) in four or more languages poses dangers to the peace and stability of the international order, given that a number of diplomatic incidents and even wars have been triggered by differences between language versions of multilingual treaties.[7] The aim of multilingual treaties is to have a common document in various languages, especially for ease of reference. The problem here starts when the drafters transplanting give a direct interpretation to the text and most of the time the text gives a new meaning in the receiving country. The Vienna Convention on the laws of treaties attempts to deal with this situation in art 33, which sets forth

---

[6]See Vienna Convention on the Law of Treaties, art 10, 23 May 1969, un Doc, A/39/27, reprinted in (1969) 63A JIL 875 (hereinafter Vienna Convention or the Convention) regarding the definition of authentic texts.
[7]A contemporary example is a dispute between the USA and the USSR regarding the 1963 Threshold Test Ban Treaty which arose because of differences in phrasing between the English and Russian versions. Anderson, 'US denies Soviet charges over nuclear test' (United Press Int, 24 August 1987).

rules for the interpretation of multilingual treaties.[8] There are various views with regards the position of a state that has entered into international legal affairs that are multilingual. One school of thought maintains that a state is bound under any circumstances (in the absence of contrary provisions in the treaty) only by the text in its own language.[9] Others agree with this position but only until the possibility of a discrepancy between the texts has been raised. Still others argue that in interpreting treaties the various texts must be compared.[10]

During the Vienna Convention, it was a matter of some controversy whether language versions should be compared during interpretation as a matter of routine or whether it was permissible to presume that all authentic versions were equivalent in meaning. Sir Humphrey Waldock was opposed to mandatory comparison, unlike Rosenne, saying that comparison would 'undermine the security of the individual texts' and the unity of the treaty by transplanting 'concepts of one language into the interpretation of a text in another language'. The present attitudes found amongst national courts regarding the routine comparison of treaty text are mixed. Most tend to rely on the treaty versions in their own native or working languages, at least when there is no contention in the text meanings. International courts and tribunals are also very far from consulting all language versions as a matter of course. Most of them consult only texts in their working language unless a divergence has been pointed out. For example, when interpreting the United Nations Charter, the International Court of Justice has almost always consulted only the English and French versions,[11] though the Chinese, Russian and Spanish versions are also authentic.

Next, I shall look at the issue of constitutional transplanting. The main thing I will concentrate on here is explaining what happens when constitutions travel across national borders and amongst various cultures. Constitutions are almost always the same in terms of their context. But because of the differences in our cultures, it becomes difficult for the drafter when the issue of borrowing emerges because the burden rests upon them to make sure that whatever they intend to borrow or however they intend to incorporate it, the end result must reflect what the policy intended to achieve. It is normally said that no one begins to write a constitution from scratch. Thus, there is a strong interest that promotes transplanting. For example, the leaders of a particular state might use legislation from another state to promote friendship. I would agree with this view because in my jurisdiction, whenever there is an issue of new legislation or an amendment to something that has been incorporated by another state, the drafters are normally hinted to take that country's legislation as a working tool, though it does not always fit our criteria. Constitutional experts also have a vested interest in borrowing or, at least, in the international exchange of ideas, because this may provide them with influence and a sense of importance. The similarity in

---

[8] Article 33 reads, '1. when a treaty has been authenticated in two or more languages, the text is equally authoritative in each language, unless the treaty provides or the parties agree that in case of divergence a particular text shall prevail'.

[9] See e.g. L Oppenheim, *International Law: A Treatise* (vol 1 1955) 956; J Starke, *An Introduction to International Law* (1967) 378.

[10] See e.g. Haraszti, *Some Fundamental Problems of the Laws of Treaties* (1973) pp 180–181.

[11] Sinclair, op. cit. p 148; Tabory idem

constitutions does not prove that borrowing has occurred. Even in sections on rights, where international standards are usually adopted, there are important departures by which the drafters manifest the unique identities of their countries.

Rett Ludwikowski gives an interesting summary of attitudes prevailing during constitution making in East Central Europe; 'The drafters of the new constitution did not have any doubts that they [would] have to borrow from the West but they wanted to borrow in their own way'.[12] With the constitution, it is sometimes difficult to differentiate between borrowing unconsciously and transplanting. I would support what Ludwikowski is saying in this statement because when drafters are doing their country's constitution of even if the leaders have sought help from constitutional experts, there is always something unique about their culture and their own style they prefer to have represented. That means, even though the drafter might have to borrow from another city or transplant certain issues, it would have to be done in a way to suit the recipient country because of the difference in their culture, geographic location and political issues. Hence, this is an area whereby we can say that borrowing or transplanting has worked because whatever it is that has gone to the receiving country would fit in.

Where transplanting concerns success, on the constitutional level, it has been seen in new institutions such as the office of the ombudsman, which was borrowed from Scandinavia for its great potential to protect the rights of the powerless.

Effects of transplanting

When we look at the modern Chinese legal system, it is based on the transplantation of foreign legal systems, especially from Western countries. After the 1980s, the topic of legal transplantation has been seriously discussed both by government and legal scholars. It is now not only possible but necessary to take advantage of good legal experience of other countries to help build a legal system in the era of economic globalisation.

Concerning China's situation, it is believed that it is necessary to transplant a foreign legal system into China's legal system. The imbalance of social development and legal development forces China to carry out legal transplantation.[13] It is normally necessary for countries to catch-up with their developed counterparts in order to promote and preserve their social developments. This is exactly what China's current situation in recent years has been. Although China re-built its economic market system and developed it very well, we have to realise that their legal system is only at the beginning stages and their legal framework is still not perfect. They had many problems, especially after joining the WTO organisation, such as the protection of intellectual property. They still have a long way to go with the protection of human rights to reach the level of developed countries. In March 2004, the Chinese government officially added a provision of private property rights to the constitution of the Peoples Republic of China. It is stipulated that 'citizens' lawful private property is inviolable'.[14] This happened

---

[12]Rett R. Ludwikowski, 'COnstitutional Culture of the New East-Central European Democracies' in M Wyrzykowski (ed) *Constitutional Cultures* (Institute of Public Affairs, Warsaw 2001).
[13]See Qinhua He, 'China Legal Science' (vol 3 2002) 90
[14]Amendment 22, Constitution of the Peoples Republic of China.

because the imbalance of social development and legal development forced China to carry out legal transplantation. In modern society, most legal changes take place via imitation, and original innovations are extremely rare. It is fair to say that the protection of private property amendment made by the Chinese government is actually an example of legal imitation; in other words transplanting.

The reasons why we could say that transplanting was successful in the Chinese situation are first, when legal transplanting is done through private contracts it is more likely to be effective because the private actors know what it is they need to transplant and to what extent. Also, because the modern Chinese system borrows from the Western countries, even though their culture is not identical, it has benefited from laws transplanted from them. This is because it helps the Chinese to catch-up with the developed countries and makes them able to take advantage of the introduction of a good legal system into their old system.

As was mentioned earlier, many foreign and international agencies and bodies that penetrate third world or developing countries are the ones who encourage legal transplants that are most times not suitable to a particular country's culture or legal system. Social conditions not only play an important role in transplanting but may even decide the success or failure of the texts or laws. Some institutions that work very well in one set of social conditions may be useless or even destructive in others. When we look into the issue of transplantation and the effect it has in the Sierra Leonean commune, it almost always comes to what I have been echoing above about transplanted laws not being able to settle in the recipient state like it did where it came from.

The reason is because the transplanted laws are not normally done to suit the culture of the people or their system but to benefit the international organisations. For example, when we take the Child Rights Act of 2007 (Sierra Leone) into consideration, there are sections that I would personally say are not workable. If we look at part vii (Institutionalised Care and Miscellaneous Matters), this section, although it has been incorporated into the Act, due to the current system in the country and other constraints, it has not been up and running thus making it a redundant chapter in the Act. Another example that could be cited from the Sierra Leonean jurisdiction is the Road Traffic Act of 2007. Like the previous Act, there are sections that have been transplanted from other jurisdictions and incorporated into it by the drafter, though we do not have any need for such sections. If we take a look at the section dealing with principal road safety provisions, part X, it deals with issues like breath testing and things like these that have not been introduced or were not being planned for but were added to the amended Act.

Conclusion

'Law is largely autonomous operating in its own sphere'.[15] This is the reason why I would say that we cannot actually get a right or wrong answer to the effects of transplanting legislation.

Sometimes the acts of drafting ideas into texts of other countries are done unconsciously by the drafters who are not conversant with the cultures of the

---

[15] A Watson, *The Evolution of Law* (The Johns Hopkins University Press, Baltimore, MA 1985) 119.

country they are contracted to draft for. That is why it is normally not convenient to use foreign drafters. At other times, there is the assumption that because it worked in one country, there should be no problems adapting it in another without thinking of their economic situation, political situation and their geographical location.

Although legal transplant is possible, as we have seen in the Chinese example, and sometimes not effective, as in the examples I gave on Sierra Leone, it is not an easy process to carry out. When legal transplantation is to be done, there are important questions we need to consider before embarking on the transplant. First, do we need to transplant the entire legal system, department laws and statutes or only the specific legal system, legal rules or legal concepts? Secondly, is the law we need to transplant closely linked to politics, the economic system and ideology or value sense? Thirdly, does the rule in question have different political purposes or social functions? And lastly, do we want to transplant international law or specific national and traditional law? If we can satisfactorily answer these questions, then we would be in a position to direct the drafter to what it is our intentions are and the aim we want to achieve.

According to Watson, '[a] successful legal transplant – like that of a human organ – will grow in its new body, and become part of that body just as the rule or institution would have continued to develop in its parent system'.

Although Watson has said that the transplanted law would grow in the recipient country, I can also disagree with that to a point because, as we have seen, the transplanted laws usually cannot achieve the same results and fulfil the same aims in their society of adoption as in their society of origin. With international conventions and treaties, they can be transplanted easily and successfully, especially those dealing with international trade, because they are usually negotiated amongst many countries and meet their needs.

As mentioned earlier, there is no right or wrong answer with regards transplanting of legal documents, but I can say that there are pros and cons to it depending on the situation at hand, it could be a success or on outright failure if the drafter is not cautious.

Notes on contributor
Rosaline Baindu Cowan received her LLB (Hons) from East London University in the UK. She was called to the Bar in Sierra Leone in 2006. She has been working at the Ministry of Justice (Attorney General's chambers) since 2007 as a legislative drafter attached to the parliamentary division. She currently resides in Sierra Leone with her three loving children Axel, Aaliyah, and Sade at their family home.

Prerogative legislation as the paradigm of bad law-making: the Chagos Islands

Roman Cormacain

Director, Sir William Dale Legislative Drafting Clinic, Institute of Advanced Legal Studies, University of London, 45 Lancaster Road, London, N4 4PJ, UK

> Legislation made by way of the Royal Prerogative is a paradigm of bad law-making. This is examined via the case study of the British Indian Ocean Territory (Constitution) Order 2004. The Order was made without reference to a legislature and without proper scrutiny or legislative drafting. It is unclear, ambiguous and imprecise. It does not use plain language or gender-neutral language. It is deliberately inaccessible, making it extremely hard for the citizen to know its contents. In form and substance, it offends against the rule of law.

1. Introduction and background

1.1. Introduction

The Chagos Islands, a British Overseas Territory, are a small archipelago of coral atolls in the Indian Ocean. In 2004, Britain enacted the British Indian Ocean Territory (Constitution) Order 2004. Section 9 prohibited the Chagossians from living in the Chagos Islands. The 2004 Order was made by way of Royal Prerogative, which means that it was made by the Crown by Order in Council, following the advice of the Privy Council. In practice, this meant that it was made by the government without recourse to parliament. The House of Lords ruled the 2004 Order valid in *Bancoult (2)*.[1]

The hypothesis of this article is that the 2004 Order is bad law because it is of low quality and is inaccessible. With regard to quality, I assess this by reference to Xanthaki's criteria of quality in legislation.[2] For example, the Order is complex and uses archaic language. I also assess whether it can be called a 'constitution' under Elkin's definition.[3] Turning next to inaccessibility, I assess

---

[1] *Bancoult v Secretary of State for Foreign and Commonwealth Affairs* [2008] UKHL 61.
[2] Helen Xanthaki, 'On Transferability of Legislative Solutions: The Functionality Test' in Constantin Stefanou and Helen Xanthaki (eds), *Drafting Legislation: A Modern Approach* (Ashgate, Aldershot 2008).
[3] Zachary Elkins and others, *The Endurance of National Constitutions* (Cambridge University Press, New York 2009).

whether BIOT legislation is accessible under Donelan's definition of accessibility.[4] I argue that the use of the Royal Prerogative meant that the Order was subject to minimal publicity. I also demonstrate the importance of accessibility by reference to judicial and academic opinion. I carry out empirical research on the locations where BIOT legislation is to be found and supplement this by a Freedom of Information request to the Foreign and Commonwealth Office (FCO).

There is an additional argument that the Order is bad law as it is *ultra vires* the power of the Crown to make legislation for colonies. Space prevents an analysis of this argument, so it is only mentioned in passing here.

An anti-democratic theme underlies many of the points made in this article. The 2004 Order is legislation without a legislature. It was not voted upon or assented to by the British parliament. It was not the subject of a referendum among the Chagossians. It was not voted upon by any representatives of the Chagossians.

1.2. Historical background

At the outset, a word on nomenclature. The Chagos Islands/Archipelago is the geographical name for the islands. British Indian Ocean Territory (BIOT) is the name first used in 1965 to demarcate the islands as a political entity. Diego Garcia is the name of the largest island. Chagossians are the inhabitants. Ilois is the historic French/Creole name used to describe them (people of the islands).

The Chagos Islands were originally part of Mauritius.[5] In 1814, Mauritius was ceded by the French to the British. By the 1960s, the main economic activity on the islands was harvesting copra from coconut plantations. The population in the 1960s was low, between 829 and 1500.[6] Some families had lived there for generations.

Storm clouds began to gather in 1964 when the UK discussed establishing a US military base on Diego Garcia. In 1965, the UK detached the islands from Mauritius. Agreement on the base was reached between the USA and the UK in 1966. In 1967, the UK bought all land from the coconut plantation company. In 1968, Mauritius became independent. From 1968 to 1971, the Chagossians left the islands. Force was not used, although it was made clear to the islanders that there was to be neither employment nor supplies on the island. The Chagossians moved to either Mauritius or the Seychelles. Their lives in those places were bleak. They were eventually paid a small amount of compensation.

Every single British judge who has considered the conduct of the British government towards the Chagossians in that period has condemned it. Sedley LJ in the Court of Appeal said that

---

[4]Edward Donelan, 'European Approaches to Improving Access to and Managing the Stock of Legislation' (2009) 30 SLR 147.
[5]See further, David Vine, *Island of Shame: The Secret History of the US Military Base at Diego Garcia* (Princeton University Press, Princeton 2009).
[6]Adam Tomkins, 'Magna Carta, Crown and Colonies' (2001) PL 571, although Madeley puts it at up to 2000, John Madeley, *Diego Garcia: A Contrast to the Falklands* (Minority Rights Group Report No. 54, 1985).

What they have received has done little to repair the wrecking of their families and communities, to restore their self-respect or to make amends for the underhand official conduct now publicly revealed by the documentary record.[7]

In the House of Lords, Lord Hoffman stated 'the removal and resettlement of the Chagossians was accomplished with a callous disregard of their interests'.[8] Lord Rodger spoke of the 'unhappy – indeed in many respects disgraceful – events of 40 years ago'.[9] Lord Carswell spoke of 'distress and indignation'.[10]

The former UK Foreign Secretary Robin Cook called government action 'sordid and morally indefensible'.[11] Bruce Kent, co-founder of the Campaign for Nuclear Disarmament said 'it is a story of ruthless military and economic imperialism, Cold War driven, and underpinned by servile British governments'.[12] Tomkins said it raised 'frankly grotesque issues of British colonial arrogance and high-handedness'.[13]

From the 1970s onwards, the Chagossians made efforts to argue for their right to return to their homeland. These were ultimately fruitless, although they were occasionally given permission for short visits, paid for by the British government. They received some further compensation. I attended a Freedom of Information Tribunal in London on 10 July 2012 at which Colin Roberts, Overseas Territories Director of the FCO, stated in cross-examination that 'government policy is to prevent resettlement of BIOT'.

1.3. Legal background

Legislation authorised all government actions. The Chagossians responded with litigation challenging the validity of the legislation (and concomitant government actions). Some of this is digested below.

1.3.1. British Indian Ocean Territories Order 1965

This Order detached the Chagos Islands from Mauritius and established the British Indian Ocean Territories as a separate legal entity. BIOT consisted of the Chagos Islands together with some other unconnected islands (which were ultimately transferred to the Seychelles). It established a Commissioner with the power to make laws for the peace, order and good governance of the territory.

1.3.2. Immigration Ordinance 1971

This Ordinance was made under the 1965 Order. Section 4(1) stated that 'no person shall enter into the Territory ... or remain in the Territory' without a permit. It formed the legal basis for the exile of the Chagossians.

---

[7] *Bancoult (2)* in the Court of Appeal.
[8] *Bancoult (2)*, House of Lords [10].
[9] Ibid., [75].
[10] Ibid., [119].
[11] Vine (n 5) 171.
[12] Bruce Kent, 'Book Review: Diego Garcia Island of Shame' (2009) <http://www.intelli-datasystems.com/bkcms/> accessed 2 August 2012.
[13] Tomkins (n 6) 572.

1.3.3. Bancoult (1) 2000

The Divisional Court in the UK gave a ruling in favour of the Chagossians.[14] The court ruled that the Immigration Ordinance 1971 was void for being *ultra vires*.

1.3.4. Immigration Ordinance 2000

As soon as the judgement in *Bancoult (1)* was made, the government enacted the Immigration Ordinance 2000. This was largely the same as the 1971 Ordinance except that the prohibitions on entry did not apply to Chagossians, that is, they were legally entitled to move to the Chagos Islands (other than Diego Garcia).

1.3.5. British Indian Ocean Territory (Constitution) Order 2004, British Indian Ocean Territory (Immigration) Order 2004

These Orders were made in the face of suspected attempts by the Chagossians to launch a protest flotilla to land on the islands. They reversed the Immigration Ordinance 2000. Both Orders were made under the Royal Prerogative. The Constitution Order is the key Order, and s 9 is the key provision. It states as follows:

No right of abode in the Territory: 9. –
(1) Whereas the Territory was constituted and is set aside to be available for the defence purposes of the Government of the United Kingdom and the Government of the United States of America, no person has the right of abode in the Territory.
(2) Accordingly, no person is entitled to enter or be present in the Territory except as authorised by or under this Order or any other law for the time being in force in the Territory.

1.3.6. Bancoult (2) 2008

The Chagossians commenced litigation against the 2004 Order. They were successful at the Divisional Court[15] and at the Court of Appeal.[16] However, their case was rejected by the House of Lords and the 2004 Order held to be valid.[17]

2. Poor quality legislation

Xanthaki sets out useful criteria for assessing the quality of legislation.[18] In this section, I assess the quality of the 2004 Order by reference to what may be termed her 'technical' drafting criteria (technical in the sense that they relate

---

[14] *Bancoult v Secretary of State for Foreign and Commonwealth Affairs* [2001] QB 1067.
[15] [2006] EWHC 1038 (Admin).
[16] [2008] QB 365.
[17] [2008] UKHL 61.
[18] Xanthaki (n 2).

solely to the words on the page, not the broader aspects of quality). These are that legislation should be clear, precise and unambiguous. At a lower level of importance in Xanthaki's hierarchy, legislation should be written in plain and gender-neutral language. This chapter also argues that the very title of the Order represents, in microcosm, its poor quality.

2.1. Clarity

Clarity means that legislation should be readily understandable. Citizens should be able to read it and quickly grasp its meaning. Butt condemned traditional drafting styles which 'ooze archaic language, complex grammatical structures and sentences of excruciating length'.[19] Bennion advocates simplicity, which means 'to put into a form which is as clear (that is intelligible and free from elaboration) to the intended reader as is practicable'.[20] Lord Simon argued that 'people who live under the Rule of Law are entitled to claim that law should be intelligible'.[21] Dickerson states that 'the importance of clarity to statutes needs little urging'.[22] In Canada, the drafters take pride in the clarity of their legislation.[23]

The 2004 Order is not clear. Many of its provisions stretch on for lines and lines of text. Take s 3(2)(a) for example. It is 117 words long (not counting the additional words contained in para (b)). It may be legally precise, but it borders on unintelligibility. It reads as follows:

(2) Without prejudice to the generality of sections 15, 16 and 17 of the Interpretation Act 1978 (as applied by section 2(1) of this Order):

   (a) the revocation of the existing Orders does not affect the continuing operation of any law made, or having effect as if made, under the existing Orders and having effect as part of the law of the Territory immediately before the commencement of this Order, but any such law shall thereafter, without prejudice to its amendment or repeal by any authority competent in that behalf, shall have effect as if made under this Order and be construed with such modifications, adaptations, qualifications and exceptions as may be necessary to bring it into conformity with this Order.

After carefully parsing this provision, I take it to mean two things. First, that existing laws continue in operation after the 2004 Order is made. Secondly, that existing laws are to be treated as if they had been made under the 2004 Order. This could be redrafted more simply as:

(2) The revocation of the existing Orders does not affect the validity of any law made under those Orders.

---

[19] Peter Butt, 'Modern Legal Drafting' (2002) 23 SLR 12.
[20] Francis Bennion, 'The Readership of Legal Texts' (1993) 27 (April) Clarity 1.
[21] Lord Simon, 'The Renton Report – Ten Years On' (1985) SLR 133.
[22] Reed Dickerson, 'The Diseases of Legislative Language' (1964) 1 Harv J on Legis 5, 5.
[23] Peter Johnson, 'Legislative Drafting Practices and Other Factors Affecting the Clarity of Canada's Laws' (1991) 12 SLR 1.

(3) But any law made under the existing Orders has effect as if it were made under this Order.

This redrafting follows Del Duca's exhortation that 'the goal of simplification is to say exactly the same thing as the original but in simplified understandable language'.[24]

Another barrier to clarity is superfluous words or phrases. For example, s 2(2) sets out definitions to be used 'unless the contrary intention appears'. Nowhere in the Order does a contrary intention appear. This form of words in a definition provision is a classic drafting technique, but it is meaningless in this context – a ritual incanted to give weight, but lacking in substance.

Further superfluities exist. Section 3(2) refers to the Interpretation Act 'as applied by section 2(1) of this Order'. This adds nothing. As s 2 applied the Act, repetition in s 3 is valueless.

Section 10 is 'subject to the provisions of this Order'. Again, this is verbiage. The Order is a single document, a single law to be read as a coherent whole. Every provision is subject to every other provision anyway. The phrase is redundant.

Other prerogative legislation suffers similar deficiencies. Some use textual amendments which are terse to the point that the reader can have no idea as to what change is being made or what the new law is, for example, the Diplomatic Service (Amendment) Order 2009.

2.2. *Precision*

Precision means that legislation should have exact and precise boundaries. Christie makes an argument for open textured or vague law, but I disagree.[25] Readers need to know exactly what is lawful and unlawful. The Renton Report even put precision as more important than simplicity – 'the draftsman must never be forced to sacrifice certainty for simplicity'.[26] The US Supreme Court stated that 'it is a basic principle of due process than an enactment is void for vagueness if its prohibitions are not clearly defined'.[27]

The 2004 Order is littered with vague provisions.

Section 2(1) states that the Interpretation Act 1978 applies to the Order with 'the necessary modifications' but does not specify what those modifications are. Section 3 talks of 'modifications, adaptations, qualifications and exceptions as may be necessary' to other laws, again without specifying what those are. Even beyond the vagueness, there is an internal inconsistency – is the 1978 Act only subject to modifications but not adaptations, qualifications and exceptions? It is unclear if a difference of meaning is intended.

Section 3(1) revokes the 'British Indian Ocean Territory Orders 1976 to 1994'. There is a footnote to the reference number of one statutory instrument, a

---

[24]Louis Del Duca, 'Is it Time for a Model Set of Drafting Principles' (2000–01) 105 Dick L Rev 205, 207.

[25]George Christie, 'Vagueness and Legal Language' (1963–64) Minn L Rev 885.

[26]Report of the Renton Committee on the Preparation of Legislation (1975, Cmnd 6053), para 11.5.

[27]*Grayned v Rockford* 408 US 104, 108 (1972)

reference to a page number (of an unspecified book) and the name of a 3rd Order. This is not precise. If legislation is to be revoked, the precise name and reference number of all legislation to be revoked should be specified. Instead, the Order has a garbled mixture of numbers and text.

Section 7 allows the Commissioner to terminate appointments 'as the Commissioner may think fit'. This is not a precise law: it is an invitation to administrative capriciousness. Hewart criticised this practice of giving wide administrative discretion to officials as being contrary to the rule of law.[28]

2.3. *Ambiguity*

Legislation is unambiguous if it can only have one meaning. Fraser argues that it is sometimes better to have ambiguity in law to allow for space for political debate.[29] Although this may hold true in politics, I profoundly disagree when it comes to legislation. The law should only admit to one meaning. Gobbi argues that if a statute is ambiguous, one can look to international treaties on the subject,[30] but in my view, the better starting point is to avoid ambiguity in the first place.

Once again, the 2004 Order fails when measured against this criterion.

Section 4 is entitled 'Establishment of office of Commissioner' and commences with 'There shall be a Commissioner'. The difficulty is that there is already a Commissioner for the Territory, originally established by the 1965 Order. Is there meant to be continuity between these Commissioners, or are they completely different entities? Does it actually mean 'There shall continue to be a Commissioner'?[31] The Order is ambiguous, although the fact that Anthony Campbell Crombie remained in post as Commissioner before and after the Order commenced indicates that the Order intended there to be continuity.[32]

The same point pertains with the Official Stamp in s 6 of the 2004 Order. That section provides that 'there shall be an Official Stamp'. Does it mean that 'there shall continue to be an Official Stamp'? Or should the old stamp under the 1965 Order be destroyed?

There is further ambiguity in s 5 when it comes to describing what the Commissioner does. Sometimes it is 'powers and duties', or 'other functions', or 'do and execute all things'. Section 8, when describing other office holders mentions 'functions attaching to office'. Once again, this is ambiguous. Using a single term like 'functions' is clear, but confusion arises once different terms are introduced.

Section 8 also introduces the concept (without definition) of 'substantive holder' of an office. Section 4(2) mentions the officer holder and someone who many temporarily be designated as an office holder. Is 'substantive holder' meant to include the first category but not the second?

---

[28] Lord Hewart, *The New Despotism* (Ernest Benn, 1929).
[29] Graham Fraser, 'In Praise of Ambiguity' (2000) Jan–Feb Policy Options 21.
[30] Mark Gobbi, 'Making sense of Ambiguity: Some Reflections on the use of Treaties to Interpret Legislation in New Zealand' (2002) 23 SLR 47.
[31] For example, 'there shall continue to be a registrar of companies', s 1060 Companies Act 2006.
[32] See List of Commissioners of BIOT on <http: www.worldstatesmen.org> accessed 3 August 2012.

Throughout the 2004 Order, the Crown is empowered to do things. Sometimes the provision empowering the Crown includes the phrase 'through a Secretary of State', but on other occasions, the power does not include this qualification. Lack of consistency is a classic example of ambiguity. When the Crown disallows a law under s 11, this must be done through a Secretary of State. But when the Crown pardons a person under s 12, it could be read as the Crown's sole decision.

Finally, under s 4, the Commissioner 'holds' office, but under s 15(3) a public officer may hold or 'act' in an office. It appears that the Commissioner holds office but does not act in that office. In practice, that cannot be correct.

2.4. *Plain language*

Eagleson described plain language as 'clear, straightforward expression, using only as many words as are necessary. It is language that avoids obscurity, inflated vocabulary and convoluted sentence structure'.[33] Kimble advocates its use in legislation[34] as does Thomas.[35] Watson-Brown thinks plain language is simply another tool in the drafter's age-old struggle to create intelligible legislation.[36] Sullivan wants to make the statute book more accessible by using plain language.[37] Tanner concluded that plain language techniques make legislation more intelligible.[38] Mowat recommended a 'massive rewriting of old laws and a consistent commitment to plain language drafting of new legislation'.[39]

Turnbull makes specific suggestions on plain language techniques to improve the quality of a draft.[40] Without repeating the entirety of his list here, I set out below the most egregious breaches of his guidelines in the 2004 Order.

The most obvious deficiency has already been mentioned in the context of clarity – long sentences. Short sentences are one of the most basic of plain language techniques and the 2004 Order fails dismally in this regard. I have already mentioned s 3(2)(a) weighing in at 117 words. Section 15(2) is 130 words long. These are paragraphs masquerading as sentences. In an Order only 15 sections long, 18 sentences contain more than 50 words. The second paragraph of The Picture of Dorian Grey is a single sentence 119 words long.[41] Oscar Wilde can pull this off: drafters cannot.

A second plain language deficiency in the 2004 Order is in the use of archaic language. The following table sets out the instances of archaic words.

---

[33] Robert Eagleson, *Writing in Plain English* (Australian Government Publishing Service, Canberra 1990).
[34] Joseph Kimble, 'Answering the Critics of Plain Language' (1994–5) 5 The Scribes Journal of Legal Writing 51.
[35] Richard Thomas, 'Plain English and the Law' (1985) SLR 139.
[36] Anthony Watson-Brown, 'Defining 'Plain English' as an Aid to Legal Drafting' (2009) 30 SLR 85.
[37] Ruth Sullivan, 'Implications of Plain Language Drafting' (2000) 22 SLR 145.
[38] Edwin Tanner, 'Legislating to Communicate: Trends in Drafting Commonwealth Legislation' (2002) 24 Sydney L Rev 529.
[39] Christine Mowat, *A Plain Language Handbook for Legal Writers* (Carswell, Calgary 1998) 79.
[40] Mark Turnbull, 'Clear Legislative Drafting: New Approaches in Australia' (1990) 11 SLR 161.
[41] Oscar Wilde, *The Picture of Dorian Grey* (Modern Library, New York, 2006).

Word	Occurrences
Forthwith	1
Thereto	1
Thereafter	5
Thereof	1
Therewith	1
Whereon	1
Hereby	5

Having read through the recent annual volumes of statutory instruments, no prerogative order commences 'immediately' they all commence 'forthwith'. See for example, the Public Appointments (Amendment) Order 2009.

The third plain language deficiency is not as pronounced – it is dividing up provisions using numbered lists. The Order does divide up sections into subsections and paragraphs. However, there is scope for more to be done. For example, s 10(2) deals with the validity of laws made by the Commissioner. It is 107 words long and concludes with four grounds on which a law may be invalid. Unfortunately, these four grounds are in a long line of text divided only by three 'ors'. The provision would read much better if a numbered list was used, that is, each ground was numbered (a), (b), (c) and (d), and each ground started on a fresh line.

A fourth plain language deficiency is one which is not as readily obvious. Turnbull suggests keeping related words together. Watson-Brown is more specific. He was concerned with provisions which set out a rule and a set of conditions which must be satisfied before the rule is to be used. His plain language suggestion is to avoid 'front-loading' conditions, that is, to clearly state the rule first, and then state the conditions after. If the provision meanders through several conditions before reaching the rule, the reader can easily lose the narrative thread of the provision. As I argued previously, 'it is difficult for readers to link the first part of the sentence to the last part of the sentence if they have to push their way through four conditions in the interim'.[42] Mackinlay refers to this more technically as 'syntactic discontinuity' – deliberate separation of two elements of the same phrase by insertion of another clause between them.[43]

This kind of syntactic discontinuity is present in s 7. Section 7 empowers the Commissioner to do three things: (a) create offices, (b) make appointments to those offices and (c) terminate those appointments. However, before reaching the second and third power, the reader must first get though the conditions of 'subject to the provisions of any law for the time being in force in the Territory and to such instructions as may from time to time be given to him by Her Majesty through a Secretary of State'. The better plain language approach would be to first state the power and then to separately state the conditions for exercise of that power. Similarly, in s 14, the reader must get through 40 words before

---

[42] Ronan Cormacain, 'A Plain Language Case Study: Business Tenancies (Northern Ireland) Order 1996' (2012) The Loophole 33, 40.
[43] Jana Mackinlay, 'Syntactic Discontinuity in the Language of UK and EU Legislation' < http://www.esp-world.info/index.html > accessed 1 August 2012.

discovering the point of the section (that the Commissioner can sell land). The first 40 words deal with pre-conditions for this exercise of power.

One final instance of a plain language deficiency is poor organisation. Turnbull suggests that legislation should have coherence. In a seminal book on drafting, Lord Thring's fourth golden rule includes a requirement that temporary provisions should be separated and placed by themselves under separate headings.[44] Transitional provisions are temporary provisions which govern the change from an old system to the new system. Thornton's advice is that 'such provisions may be important but they are of temporary concern and should not be scattered about in the substantive provisions'.[45] Unfortunately, s 13(2) of the 2004 contravenes this. Alongside powers of the Chief Justice to direct the court to sit in the UK are provisions on cases which started before commencement of the Order but are to be heard after commencement – this kind of transitional provision should be in a schedule.

2.5. *Gender-neutral language*

Legislation is gender neutral if it formally and substantively applies equally to all genders. This article does not seek to weigh up the arguments for and against gender-neutral drafting. Rather, it proceeds on the basis that gender-neutral drafting is a good thing. There is nothing radical in this. Schweikart supports it.[46] In Australia, it is argued that sexist language denigrates women.[47] Peter Quiggin, First Parliamentary Counsel, Australia, stated that 'I think that it is easy to underestimate the negative effect of using language that excludes 50% of the population'.[48] Hill argues in favour of gender-neutral language in court.[49] For Petersson, the case for gender-neutral language is so strong that she argues that old statutes should be revised to strip them of gendered language.[50]

This is not a dry esoteric point, it has a real impact on everyday life. In *Bebb v Law Society*,[51] it was argued that a woman was entitled to be admitted as a solicitor as a woman was a 'person' within the meaning of the law. The actual ruling of the Court of Appeal was that a woman was not a 'person'.[52]

The 2004 Order is not gender neutral. References to the Commissioner are to 'he' and 'his' powers. The masculine is also used to refer to public officers. Basic gender-neutral drafting techniques could solve these problems. Even the

---

[44]Henry Thring, *Practical Legislation: The Composition and Language of Acts of Parliament and Business Documents* (John Murrary, London 1902) 42.
[45]G Thornton, *Legislative Drafting* (4th edn Butterworths, Cape Town 1996) 385.
[46]Debora Schweikart, 'Gender Neutral Pronoun Redefined' (1998–99) 20 Women's Rts L Rep 1.
[47]Unknown, 'Avoidance of Sexist Language in Legislation' (1985) 11 CL Bull 590.
[48]Comment on Commonwealth Association of Legislative Counsel private message board, accessed on 19 March 2013, reproduced with permission of Peter Quiggin.
[49]William Hill, 'A Need for the Use of Non-Sexist Language in the Courts' (1992) 49 Wash and Lee L Rev 275.
[50]S Petersson, 'Gender Neutral Drafting: Recent Commonwealth Developments' (1990) 20 SLR 35.
[51][1914] 1 C 286.
[52]Rosemary Auchmuty, 'Whatever happened to Miss Bebb? The Law Society and Women's Legal History' (2011) 31 LS 199.

classical references to 'Her Majesty' can be made gender neutral by the simple expedient, used in New Zealand legislation, of referring instead to 'the Crown'.

2.6. Misleading title

There are two objections to the title British Indian Ocean Territory (Constitution) Order. First, 'British Indian Ocean Territory' is disingenuous. Secondly, the Order is not a constitution.

An Act's title should reflect its contents. In researching the use of personalised Bill titles, Jones quotes a drafter as saying that 'a short title is meant to be a description of what is in the Bill'.[53] The title should be sober and neutral, not tendentious or controversial. In Scotland, this is mandated by Standing Orders of the Scottish parliament:

> The text of a Bill – including both its short and long titles – should be in neutral terms and should not contain material that is intended to promote or justify the policy behind the Bill, or to explain its effect.[54]

2.6.1. 'British Indian Ocean territory'

In the indexes of the digested cases from Mauritius before BIOT was detached from it in 1965, there is no reference to an entity called BIOT.[55] The term BIOT did not exist before 1965. Britain is responsible for 13 other Overseas Territories:

- Anguilla
- British Antarctic Territory
- Bermuda
- British Virgin Islands
- Cayman Islands
- Falkland Islands
- Gibraltar
- Montserrat
- Pitcairn Island
- St Helena, Ascension Island and Tristan da Cunha
- South Georgia and Sandwich Islands
- Sovereign Base Area on Cyprus

BIOT is an artificial construct. 'Chagos Islands' is precise and geographically accurate. BIOT is vague and insipid. Furthermore, BIOT gives the impression of some remote, unoccupied land, untouched by human hand and unnamed by human

---

[53] Brian Jones, 'Transatlantic Perspectives on Humanised Public Law Campaigns: Personalising and Depersonalising the Legislative Process' (2012) 6 Legisprudence 57,70.
[54] s 9.2.3.
[55] W Greene, *Digest of the Reported Criminal Jurisprudence of the Supreme Court of Mauritius 1843–1883* (Port Louis, 1884), L Hughes, *Digest of the Reported Decisions of the Supreme Court of Mauritius 1861–1901* (Central Printing Establishment, 1905), G Nairac, *Digest of the Mauritius Law Reports 1902–1925* (PG Bumstead, 1927), Gerard Lalouette, *A Digest of the Decisions of the Supreme Court of Mauritius 1926–1945* (Eliel Felix, 1947).

tongue. The only similarly named Overseas Territory is British Antarctic Territory – a place with no permanent inhabitants. Chagos Islands are peopled by Chagossians, but there is no obvious noun to describe the people who belong to BIOT.

It might be thought that this argument is a fanciful conspiracy theory. However, the propaganda drive of the UK when making the original 1965 Order was express (although covert). The government of the day deliberately misrepresented the facts to the outside world, pretending that the islands were only inhabited by a few migrant labourers. Vine cites the following comments by various senior British officials:

> The legal position of the inhabitants would be greatly simplified from our point of view – though not necessarily from theirs – if we decided to treat them as a floating population.
>
> This device, though rather transparent, would at least give us a defensible position.
>
> To certify, more or less fraudulently [the Chagossians] as belonging to somewhere else.[56]

This disingenuous approach is not limited to the colonial past. On 15 June 2004, the Under-Secretary of State for the FCO, Bill Rammell, informed parliament of developments in BIOT. He referred to the Chagossians who 'were in due course relocated to Mauritius and Seychelles, from where they or their families originated'.[57] This is not actually a lie, but it certainly is misleading. 'Relocation' is a euphemism for the more accurate exiled/tricked/intimidated. A grandparent may have 'originated' in Mauritius, but many of the Chagossians were born and bred in the Chagos Islands. David Snoxell was the British High Commissioner to Mauritius when the 2004 Order was made; he described the actions of his own government as 'three decades of dissimulation and subterfuge'.[58]

Calling the Chagos Islands BIOT is as disingenuous as calling the UK the Eastern Atlantic Archipelago and as propagandist as naming it Airstrip One.[59]

2.6.2. 'Constitution'

Finer describes constitutions as

> Codes of rules which aspire to regulate the allocation of functions, powers and duties among the various agencies and offices of government, and define the relationship between these and the public.[60]

---

[56]Vine (n 5) 91 for all quotes.
[57]Written Ministerial Statement 15 June 2004, col 32WS.
[58]'Political Context (the *Bancoult* case) and Possible Solutions' (Colloquium: The Common Law, the Royal Prerogative and Executive Legislation, fCambridge, 19 January 2008).
[59]George Orwell, *1984* (Secker & Warburg, London 1949).
[60]S Finer, *Five Constitutions* (Humanities Press, Sussex 1979) 15.

Elkins sets out three purposes of constitutions.

(1) Limit the behaviour of government.
(2) The symbolic function of defining the nation and its goals.
(3) Defining patterns of authority and setting up government institutions.[61]

The 2004 Order does fulfil the third purpose as it does set out executive, legislative and judicial power structures.

The 2004 Order fails absolutely at the first purpose. This purpose can be traced back at least as far to Thomas Paine who said that the fundamental function of a constitution is to restrain government.[62] The Order does not grant rights to people over government, it simply exiles the people. Not quite Lincoln's paradigm of 'of the people, by the people, for the people',[63] rather it is government against the people. Another American perspective on British colonial constitutions is that 'Britain's history with its colonies shows it can and does sweep away rights when it is convenient'.[64] Plender stated that 'A significant number of modern national constitutions characterise the right to enter one's country as a fundamental or human right'.[65] But the only part of the 'constitution' which deals with human rights takes them away rather than protects them. As Lord Mance said, 'a constitution which exiles a territory's inhabitants is a contradiction in terms'.[66]

The Order also fails at the second purpose. Murphy paraphrases this purpose thus, that it 'serves as a binding statement of a people's aspiration for themselves as a nation'.[67] There is nothing in the 2004 Order which is uplifting or aspirational. Instead, there is the terse statement in s 9 that the territory was 'constituted and set aside for the defence purposes of the Government of the United Kingdom and the Government of the United States of America'. This is not a preamble but 'an apologia'.[68] In addition, the apologia is simply wrong, as the former British High Commissioner to Mauritius said, 'I have never seen a convincing explanation as to why limited resettlement of UK nationals, on the Outer Islands, would pose a threat to the security of the base [Diego Garcia], 150 miles away'.[69]

Not only does the 2004 Order fail as a constitution by the external standards set out above, it also fails by the government's own standards. Hendry and Dickson are two lawyers at the FCO. In their book, they state that

---

[61] Elkins (n 3).
[62] *Common Sense and Other Writings* (Modern Library, New York 2003).
[63] Abraham Lincoln, Gettysburg Address, 1863.
[64] Michael Eshelman, 'New Pitcairn Islands Constitution: Strong, Empty Words for Britain's Smallest Colony' (2012) 24 Pace Int L Rev 21, 23.
[65] Richard Plender, *International Migration Law* (2nd edn Martinus Nijhoff, Dordrecht/Boston 1988) 135.
[66] *Bancoult (2)* [157].
[67] W Murphy, 'Constitutions, Constitutionalism and Democracy' in Douglas Greenberg and others (eds) *Constitutionalism and Democracy: Transitions in the Contemporary World* (Oxford University Press, London 1993).
[68] *Bancoult (2)* [150].
[69] Snoxell, 3.

The policy of the UK Government has been to seek evidence of popular acceptance in the territory of a politically agreed [constitutional] text, whether by resolution of the locally elected body, by referendum, or by less formal means of public consultation.[70]

Far from being consulted, the Chagossians were kept in the dark about their forthcoming exile from their homeland.

The UK government discussed human rights in Overseas Territories and stated in a White Paper that 'Overseas Territories legislation should comply with the same international obligations to which Britain is subject, such as the European Convention on Human Rights and the UN International Covenant on Civil and Political Rights'.[71] Hendry and Dickson discuss the White Paper and state that 'the UK's position was that it would not agree to a new territory constitution which did not contain a fundamental rights chapter'.[72] Although this was true for the constitutions of the Virgin Islands, Cayman Islands, St Helena, Ascension and Tristan da Cunha, Pitcairn, Falkland Islands, Turks and Caicos Islands, Gibraltar and Montserrat, it is not true for the Chagos Islands.

Contrast the treatment of the Chagos Islands with the treatment of Mauritius. The UK, by Order in Council under the Royal Prerogative, gave Mauritius a constitution in the Mauritius Independence Order 1968. That 1968 Constitution does comply with the requirements set out by Finer and Elkins. It commences with the phrase that 'Mauritius shall be a sovereign democratic state' and continues with 'the right of the individual to life, liberty and security of the person and the protection of the law'. There are 17 sections in the chapter entitled 'protection of the fundamental rights and freedoms of the individual'. There are chapters on citizenship, parliament, the executive, the judicature, the public service, the ombudsman and finance. That constitution is 122 sections long. It bears no comparison to the purported constitution contained in the 2004 Order. As Finer notes 'some [constitutions] are never meant to be taken seriously'.[73]

3. Inaccessible law

3.1. *Importance of accessibility*

Donelan defines accessibility – 'in the context of legislation, means that it is easy to access online or in published texts'.[74]

Accessibility is important for many reasons. First, it is a fundamental component of the rule of law, 'the acceptance of the rule of law as a constitutional principle requires that a citizen, before committing himself to any course of action, should be able to know in advance what are the legal consequences that will flow from it'.[75] Secondly, it is elementary fairness that people are told of the

---

[70] Ian Hendry and Susan Dickson, *British Overseas Territory Law* (Hart Publishing, Oxford 2011) 31.
[71] *Partnership for Progress and Prosperity: Britain and the Overseas Territories* (Cm 4264, 1999).
[72] Hendry and Dickson, 151.
[73] S Finer and others, *Comparing Constitutions* (Clarendon Press, Oxford 1995) 6.
[74] Donelan (n 4) 182.
[75] *Black Clawson v Papierwerke Waldhof* (1975) AC 591, 638.

rules they are expected to obey. Thirdly, it grants democratic legitimacy to law. Carr said that laws should be published 'so that the public, in being informed of its ante-natal opportunity to criticise and the place where copies of the proposed rules can be obtained, is indirectly informed that legislation is impending'.[76] Fourthly, it acts as a check upon executive abuse of power. Ronald, discussing executive legislation, regarded 'publicity as a safeguard for holding the rule-making officials in check'.[77] Finally, in practical terms, it increases the chance of a law being obeyed.

In elucidating the meaning of the rule of law, Bingham begins with 'accessibility of the law'.[78] Greenberg says that 'it is of enormous importance that laws are made accessible to the public as soon as possible'.[79] For Fuller, one of the ways that a system of law can fail is if there is a failure to publicise or make available the law to the affected parties.[80] The Venice Commission stated that

> The principle of legal certainty is essential to the confidence in the judicial system and the rule of law ... To achieve this confidence, the state must make the text of the law easily accessible[81]

The European Court of Human Rights stated that 'the law must be adequately accessible'.[82] In Australia, Gleeson said that 'the content of the law must be adequately accessible'.[83] In the European Union, the same point is made by Donelan, 'all participants in a society, an economy or government need to be able to find the legislation'.[84] The SIGMA initiative reinforces this point for Europe – 'a principal aim of legislation is to enable those affected by it to organise and regulate their activities in accordance with its normative requirements ... ready access to that legislation is a necessary concomitant'.[85] The courts in Canada take the same view, 'to bind the citizen by a law, the terms of which he has no means of knowing, would be a mark of tyranny'.[86] Canadian drafter Keyes agrees, 'if the law is to command respect and function as it is intended, it must be adequately promulgated'.[87]

In New Zealand, the subject is of such importance that the government created the Public Access to Legislation project.[88] Anthony says this was done

---

[76] Cecil Carr, *Delegated Legislation* (Cambridge University Press, Cambridge 1921) 36.
[77] James Ronald, 'Publication of Federal Administrative Legislation' (1938) 7 Geo Wash L Rev 52, 61.
[78] Tom Bingham, *The Rule of Law* (Penguin, London 2011) 37.
[79] Daniel Greenberg, *Craies on Legislation* (9th edn, Sweet and Maxwell, London 2008) 374.
[80] Lon Fuller, *The Morality of Law* (Yale University Press, New Haven 1969)
[81] Venice Commission, *Report on the Rule of Law* (March 2011) para 44.
[82] *Sunday Times v UK* (1979) 2 EHRR 245, 271.
[83] Murrary Gleeson, 'Courts and the Rule of Law' (Melbourne University, 7 November 2001).
[84] Donelan (n 4) 149.
[85] SIGMA, *Law Drafting and Regulatory Management in Central and Eastern Europe* SIGMA Papers No. 18.
[86] *Watson v Lee* (1979) 26 ALR 461, 465.
[87] John Mark Keyes, 'Perils of the Unknown – Fair Notice and the Promulgation of Legislation' (1993) 25 Ottawa L Rev 579, 606.
[88] Geoff Lawn, 'Improving Public Access to Legislation: The New Zealand Experience so far' (2004) 6 UTS L Rev 49.

'to improve the way in which New Zealand legislation is made available to the public'.[89] In Wales, Hughes and Davies strongly support additional resources being made available in order that the public may have access to up to date versions of Welsh legislation.[90]

The specific issue of access to legislation has come before the UK courts twice recently. In *R v Chamber*,[91] the defendant only avoided a criminal conviction when it was realised, at the last moment, that he was being prosecuted under a long-revoked law. The court found it troubling that the case had advanced so far on foundations of straw. It bemoaned the fact that 'there is no comprehensive statute law database with hyperlinks which would enable an intelligent person, by using a search engine, to find out all the legislation on a subject'.[92]

The legislation in that case was at least available online, albeit that it was lost amidst a welter of other regulations. The issue in *ZL and VL* was more concerned with the lack of publication of the statute.[93] An Act received Royal Assent on 7 November 2002 and came into force immediately. Before being printed on the 28 November, the government attempted to use the Act against ZL and VL. The Court of Appeal found in favour of the government – 'it is beyond argument that an Act of Parliament takes legal effect on the giving of Royal Assent, irrespective of publication'.[94] However, the court was critical of the government's approach and warned that it was not guaranteed of success the next time. It left open the question on 'a consideration of the validity of the exercise of executive powers which invade a Convention right in reliance on an inaccessible law'.[95]

3.2. *Official UK position on promulgation of legislation*

What then is the official position in the UK on the promulgation of legislation? Greenberg cites two parliamentary statements on the subject. First, the Attorney General

> The Lord Chancellor recognises that he has a responsibility, on behalf of the government, to ensure that satisfactory arrangements are made for the publication of the statute book, in order that the citizen may know by what laws he is bound.[96]

Secondly, in response to the *ZL* case, the House of Lords stated that 'all Acts are published simultaneously on the internet and in print as soon as possible after Royal Assent'.[97]

---

[89]Kate Anthony, 'The Public Access to Legislation Project: Served with Accompaniments' (2008) 16 Austl L Libr 21, 21.
[90]Dylan Hughes and Huw Davies, 'Accessible Bilingual Legislation for Wales' (2012) 33 SLR 103.
[91][2008] EWCA Crim 2467.
[92]*Chambers*, [28].
[93]*ZL and VL v Secretary of State* [2003] EWCA Civ 25.
[94]*ZL*, [17].
[95]*ZL*, [23].
[96]HC Deb. June 13 1991 WA 613–614.
[97]HL Deb February 10, 2003 cc 464–466.

It is more difficult to ascertain the official position on promulgation of prerogative legislation. Greenberg states that it is available from two sources. First, as prerogative orders are made on the advice of the Privy Council, 'they are however readily available from the Privy Council'.[98] Secondly, even though they are not statutory instruments within the meaning of the Statutory Instruments Act 1946, 'some are also printed at the end of the annual volumes of statutory instruments published by Her Majesty's Stationery Office'.[99] In correspondence, the Statutory Publications Office in Northern Ireland has stated that prerogative orders relating to Northern Ireland are also included in the annual volumes of Statutory Rules, even though they are not actually statutory rules within the meaning of the Statutory Rules (Northern Ireland) Order 1979.[100]

3.3. Access to Chagos Island legislation

It is immediately obvious to anyone researching Chagos Island legislation that it is extremely difficult to access. Tomkins describes it as 'unaccountable, indeed wholly secret rule-making'.[101]

There is no official website with authoritative copies of the legislation. The official government website for legislation has a small number of BIOT statutes, but none made under the Royal Prerogative (and the prerogative orders, including the 2004 Order, are the key texts). The FCO, as the official government body responsible for Overseas Territories, does not have the 2004 Order on its website. National Archives have some BIOT Gazettes (see further below), but none from 1990 onwards.[102] Although Greenberg suggests that prerogative orders are readily available from the Privy Council, the reality is not quite as rosy. In correspondence, the Privy Council stated that

> On our website Privy Council meetings from June 2010 include links to the full texts of Orders made that are not otherwise published on the legislation.gov.uk website. Unfortunately we do not have the staff resources to do this retrospectively, and inquirers are advised to contact us direct if they require copies.[103]

If one knows the date an order is made, the Privy Council will promptly send it out. However, if one does not know the date and name of an order and is just doing a generalised search, it is difficult to get anything.

The other source that Greenberg gives as a possibility is the annual volume of statutory rules. Again, this draws a blank for BIOT prerogative Orders. The 2004 volume of statutory instruments is 10,236 pages long. It does not contain the 2004 Order. There are some entries relating to Overseas Territories, but these relate to 'proper' statutory instruments, that is, those made in the proper way under the authority of (and subject to the scrutiny of) parliament. The original

---

[98] Greenberg (n 79) 390.
[99] Ibid.
[100] Email from Christine Scott to author (15 July 2012).
[101] Tomkins (n 6) 573.
[102] Email from Dr Edward Hampshire to author (27 July 2012).
[103] Email from Margaret Newell to author (6 August 2012).

1965 Order likewise does not appear in the 1965 volume of statutory instruments. In fact, it is noticeable by its absence, as the 1965 volume does contain other prerogative orders in council. For example, it has the Royal Instructions relating to BIOT, as well as prerogative orders relating to Fiji, Basutoland and Mauritius.

I submitted a request to the FCO under the Freedom of Information Act 2000 on 11/7/2012. The request concerned promulgation of BIOT legislation. In response the FCO claimed that Freedom of Information did not extend to Chagos Islands and that therefore they were not bound to answer any questions. This is in spite of the fact that BIOT legislation is made by the Queen, in right of the UK, in the UK after being drafted in the UK by UK civil servants. To give credit to the FCO, they did provide me with some information on a concessionary basis.

The one place that BIOT legislation is published is in the British Indian Ocean Territory Gazette. Once again, the Gazette is not available online. According to the FOI response from the FCO, the current total global distribution list of the Gazette is 20. Of these, 16 go to an emanation of the government. The remaining 4 on the list are all British law libraries: the British Legal Library, Bodleian Law Library, Squire Law Library and the Library at the Institute of Advanced Legal Studies. One copy does go to Mauritius, but it is to the British High Commission there.

Richard Dunne and I have catalogued the holdings at these libraries other than the Bodleian. The results are set out in Appendix 1. In summary, between 1965 and 1992, these holdings are virtually non-existent. After 1992, these holdings are largely complete, although there are several missing volumes. The librarian at the Institute of Advanced Legal Studies stated that if they do not receive a copy, they contact the supplier, 'we are not always successful and we do not always know the reason why'.[104] If these law libraries, on the FCO distribution list, do not have the legislation, how can anyone be expected to access it? In response to complaints about the lack of Gazettes at these libraries, the FCO replied 'the material you request should be in the public domain (even if for reasons beyond the control of present members of the BIOT Administration it is not)'.[105]

There are few non-governmental sources of BIOT Orders. Westlaw has none of the key BIOT Orders. LexisNexis is only marginally better. Raworth's Constitutions of Dependencies and Territories list three Orders, but the 2002 edition does not have the key 1965 Order or the 1971 Immigration Ordinance.[106] The top ranked Google search result for the 2004 Order gives a text which has spelling and grammatical mistakes as well as missing out a section. It has only been through making personal contact with the legal team for the Chagossians that I was eventually able to get a full list of the statutes.

Even parliament cannot ensure they have proper access to BIOT legislation. The FCO had previously indicated that they would send draft copies to the Foreign

---

[104]Email of 30/8/2012 from Lesley Young to author.
[105]Email of 11/11/2010 from FCO to Richard Dunne.
[106]Philip Raworth, *Constitutions of Dependencies and Territories* (Oceana, Dobbs Ferry 2002).

and Commonwealth Affairs Committee in advance of them being made. However, no draft copies of the 2004 Order were sent to the Committee. The Secretary of State for the FCO attempted to justify this to the Committee – 'we needed to preserve complete confidentiality if we were to avoid the risk of an attempt by the Chagossians to circumvent the Orders before they came into force'.[107]

By way of historical comparison, access to legislation was much better before BIOT was detached from Mauritius. *Colonial Government v Vitry* (1899) concerned the promulgation of an 1898 Ordinance.[108] The Ordinance was published in the Official Gazette and also in eight newspapers. The court held that this 'was sufficient publication under our law, and consequently, that this Ordinance came into force on the last mentioned day and hour [of the final publication]'.[109]

It could be thought that the lack of official promulgation of this legislation is accidental. However, it is clear that official government policy is to make the BIOT legislation inaccessible. The Secretary of State sent a confidential telegram to the Governor of the Seychelles on the subject of what was to become the Immigration Ordinance 1971. In para 3, he stated 'our concern is that publication of Ordinance and any regulations there under should be limited to minimum by law so as to attract as little attention as possible'.[110] The Governor responded 'Ordinance would be published in BIOT Gazette which has only very limited circulation both here and overseas after signature by Commissioner. Publicity will therefore be minimal'.[111]

Other prerogative legislation is equally difficult to track down. The legislation governing the Northern Ireland Civil Service is the Civil Service Commissioners (Northern Ireland) Order 1999 as amended in 2003 and 2007. It is extremely difficult to access an up to date version of the 1999 Order. In fact, it is extremely difficult to even find out that there is an Order and that it was amended in 2003 and 2007. The Commissioners do not publish all the Orders. The official government websites do not have them. The official government printers and newspapers of record do not have them. Commercial databases do not have them.

Whether deliberate or accidental, it is well nigh impossible to access authentic copies of BIOT legislation and this makes the legislation fundamentally bad law. Millennia ago Suetonius wrote the following of Caligula's laws:

> These taxes being imposed, but the act by which they were levied never submitted to public inspection, great grievances were experienced from the want of sufficient knowledge of the law. At length, on the urgent demands of the Roman people, he published the law, but it was written in a very small hand and posted up in a corner so that no one could make a copy of it.[112]

In the internet age, publication via the Gazette is the equivalent to written in a very small hand and posted up in a corner.

---

[107] Jack Straw letter of 9 July 2004.
[108] Reported in the 1861–1901 Mauritian Digest at 53.
[109] Paragraph 14.
[110] Telegram of 22/12/1970.
[111] Telegram of 11/1/1971.
[112] Suetonius, *Lives of the 12 Caesars* (Alexander Thomson trans, 1883) 278.

4. Conclusion

The Chagossians were exiled from their homeland by prerogative legislation – legislation made, not by a legislature but by the executive. I have sought to show that the 2004 Order is bad law because it is of low quality and because it is inaccessible.

I have shown that the 2004 Order is of low quality when measured by Xanthaki's criteria. It is not clear, precise or unambiguous. It is not written in gender-neutral or plain language. Its title is disingenuous.

If the Order had been made as an Act of Parliament, it is submitted that most of these defects would have been removed. It would have been drafted by trained legislative counsel familiar with the principles of sound legislative drafting. Proper scrutiny would have improved quality. It would correctly have been entitled the Chagos Islands (Exile) Act.

I have shown that the inaccessibility of the 2004 Order seriously undermines its legitimacy. Accessibility is fundamental to the legality of a law. A law which is only accessible by literally trawling through dusty shelves in the basement of a London law library is not a good law. If the law had been made properly, rather than by the prerogative, accessibility would have vastly improved. It would be on the statute book, on parliament's website, on the official legislation website and available on multiple databases. Cohn states that prerogative orders are 'less visible and accessible and provide a weaker basis for accountability and review processes'.[113] It is hard to argue with her view that this is precisely what makes this mode of law-making attractive to government.

Although the 2004 Order may be the nadir of bad law, I have shown that other prerogative legislation also suffers from defects in terms of quality and accessibility. As Cohn summarises, prerogative legislation allows government to make laws 'without passing the cumbersome legislative process, to design and apply rules without necessarily publishing them, thereby evading subjection to accountability mechanisms'.[114] Moules also attacks prerogative legislation on this ground, as an attempt by the executive to deny parliamentary and judicial scrutiny simply by choosing a particular mode of enactment.[115]

British parliamentarians have turned their minds to this issue and have spoken clearly against the policy. Discussing the Chagossians, Jeremy Corbyn MP said

> The Prime Minister's Office has inherited the power of the royal prerogative and this can and is used to bypass Parliament. It is high time that all prime ministerial decisions were brought under parliamentary scrutiny.[116]

As has been demonstrated in relation to the Chagos Islands, prerogative law-making is the paradigm of bad law-making. In my opinion, this law is so fundamentally flawed, so oppressive and draconian that it should never have been made.

---

[113] Margit Cohn, 'Judicial Review of Non-Statutory Executive Powers after *Bancoult*: a Unified Anxious Model' [2009] PL 260, 262.
[114] Ibid., 265.
[115] Richard Moules, 'Judicial Review of Prerogative Orders in Council: Recognising the Constitutional Reality of Executive Legislation' (2008) 67 CLJ 12.
[116] Website of Jeremy Corbyn MP <http://www.jeremycorbyn.org.uk/?p=1060> accessed on 22 August 2012.

Notes on contributor

Ronan Cormacain is a consultant legislative counsel and has been drafting legislation for over 12 years. He drafts primarily in the UK, Northern Ireland, Crown Dependencies and Overseas Territories. He is a director at the Sir William Dale Legislative Drafting Clinic at the University of London where is also studying for a PhD in legislative drafting and the rule of law.

Appendix 1. Copies of BIOT Gazette in British law libraries

Gazette	Issue	Institute of advanced legal studies library	British library	Squire law library	Cambridge university library
1965			Yes		Yes
1966		Deficient			Yes
1967					Yes
1968					
1969					
1970					
1971					
1972					
1973					
1974					
1975					
1976					
1977					
1978					
1979					
1980					
1981					
1982			Yes		
1983					
1984					
1985					
1986					
1987					
1988					
1989					
1990					
1991					
1992			Yes		
1993		Yes	Yes		
1994	1	Yes	Yes		
	2	Yes	Yes		
	3	Yes	Yes		
	4		Yes		
1995	1	Yes	Yes		
	2	Yes	Yes		
1996	1	Yes	Yes		
	2		Deficient		
1997	1	Yes	Deficient		
	2	Yes	Yes		
1998	1	Yes	Yes		
	2	Yes	Yes		
	3	Yes	Yes		

(Continued)

Appendix 1. (*Continued*)

Gazette	Issue	Institute of advanced legal studies library	British library	Squire law library	Cambridge university library
1999	1	Yes	Yes		
	2	Yes	Yes		
2000	1	Yes	Yes		
	2	Yes	Yes		
2001	1	Yes	Yes		
	2	Yes	Yes		
2002	1	Yes	Yes		
	2		Deficient		
2003	1	Yes	Yes		
	2		Deficient		
2004	1	Yes	Yes		
	2	Yes	Yes		
2005	1	Yes	Yes		
	2			Yes	
2006	1	Yes	Yes	Yes	
	2	Yes	Yes	Yes	
2007	1	Yes	Yes	Yes	
	2			Yes	
2008	1	Yes	Yes	Yes	
	2	Yes	Yes	Yes	
2009		Yes	Yes	Yes	
2010			Yes	Yes	
2011	1	Yes	Claimed		
	2		Claimed		

Incorporation of international and regional human rights instruments: comparative analyses of methods of incorporation and the impact that human rights instruments have in a national legal order

Reyneck Matemba

Assistant Chief Legislative Counsel, Ministry of Justice, Malawi

> This article looks at the incorporation into a country's domestic law of human rights principles and obligations as enshrined in four selected international human rights instruments as the most effective way of ensuring that those instruments have a significant impact in a national legal order. The article makes a comparative analysis of the impact that the selected instruments have had in the Republic of Malawi and the Republic of South Africa, and observes that although the two countries have not domesticated the instruments, the instruments have nevertheless had a significant and recognisable impact through constitutional reforms and judicial decisions.

1. Introduction

Human rights have generally been in peril on the African continent.[1] This dates back to the colonial and apartheid eras in the second half of the twentieth century when the peoples of Africa began the struggle for the realisation of their basic human rights and fundamental freedoms.[2]

Starting from the late 1950s, colonial territories in Africa began to be granted independence. Many of the independent states adopted independence constitutions, some of which contained human rights provisions. The states also acceded to various international and regional human rights instruments, proclaiming and guaranteeing their citizens basic rights and fundamental freedoms.[3]

Following the political transformation on the African continent in the 1990s, several African states became multiparty democracies, and again adopted new constitutions in order to govern the democratic systems of government that had been embraced. In addition to containing a Bill of Rights, most of the newly adopted constitutions made detailed provision for the ratification and domestic

---

[1] NJ Udombana, 'The African Commission on Human and Peoples' Rights and the Development of Fair Trial Norms in Africa' (2006) 6 Afr Hum Rts LJ 299.
[2] BT Nyanduga, 'Conference Paper: Perspectives on the African Commission on Human and Peoples' Rights on the Occasion of the 20th Anniversary of the Entry into Force of the African Charter on Human and Peoples' Rights' (2006) 6 Afr Hum Rts LJ 256.
[3] Ibid. 256.

incorporation of treaties, which are the primary source of international and regional human rights law.[4]

Through ratification and incorporation, human rights instruments become part and parcel of domestic law.[5] However, the success or failure of any international or regional human rights system is evaluated in accordance with its impact on human rights practices at the domestic level. Ratification of human rights instruments in itself is largely a formal and in some cases an empty gesture.[6]

Therefore, whether a state automatically recognises human rights instruments as forming part of its domestic laws upon ratification without the need for formal incorporation into domestic law, or formally incorporates them into domestic laws in order to become enforceable in domestic courts, the challenge really lies in ensuring that the human rights principles and obligations enshrined in those instruments are realised and ultimately make a significant impact at the domestic level. It is in view of these observations that this article examines the incorporation of international and regional human rights instruments, and makes comparative analyses of methods of incorporation and the impact that human rights instruments have in a national legal order.

2. Methodology

The hypothesis in this article is that incorporation of human rights principles and obligations enshrined in international and regional human rights instruments into domestic law is the most effective way of ensuring that the instruments have a significant impact in a national legal order.

In proving this hypothesis, the article will refer to various forms of literature such as books, journal articles, pieces of legislation, articles and conference papers. These sources of literature generally offer insights on the subjects of international law and international human rights law that are relevant to the better understanding and analysis of the hypothesis.

Specifically, in making a comparative analysis of the methods of incorporating human rights instruments, the article will examine the specific constitutional provisions providing for the incorporation of international agreements in the 1994 Constitution of the Republic of Malawi[7] and the 1996 Constitution of the Republic of South Africa.[8] This examination will be done with reference to monism and dualism, the two theories that help articulate the precise status and role of international and regional human rights law in a national legal order.[9]

---

[4] RKM Smith, *Texts and Materials on International Human Rights* (Routledge–Cavendish, London 2007), 22.
[5] K Hayes, 'General Principles: Judicial Implementation of International Human Rights Norms' in: W Maina and W Wahiu (eds), *Human Rights Litigation and the Domestication of Human Rights Standards in Sub Saharan Africa* (AHRAJ Casebook Series vol 1 International Commission of Jurists, Nairobi 2007), 17.
[6] C Heyns and F Viljoen, *The Impact of the United Nations Human Rights Treaties on the Domestic Level* (Kluwer Law International, The Hague 2002), 1.
[7] Act No 20 of 1994.
[8] Act No 108 of 1996.
[9] O Tshosa, *National Law and International Human Rights Law: Cases of Botswana, Namibia and Zimbabwe* (Ashgate Publishing Ltd, Aldershot 2001), p. 3.

Again, in making a comparative analysis of the impact of human rights instruments in a national legal order, the article will examine the Bills of Rights in the Constitution of Malawi and the Constitution of the Republic of South Africa (RSA), as well as judicial decisions by courts in the two countries. Here, the article will primarily focus on the impact that the Universal Declaration of Human Rights (UDHR), the Convention on the Rights of a Child (CRC), the African Charter on Human and Peoples' Rights (ACHPR) and the African Charter on the Rights and Welfare of the Child (ACRWC) have had in Malawi and RSA.

The article will focus on the Republic of Malawi and the RSA, former British colonies and therefore sharing aspects of a legal system that is based on the common law tradition. Again, both countries generally emerge from a period characterised by gross violations of human rights,[10] and were therefore keen to embrace international and regional human rights systems in an attempt to prevent the violations' recurrence in society, besides consolidating their democracies.[11]

3. The relationship between international law and national law

3.1. Monism and dualism

Monism and dualism are the two theories concerning the relationship between international law and national law that are usually juxtaposed.[12]

Under the monist tradition, international law and domestic law are inextricably linked, such that international law automatically becomes part of the domestic legal order upon ratification,[13] it is also enforced like any other domestic law.[14]

However, dualism sees international law and domestic law as operating on separate planes; the former stipulates norms governing the relations between nation states, and the latter those norms governing the relationship between individuals within the state or between individuals and the state.[15] Since the two legal orders are regarded as two separate and self-contained spheres of legal action, international law plays no role in the domestic legal order except in so far as domestic law adopts the international law.[16]

Again, the monist approach is mainly common in civil law countries and it is associated with self-executing treaties which are enforceable in the domestic realm without the need of domestic legislation.[17] Whereas the dualist approach is

---

[10] Heyns and Viljoen (n 6) 539.
[11] JC Mubangizi, 'Protecting Human Rights Amidst Poverty and Inequality: The South African Post-Apartheid Experience on the Right of Access to Housing' (2008) 2 Afr J Leg Stud 131.
[12] I Brownlie, *Principles of Public International Law* (6th edn. OUP, Oxford 2007) 31.
[13] F Viljoen, *International Human Rights Law in Africa* (OUP, Oxford 2007), 18.
[14] D Donoho, 'Human Rights Enforcement in the Twenty-First Century' (2006) 35 GA J Int'l & Comp L 13.
[15] BR Opeskin, 'Constitutional Modelling: The Domestic Effect of International Law in Commonwealth Countries: Part I' (2000) PL 5.
[16] Ibid. 5, 6.
[17] AO Enabulele, 'Implementation of Treaties in Nigeria and the Status Question: Whither Nigerian Courts?' (2009) AJICL 1.

usually adopted by common law countries and it is associated with non-self-executing treaties.[18]

4. The analyses

4.1. Methods of incorporating human rights instruments into domestic law

Going by the discussion in clause 3, international and regional human rights instruments are expected to become an integral part of domestic law upon ratification in states following the monist tradition; and, in principle, need to be domesticated before they become part of domestic law in dualist states.[19]

However, state practice in Malawi and RSA, both dualist states, indicate that they do not strictly adhere to one method when incorporating human rights instruments into domestic law because their Constitutions provide for both methods (see Table 1).

(A) International agreements

At international law, Malawi becomes bound by an international agreement upon ratification by parliament, but the agreement does not become part of the laws of Malawi unless it has been enacted or incorporated into the laws of Malawi by an Act of Parliament.[20]

Similarly, at international law an international agreement binds the RSA only after it has been ratified or approved by a resolution of both the National Assembly and the National Council of the Provinces; and becomes law in RSA only when it has been incorporated into law by national legislation.[21]

Clearly, this method of incorporating international agreements into domestic law as provided for in the Constitutions of the two countries is based on the dualist notion.

However, the Constitution of the RSA in section 231 (4) exempts from enactment into law a self-executing provision of an agreement that has been approved by Parliament;[22] this position is not available under the Malawi Constitution.

Effectively, therefore, a provision of an agreement that is self-executing is law in the RSA and may be implemented directly without the need for incorporation into domestic legislation, so long as it is not inconsistent with the Constitution or an Act of Parliament. One can therefore argue that as far as the domestic incorporation of self-executing provisions of an international agreement that has been approved by Parliament is concerned, the RSA follows a monist approach.

---

[18]B Conforti, 'National Courts and the International Law of Human Rights' in: B Conforti and F Francioni (eds), *Enforcing International Human Rights in Domestic Courts* (Kluwer Law International, The Hague 1997), 7.
[19]Viljoen (n 13) 530.
[20]S 211 (1) of the Malawi Constitution (1994).
[21]Ss 231 (2) & (4) of the Constitution of RSA (1996).
[22]ME Olivier, 'Exploring the Doctrine of Self-Execution as Enforcement Mechanism of International Obligations' (2002) 12 SAYIL 117–18.

Table 1. Constitutional provisions containing methods for incorporating human rights instruments.

Country	Constitutional provision for incorporation of instrument	Method for incorporation of instrument
Malawi	Section 211 (3)	Monist
	Section 211 (1)	Dualist
RSA	Section 231 (4) and Section 232	Monist
	Section 231 (2) Section 231 (4)	Dualist

Table 2. Parts of the CRC and the ACRWC that have made a significant impact in the Bills of Rights of the Constitutions of Malawi and RSA.

Country	International instrument	Regional instrument	Constitutional provision incorporating treaty norms
Malawi	CRC (Part One: Articles 1–40)	ACRWC (Chapter One: Articles 1–29)	Section 23
RSA	CRC (Part One: Articles 1–40)	ACRWC (Chapter One: Article 1–29)	Section 28

(B) Customary international law

While the Constitution of Malawi and that of the RSA recognise a dualist approach in relation to international agreements, the opposite is true in relation to customary international law. The Constitutions employ a monist approach in that no Act of Parliament is required in order for international law to become part of domestic law.

Thus, customary international law is law in Malawi and the RSA unless it is inconsistent with the Constitution or an Act of Parliament.[23]

4.2. *Impact of human rights instruments in a national legal order*

(A) Constitutional provisions incorporating treaty norms

The impact of most human rights instruments is more pronounced if the treaty norms they espouse are recognised on the domestic level. One way of making treaty norms recognisable on the domestic level is by incorporating them into a Bill of Rights of a Constitution.

Table 2 shows parts of the CRC and the ACRWC that have made a significant impact on the contents of the corresponding constitutional provisions on the rights of children in the Bills of Rights of the Constitutions of Malawi and RSA.

ACRWC and CRC. As shown in Table 2, both Malawi and the RSA dedicate a special section to children in their Constitution. An examination of the rights contained in the two sections shows that the Constitution of each of the two

---

[23] See s 211 (3) of the Malawi Constitution and s 232 of the Constitution of the RSA.

Table 3. The legal status of the UDHR, CRC, ACHPR and the ACRWC in Malawi and RSA.

Country	International instrument	Regional instrument	Date of signature	Date of accession	Date of ratification	Entry into force of instrument
Malawi	UDHR		–	–	–	–
		ACHPR	23/02/90	–	17/11/89	21/10/86
	CRC		–	02/01/91	–	02/09/90
		ACRWC	13/07/99	–	16/09/99	29/11/99
RSA	UDHR		–	–	–	–
		ACHPR	09/07/96	–	09/07/96	21/10/86
	CRC		29/01/93	–	16/06/95	02/09/90
		ACRWC	10/10/97	–	07/01/00	29/11/99

Source: See <http://www.un.org/en/documents/udhr/>; <http://www.africa-union.org>; <http://treaties.un.org/>

countries has incorporated a whole range of rights accorded to children, derived from chapter one of the ACRWC and part one of the CRC. Effectively, what section 23 of the Malawi Constitution and section 28 of the Constitution of the RSA do is reaffirm and endorse the human rights principles and obligations relating to children as expressed in the ACRWC and the CRC.

It is worth mentioning however that, unlike the CRC which entered into force in 1990 and was acceded to by Malawi in 1991 (before its 1994 Constitution) and ratified by RSA in 1995 (before its 1996 Constitution), the ACRWC came into force in 1999 and got ratified by Malawi in 1999 and the RSA in 2000, years after the Constitutions of the two countries had already come into force (see Table 3).

The question that one would ask therefore is how could the Constitutions of the two countries reaffirm and endorse human rights principles of a treaty that was not in force at the time the Constitutions were drafted or came into force?

Well, the ACRWC emerged out of the sentiment that the CRC ignored vital socio-cultural and economic realities particular to Africa. Therefore, unlike the CRC, the ACRWC stresses the need to consider African cultural peculiarities in matters relating to the rights of children.[24] Besides this minor difference, the human rights principles and norms enunciated in the ACRWC are substantially similar to those in the CRC. Actually, the ACRWC was also adopted as one way of promoting the CRC.[25] Hence, the human rights principles enshrined in the ACRWC did not negate those in the CRC; or sections 23 and 28 of the Constitution of Malawi and the RSA, respectively. That is why even after Malawi and the RSA had ratified the ACRWC, no amendments were made to sections 23 and 28.

Again, even though Malawi and the RSA have not specifically domesticated the CRC and the ACRWC into national law by an Act of Parliament as required by their Constitutions, incorporation of the fundamental human rights principles

---

[24] D Olowu, 'The Regional System of Protection of Human Rights in Africa' in: J Sloth-Nielsen (ed), *Children's Rights in Africa: A Legal Perspective* (Ashgate Publishing Ltd, Hampshire, 2008), p. 23.
[25] R Murray, *Human Rights in Africa: From the OAU to the African Union* (CUP, Cambridge 2004), 26.

Table 4. Relevant articles in the UDHR and the ACHPR that made a significant impact in the Bills of Rights in the Constitutions of Malawi and RSA.

Country	International instrument	Regional instrument	Chapter in the constitution containing treaty norms
Malawi	UDHR (Articles 1–21)	ACHPR (Articles 2–12)	Chapter IV (Bill of Rights)
RSA	UDHR (Articles 1–21)	ACHPR (Articles 2–12)	Chapter II (Bill of Rights)

enshrined in the two treaties into their Constitutions indicates the extent of the impact that the treaties have had in the national legal orders of the two countries.

It may be argued however that mere incorporation of these treaty norms into the Constitution offers no guarantees with respect to their enjoyment.[26] Considering that the significance of any constitutionally recognised right quickly diminishes when no means of enforcement is provided for,[27] the framers of the Constitution of Malawi and that of the RSA strategically positioned sections 23 and 28 respectively in Bills of Rights that are justiciable, thereby enabling an aggrieved individual to seek legal redress in a court of law. The incorporated treaty norms are therefore enforceable and can be protected at the domestic level.

UDHR and ACHPR. Table 4 shows the relevant articles in the UDHR and the ACHPR that made a significant impact on the contents of the Bills of Rights in the Constitutions of Malawi and RSA.

In terms of its conceptualisation, the ACHPR bears greater resemblance to the contents of the UDHR,[28] except that the ACHPR was designed to respond to various dimensions of human rights in Africa. Similar to the relationship between the CRC and the ACRWC, the human rights principles and norms enshrined in the ACHPR are therefore substantially similar to those enshrined in the UDHR.[29] Actually, the ACHPR ties the African drive with the UDHR to promote and ensure respect for human rights.[30]

Even though Malawi and the RSA have not specifically domesticated the UDHR and the ACHPR into national law by an Act of Parliament as required by their Constitutions, an examination of chapter IV (Bill of Rights) in the Constitution of Malawi and chapter II (Bill of Rights) in the Constitution of the RSA clearly reflect the significant impact and influence that the UDHR and the ACHPR have had on the national legal orders of the two countries in terms of constitutional reforms. The two Bills of Rights in significant respects mirror or replicate the human rights principles and obligations enshrined in the UDHR and the ACHPR. This is because drafters of the two Bills of Rights incorporated

---

[26] J Tobin, 'Increasingly Seen and Heard: The Constitutional Recognition of Children's Rights' (2005) 21 S Afr J on Hum Rts 86.
[27] Ibid. 118.
[28] Olowu (n 25) 16.
[29] VOO Nmehielle, *The African Human Rights System: Its Laws, Practice, and Institutions*, 35.
[30] IA Badawi El-Sheikh, 'The African Regional System of Human Rights: Notes and Comments' in: M Cherif Bassiouni and Z Motala (eds), *The Protection of Human Rights in African Criminal Proceedings* (Kluwer Academic Publishers, The Hague, 1995), 24.

the human rights principles and obligations enshrined in the two instruments, especially the civil and political rights provided for in articles 1 to 21 of the UDHR and articles 2 to 12 of the ACHPR.

It is worth pointing out that (as shown in Table 3) Malawi ratified the ACHPR in 1989 and is therefore a party to and bound by the ACHPR. Malawi has not, however, ratified or acceded to the UDHR, which of course is a declaration not a treaty, and therefore lacks formal binding force. Nevertheless, this Declaration has been widely recognised as binding due to the obligations contained in the Charter of the United Nations and also because its parts have become part of customary international law.[31]

The UDHR was expressly made part of the laws of Malawi pursuant to section 2 (1) (iii) of the 1966 Constitution of Malawi, which provided that the government and the people of Malawi shall continue to recognise the sanctity of the personal liberties enshrined in the UDHR. However, one can argue that this Declaration no longer forms part of the laws of Malawi because the 1966 Constitution was repealed, and again because section 200 of the 1994 Constitution, which is a saving clause for all laws that were in force on the appointed date, does not make any reference to international law.[32]

The human rights norms enshrined in the UDHR are some of the parts of this Declaration that have precipitated into customary international law; and, according to section 211 (3) of the 1994 Constitution, customary international law forms part of the laws of Malawi unless it is inconsistent with the Constitution or an Act of Parliament. Therefore, even though the 1966 Constitution was repealed and section 200 of the 1994 Constitution does not save international law, the UDHR forms part of the laws of Malawi by virtue of section 211 (3).

Just like Malawi, the RSA is a party to and bound by the ACHPR having ratified it in 1996. However, the RSA has not ratified or acceded to the UDHR. Though, as we have seen, the human rights norms enshrined in the UDHR are also reflected in the Constitution of the RSA. This is because, just like in Malawi, the UDHR is considered as part of the law of the RSA as customary international law. Besides this, as alluded to above, both the UDHR and the ACHPR played a significant role during the drafting processes of the Bill of Rights both in the interim (1993) and the final (1996) Constitutions of the RSA.

(B) Judicial decisions

An examination of judicial decisions in Malawi and the RSA shows that courts prefer to enforce domestic laws over human rights instruments that have been ratified but not domesticated into national law by an Act of Parliament when deciding cases brought before them.

In *Chihana v The Republic*,[33] the appellant argued that some of his fundamental rights enshrined in the UDHR and the ACHPR had been violated by the

---

[31] JC Mubangizi, *The Protection of Human Rights in South Africa: A Legal and Practical Guide* (Juta and Co Ltd, Durban 2004), 13.
[32] DM Chirwa, 'A Full Loaf is Better than Half: The Constitutional Protection of Economic, Social and Cultural Rights in Malawi' (2005) 49 J Afr L 52.
[33] Malawi Supreme Court of Appeal Criminal Appeal No. 9 of 1992 <http://www.malawilii.org/cgi-bin/malawi>.

state. The Malawi Supreme Court agreed with the appellant and stated that the content of the UDHR had been incorporated into Malawi law by virtue of section 2 (1) (iii) of the 1966 Constitution. However, in rejecting the enforceability of the ACHPR, the Court said:

> This Charter must be placed on a different plane from the UDHR. Whereas the latter is part of the law of Malawi, the African Charter is not. Malawi may well be a signatory to the Charter but until Malawi takes legislative measures to adopt it, the Charter is not part of the municipal law of Malawi and we doubt whether in the absence of any local statute incorporating its provisions the Charter would be enforceable in our Courts.[34]

Similarly, the Supreme Court of RSA in *S v Adams; S v Werner*[35] made the following observations in relation to the Charter of the United Nations (which is the foundation of the UDHR):

> The Charter of the UN has not been incorporated into the municipal law by an Act of Parliament. Consequently, it cannot be directly enforced by South African courts ... Where a South African statute clearly and unambiguously violates a treaty to which South Africa is a party, a South African court has no alternative but to apply the statute even if by so doing it results in a violation of South Africa's international obligations.[36]

Just recently, in *Re: The Adoption of CJ (a Female Infant)*,[37] a case where pop music star Madonna was challenging the decision of the Malawi High Court in declining to grant her an application to adopt a female infant CJ, the Malawi Supreme Court, in opting to decide the appeal using the Malawi Constitution and the Adoption of Children Act (Cap. 26:01) rather than the CRC and the ACRWC, said:

> In all cases the courts will have to look at our Constitution and our statutes and see if the international agreement is consistent with the law of the land ... In doing so, the courts will try as much as possible to avoid a clash between what our laws say on the subject and what the international agreements ... are saying on the subject, but where this is not possible, the provisions of our Constitution and the laws made under it will carry the day.

The Court further observed that:

> ... when we look at our Constitution and the Act there is no clash between what is provided for in our own laws and what is provided for in the various conventions that have been referred to us. We will therefore use our own Act and Constitution which are sufficient in deciding this Appeal.[38]

---

[34] Ibid. 13.
[35] (1981) (1) SA 187 (AD).
[36] Ibid. 23.
[37] Malawi Supreme Court of Appeal Adoption Appeal No. 28 of 2009 <http://www.malawilii.org/cgi-bin/malawi>.
[38] Ibid. 11.

5. Conclusion

First, this article looked at the methods of incorporating international and regional human rights instruments into domestic laws in Malawi and RSA. The article has found that actual state practice in Malawi and the RSA, though both dualist states, is that they do not strictly adhere to one method when incorporating human rights instruments into domestic law because their respective Constitutions provide for methods that reflect both monist and dualist approaches.

Second, the article looked at the impact that the UDHR, ACHPR, CRC and the ACRWC have had in Malawi and the RSA. The article found that even though the two countries have not specifically domesticated the four instruments into national law through an Act of Parliament as required by their respective Constitutions, the four instruments have had a significant and recognisable impact through constitutional reforms in the two countries in that both countries have incorporated the human rights principles and obligations enshrined in the four instruments into the Bill of Rights of their Constitutions.

Again, this article has observed that the impact of the instruments has also been reflected in a number of judicial decisions made by courts in the two jurisdictions, and has found that national courts are more willing to apply domestic law rather than international or regional human rights instruments that have merely been ratified, but not specifically domesticated into national law by an Act of Parliament. Several reasons can be advanced in support of the courts' approaches. First, both countries regard the Constitution as their supreme law and incorporation of treaty norms into a Constitution makes them become an integral part of a law that is superior to all other laws.[39] Second, international human rights law does not enjoy a prominent status over domestic legislation in the legal hierarchies of the two countries because the Constitution of each of the countries ascribes a status to an international agreement similar to that of an Act of Parliament, but where there is conflict between the two, an Act prevails.[40] Third, the way in which treaties are negotiated involves a lot of give and take; treaties are therefore a product of compromise arising out of hard bargaining by the contracting parties[41]

The above findings therefore lend credence to the hypothesis that incorporation of human rights principles and obligations enshrined in international and regional human rights instruments into domestic law is the most effective way of ensuring that the instruments have a significant impact in a national legal order.

Notes on contributor

Reyneck Matemba is an Assistant Chief Legislative Counsel at the Ministry of Justice, Malawi. He is a member of the Malawi Law Society and the Commonwealth Association of Legislative Counsel (CALC).

---

[39] See s 5 of the Malawi Constitution and s 2 of the Constitution of RSA.
[40] See s 211 of the Malawi Constitution and s 231 of the Constitution of RSA.
[41] In Re: *The Adoption of CJ (a Female Infant)* MSCA Adoption Appeal No.28 of 2009, 2009, 10.

Properly drafted arbitration agreement as a safeguard to its adequate interpretation: Rwanda case study

Froduard Munyangabe

Ministry of Justice, P.O Box 160, Kigali, Rwanda

> Under Rwandan law, wrong interpretation is not the reason for setting aside an arbitral award (art 47 of Law No. 005/2008 of 14/02/2008 on arbitration and conciliation in commercial matters). This work intends to consider whether or not improper drafting of the arbitration agreement can have a bad impact during its interpretation by the arbitrators and on its enforcement; this remains an issue to examine. The work relates to the experiences of countries where arbitration has been applied. It concludes by confirmation on whether or not the above-mentioned law should be amended.

1. Introduction

It has become frequent to observe parties preferring to submit their disputes to a third party they agree upon. They do so by means of an arbitration agreement, which is defined as an agreement by which two or more determined or determinable parties agree in a binding way to submit one or more existing or determined future disputes to an arbitral tribunal by excluding the original state jurisdiction; this in accordance with a legal order which is determined directly or indirectly.[1]

In general, parties are free to agree on how the arbitration proceedings will be conducted. This is referred to 'as party autonomy'[2] and based on consent.[3] If the parties have agreed to solve their disputes by arbitration, the courts will not be permitted to exercise jurisdiction over the dispute.[4]

---

[1] Christoph Müller, *International Arbitration* (Bruylant, Brussels 2004) 28; Gabrielle Kaufman-Kohler and Blaise Stucki, *International Arbitration in Switzerland* (Kluwer Law International, Zurich 2004) 15.
[2] Michael J Moser and Teresa YW Cheng SCJP, *Hong Kong Arbitration* (Kluwer Law International, The Hague 2004) 1.
[3] Richard Garnett and others, *A Practical Guide to International Commercial Arbitration* (Oceana Publications, Inc, New York 2000) 3.
[4] Michael J Moser and Teresa YW Cheng SCJP, op cit 31; Matti S. Kurkela and Hannes Snellman, *Due Process in International Commercial Arbitration* (Oceana, Helsinki 2005) 20; Gabrielle Kaufman-Kohler and Blaise Stucki, op cit 15.

Considering art 47 of Law No. 005/2008 of 14/02/2008 on arbitration and conciliation in commercial matters,[5] it appears that with the Rwandan law, wrong interpretation of an arbitration agreement by arbitrators does not retain the attention of the Rwandan legislator. Indeed, wrong interpretation is not mentioned among the reasons of setting aside an arbitral award decided by arbitrators.

This article intends to consider whether or not improper drafting of the arbitration agreement can have an impact during its interpretation by the arbitrators. In this case, whether bad interpretation is likely to cause any problems at the time of its enforcement, this remains a major issue to examine.

It is also important to relate to the experiences of other countries where arbitration has been applied, and to focus on whether properly or improperly drafted arbitration agreements do really have any impact on the interpretation of arbitration agreements and their enforcement in different countries.

This article with reference to a number of literatures, especially books, will examine the impact of an improper drafted arbitration agreement on its interpretation, take into account some courts' decisions, examine the impact during its interpretation by the arbitrators, in this case whether bad interpretation is likely to cause any problems at the time of its enforcement.

Besides, by examining relevant theoretical materials, this article will examine whether there is a need for the appeal against badly interpreted arbitration agreement and why or why not if at all it is not necessary.

The Rwandan arbitration institution is a recent creation. In order to be more strengthened and effective, it could be argued that it would hugely benefit from experiences of other existing systems of arbitration at the international level.

In this view, this article intends to examine whether an improperly drafted arbitration agreement could have any impact on the interpretation of the agreement and its enforcement.

2 Drafting of arbitration agreement

Most arbitration agreements are contained in an arbitration clause typically included in contracts before any dispute arises. Pre-dispute arbitration agreements

---

[5]Article 47 states that 'An arbitral award decided by an arbitration may be set aside by the court specified in art. 8 of this Law only if: (1) the party seeking cassation furnishes proof that: (a) a party to the arbitration agreement (…) was under some incapacity; or the said agreement is not valid under the Law to which the parties have subjected it or, failing any indication thereon, under the Rwandan Law; (b) the party making the application was not given proper notice of the appointment of an arbitrator or of the arbitral proceedings or was otherwise unable to present his or her case; (c) the award deals with a dispute not contemplated by or not falling within the terms of the submission to arbitration or contains decisions on matters beyond the scope of the submission to arbitration, provided that, if the decisions on matters submitted to arbitration can be separated from those not so submitted, only that part of the award which contains decisions on matters not submitted to arbitration may be set aside; (d) the composition of the arbitral tribunal or the arbitral procedure was not in accordance with the agreement of the parties, unless such an agreement is in conflict with provisions of this Law from which the parties cannot derogate, or, failing such agreement, was not in accordance with this Law, (2) the Court finds that: (a) the subject matter of the dispute is not capable of settlement by arbitration under the Rwandan Law; the award is in conflict with the public security of the Republic of Rwanda.

can also constitute stand-alone contracts. Parties may also decide to enter into arbitration agreement after a dispute arises, in which case their agreement is called a 'submission agreement'.[6]

In order to be well drafted, a number of drafting considerations must be taken into account. Indeed, various drafting considerations affect the content of arbitral agreements and their effectiveness. In this regard, a number of contents have been considered as necessary when arbitration agreements are drafted. Other elements are not deemed necessary, but have been suggested as recommended.

2.1 Necessary elements

The necessary elements to an arbitration clause are those elements without which an arbitration clause will be ineffective and unenforceable, if a party seeks enforcement through the judicial process.[7] Consecutively, they are analysed below.

2.1.1 Scope

From a reading, it is fundamental that an arbitration clause that provides ambiguously for arbitration of a set that is less than the universe of disputes arising out of or in connection with the contract is an invitation to litigation about the scope of the arbitrators' jurisdiction.[8] Therefore, while drafting an arbitration agreement, it is necessary to clearly indicate the subject matter to be submitted to arbitration.

> In most contracts that provide for arbitration, the parties intend that all disputes arising out of or in connection with the contract be subject to arbitration, and the phrase all disputes 'in connection with' the agreement has become the model for broad arbitration clauses. Equally workable is the phrase 'arising out of or relating to' (...). By using a more limited description – for example, one that covers only disputes 'arising out of the contract – the parties create the risk that a court will conclude that the parties did not intend the clause to be broad.[9]

In *Vecto Sales, Inc v Vinar,* for example, it was found that 'arising out of' indicated that 'the parties intended to limit the applicability of this clause', and held that 'claims for breach of a related agreement were outside the scope of the arbitration clause'.[10]

As suggested by Herbert Kronke and others the uncertainty regarding the scope of the arbitration agreement leads to a liberal and broad interpretation made by courts.[11] In this perspective, he wrote that in *Rederij Empire CV v*

---

[6] Paul D Friedland, *Arbitration Clauses for International Contracts* (2nd edn Jurinet LLC, New York 2007) 57.
[7] Paul D Friedland, op cit 61.
[8] Ibid 62; Rene David, *Arbitration in International Trade* (Kluwer Law And Taxation Publication, Deventer/Boston 1985) 186.
[9] Paul Friedland, op cit 61; Stewart McClendon and Rosabel E Everard Goodman, *International Arbitration in New York* (Transnational Publisher, New York 1986) 50.
[10] *Vecto Sales, Inc v Vinar*, 98 F. App'x 266, 266–67 (5th Cir 2004) as cited by Paul Friedland, op cit 61.
[11] Herbert Kronke and others, op cit 59.

Arrocerias Herba SA, the Spanish Supreme Court did not refer the parties to arbitration because it was held that '[n]owhere can we find the necessary indication of which disputes that could arise between the parties should be referred to arbitration ...'.[12]

As proposed by Friedland, to avoid defective clauses when a narrow scope is intended, parties can use the following clause:

> Except for those matters which are specifically excluded from arbitration hereunder, all disputes...

The following matters are specifically excluded from arbitration hereunder: —.[13]

2.1.2 Exclusivity

An effective arbitration clause indicates clearly that parties on agreement agree that not a national court, but rather a private tribunal is to render a final and a binding decision on their dispute.[14]

In Rwanda's case, considering art 7 of Law No. 005/2008 of 14/02/2008 on arbitration and conciliation in commercial matters, it is clear that subject to some exceptions, courts are not allowed to intervene on issues submitted to arbitration.[15] In this case, even where parties leave room for doubt to know whether an arbitral tribunal's decisions are to be deemed final or not, the assumption will be that courts are not competent.

2.1.3 Designated dispute resolution method

As observed by Friedland, 'a surprising number of international arbitration clauses fail either actually to require arbitration or to set out correctly the name of the intended arbitral institution'.[16]

A good example that can illustrate that the failure to clarify the intended arbitral institution can lead to ambiguity is the case where the drafter of an arbitration clause confuses expert and arbitrator. Indeed, Friedland suggests that expert determination is to be distinguished from arbitration in a number of ways.[17] He argues,

> While an arbitrator is chosen to exercise a judicial function and to resolve a dispute based upon submissions by the parties, an expert is chosen for his or her expertise in a certain subject matter and often does his or her own investigation or appreciation of the issue ... Awards are enforced in respect of conventions and other laws

---

[12]Ibid.
[13]Paul Friedland, op cit 63.
[14]Herbert Kronke and others, *Recognition and Enforcement of Foreign Arbitral Award: A Global Commentary on the New York Convention* (Wolters Kluwert, Rijnland 2010) 50. See also Jack J Coe Jr, *International Commercial Arbitration: American Principles and Practice in a Global Context* (Transnational Publishers, Inc. 1997) 160; Paul Friedland, op cit 63.
[15]It states that 'in all matters governed by that Law, no court shall intervene except where so provided in this Law'.
[16]Paul Friedland, op cit 63.
[17]Paul Friedland, op cit 143.

governing arbitration in relevant jurisdictions while experts' decisions, unless re-qualified as an arbitration are not governed those legal instruments.[18]

Considering the opinions as given by several authors, it can be observed that they have different perspectives while relating to expert and arbitrator. In Fouchard, it is argued that

> [if] the parties confer a power of decision (to decide a technical dispute or to evaluate an item of property or loss) on a third party to whom they refer as an expert, that third party is in fact either an arbitrator or, in the absence of a dispute, an agent appointed by both parties.[19]

According to Friedland, 'pursuant to this view, if the expert decides an international dispute in a final and binding decision, the expert's decision is an arbitral award governed by the New York Convention'.[20] By contrast, John Kendall considers that expert determination is distinct and to be distinguished from arbitration and that the expert decision is not an arbitral award and therefore not subject to the New York Convention.[21]

Herbert Kronke and others suggest that when a contract provides for arbitration as a general dispute resolution method and at the same time provides for other procedures such as expert determination of certain specific issues, the delimitation of the two procedures can sometime be problematic and require interpretation of the dispute resolution clauses.[22]

In the case of Rwanda, according to art 7 of Law No. 005/2008 of 14/02/2008 on arbitration and conciliation in commercial matters, since the law does not allow the intervention of courts in issues submitted to arbitration, the confusion remains linked to the demarcation between arbitration and conciliation.

In art 2 of the same law, it is indeed stated that 'conciliation does not apply to cases submitted to a judge or to an arbitrator, in the course of judicial or arbitral proceedings in attempts to facilitate a settlement between the parties'. If this is the case, the fact of the matter remains clear on how the content and the intention of parties are expressed while drafting an arbitration agreement. Parties could intend to make an arbitration agreement, but expressing it ambiguously with room for confusion could be a way where one party could claim a conciliation mechanism.

A decided case illustrates how a defective arbitration agreement can lead to an ambiguity that requires courts' interpretation. In *Schofield v International Development Group Co*, it has been decided that 'the parties agreed to arbitration

---

[18] Ibid.
[19] Fouchard and others, in Emmanuel Gillard and John Savage (eds) *Goldman on International Commercial Arbitration* (Kluwer Law International, The Hague 1999) 26 as cited by Paul Friedland, op cit 143.
[20] Paul Friedland, op cit 143.
[21] John Kendall, *Expert Determination* (3rd edn 2001) 160–1 as cited by Paul Friedland, op cit 143.
[22] Herbert Kronke and others op cit 59.

even though the dispute resolution clause made reference to an independent auditor'.[23]

2.2 Recommended elements

Even if failure to include them in an arbitration clause does not render a clause unenforceable, three elements are considered as recommended when drafting an arbitration clause in order to avoid the necessity of filling the gap inherent to their absence when a dispute arise and is bought to courts. Those elements that should be addressed in any international arbitration clause are the place of arbitration, the method of selection and number of arbitrators, and the language of the arbitration.[24]

Taking into account the necessary elements pointed out in section 2.1, this has sufficiently proved clearly that poorly drafted arbitration clauses affect the quality of arbitration agreements; it is, however, important to examine the place dedicated to the interpretation of arbitration agreements.

3 Interpretation of arbitration agreements

3.1 Arbitration agreements as interpreted internationally

There is a general trend in national laws against judicial intervention in pending arbitral proceedings.[25]

The competence of an arbitration tribunal to interpret an award has been controversial. The interpretation of arbitration agreement is only permitted for the purposes of correcting some errors affecting the arbitration agreement.[26]

Those in opposition to the modification express fear that the power given to a party to request interpretation of an award could be used as a weapon for confusion and delay in the hands of a party disappointed by the outcome of the arbitral proceedings as reflected in the arbitral award. Modern arbitration rules are mixed in permitting this power of interpretation (the UNCITRAL, AAA International Rules, ICSID Rules and Stockholn Rules do provide for interpretation; the LCIA, AAA Commercial and WIPO Rules do not).[27] Protection from abuse is provided by stipulation of a short period of application for interpretation and for parties to make their views and comments, and a short period within which the tribunal must render a decision interpreting the award.[28]

One of the main reasons for parties to choose the arbitration mechanism is to avoid cost and loss of time inherent to litigation procedure. However, practically

---

[23] *Schofield v International Development Group Co*, No. SA-05-CA-110-RF, 2006 WL 504058 (at 2) (decided 2006) YCA XXXI (2006), 1414 (at 1417–1418 (US District Court for the Western District of Texas, US) as cited by Herbet Kronke, op cit 50.
[24] Paul Friedland, op cit 65.
[25] Richard Garnet and others, *A Practical Guide to International Commercial Arbitration* (Oceana, New York 2000) 113
[26] See for example art 29 (1) of the Internal Rules of the International Chamber of Commerce Court of Arbitration.
[27] Laurence Graig and others, *Annotated Guide to the 1998 ICC Arbitration Rules with Commentary* (Oceana, New York 1998) 159.
[28] Ibid.

in some circumstances, it does happen that parties make recourse to courts because the arbitration itself cannot adequately give responses to all their concerns. For example, parties can agree on 'a clause providing for expended judicial review in the view of obtaining the informality, flexibility and cost benefits of arbitration combined with the assurance that the judicial system will correct any errors of law'.[29] In the same perspective, it has been suggested that 'even when the parties desire to settle the whole range of disputes through arbitration, local Law may prevent the submission of certain categories of disputes to arbitration'.[30]

Also as indicated through courts' decisions cited in this article, courts intervene to interpret unclear or defective clauses. In Kronke's words, 'the interpretation of the arbitration agreement is particularly important when one is faced with pathological arbitration clauses. These are poorly drafted agreements that are incomplete, unclear or contradictory, and thus lead to confusion as to the parties' intent'.[31] Based on Kronke's argument, interpretation of pathological arbitration clause is done by courts.

Also, it is clear that there are a number of conventions that make provision for scrutiny of award before being signed. This is the case for ICC, and it has been suggested that the scrutiny by the court is useful in preventing ambiguous language that could subsequently require interpretation.[32]

3.2 Rwandan case

In Rwanda, according to art 7 of Law No. 005/2008 of 14/02/2008 on arbitration and conciliation in commercial matters, no court shall intervene in issues submitted to arbitration.

Arbitrators can interpret the award of an arbitration agreement according to art 45 of the above law.

The Rwandan law does not recognise the interpretation of arbitration agreements. Based on the findings in countries where the arbitration procedure has attained significant development, it is not rare to assist to arbitration awards contested by parties on agreement. It appears that the outstanding problem is linked to the way of drafting arbitration agreements and consequently their interpretation. It can be realised that poorly drafted arbitration clauses affect the content of the arbitration agreement and this can lead to the need of their interpretation by courts.

Considering that there could be cases in which parties may not have a common understanding on the way what they had agreed upon in their arbitration agreement has been drafted, and taking into account that the Rwandan law recognises only the interpretation of the arbitration award, it could be argued

---

[29]Ibid., 106.
[30]J Stewwart McClendon and Rosabel E Everard Goodman, *International Arbitration in New York* (Transnational Publisher, New York 1986) 34.
[31]Herbert Kronke, op cit 58. See also Jack J Coe Jr, op cit 161; Paul Friedland, op cit 63.
[32]Isaak I. Dore, *International Arbitration Law Library, The UNCITRAL Framework for Arbitration in Contemporary Perspective* (Graham & Trotman/Martinus Nijhoff, London 1993) 41.

that the Rwandan law would be more complete and effective if it allows that parties on arbitration agreement to submit their claim to court in order to challenge the interpretation made by arbitrators when what they have intended in the arbitration agreement is misunderstood. For this to be done, art 47 of Law No. 005/2008 of 14/02/2008 on arbitration and conciliation in commercial matters would be amended and include the wrongly interpreted agreement made by arbitrators in causes justifying the appeal.

4 Conclusions

This article demonstrated that defective clauses of arbitration agreements lead to wrong interpretation. It revealed that in many jurisdictions, interpretation of arbitration agreements is done by arbitrators and in some circumstances parties on arbitration agreement make recourse to courts to get a solution that covers all their concerns where the law allows it. It has also highlighted that at the international level the interpretation of ambiguously drafted arbitration clauses supersedes the competence of arbitrators and necessitates the intervention of state courts.

Having observed that in Rwanda's context the wrongly interpreted arbitration agreement by arbitrators is not a cause of setting it aside and that parties may need to be given the opportunity to submit their claims before courts, this article proposes the amendment of Law No. 005/2008 of 14/02/2008 on arbitration and conciliation in commercial matters. This position is based on the fact that in other countries where arbitration has been applied practically for a long time, courts have been intervening to give a clear understanding of unclear arbitration clauses.

All in all, by analysing the hypothesis and while carrying out this theoretical study, although there were different books from which to relate, it can be stated that there was limited theoretical material to be used as regards Rwanda's arbitration procedure respectively, due to the fact that arbitration in Rwanda is a recent creation.

Notes on contributor

Froduard Munyangabe is currently a principal state attorney in the Ministry of Justice/Rwanda. He has a master's degree in Advanced Legislative studies from the University of London, Institute of Advanced Legal studies and a master's degree in Business Law from the National University of Rwanda. From 2000 to 2003, he served as a prosecutor in the Rwandan Prosecution Authority. From 2003 to 2008, he worked in the Parliament of Rwanda, first, as technical director of the Human Rights, Unity and Reconciliation Parliamentary Committee and, subsequently, as the director of Committee Support Unit in the Senate of Rwanda. From 2008, he has served in the Ministry of Justice.

Index

Note: Page numbers in **bold** type refer to **figures**
Page numbers in *italic* type refer to *tables*
Page numbers followed by 'n' refer to notes

AAA Commercial 145
AAA International Rules 145
abusers 67–8
accessibility 109, 121–6, 127
accountability 88
accuracy 54, 76
Act of Parliament 4, 12, 123
Acts 15, 19, 21, 47; language style 46; publication 123; structure 83; title 118
Adam 59
Adlers, Z. 65
Africa 101–2, 130, 135; constitutions 130; customary laws 2; human rights 136
African Charter on Human and Peoples' Rights (ACHPR) 132, 135, *135*, 136, *136*, 137, 138, 139
African Charter on the Rights and Welfare of the Child (ACRWC) 132, 135, *135*, 139
Aitken v South Hams District Council (1995) 95
ambiguity 24, 25, 35, 36, 39, 44, 84, 95, 97; British Indian Ocean Territory (Constitution) Order (2004) 114–15; definition 16; semantic 11; syntactic 11
Anthony, K. 122–3
arbitration 140–7, 144–5, 146
arbitration agreements 2; designated dispute resolution method 143–5; drafting 141–5; exclusivity 143; improperly drafted 140–7; international interpretation 145–6; interpretation 145–7; recommended elements 145; Rwanda 146–7; scope 142–3
Aristotle 5
Asprey, M.M. 26–7, 30
Associated Newspapers Ltd v Wilson (1995) 18
Attorney General 80, 123
audience 15, 18, 26, 43, 45, 54
Augustin, M. 2, 42–9
Australia 19, 29; Act of the Victorian Parliament 20; Federal Court 47–8; gender-neutral language 52; Law Reform Commission of Victoria 17, 21; New South Wales Parliamentary Counsel 27; Social Security Act (1991) 47–8; Victoria Supreme Court 20
Australian Commonwealth 45
autocratic regimes 11

B v B (1995) 96
bad law-making 108–29
Baindu Cowan, R. 2, 101–7
Bancoult v Secretary of State for Foreign and Commonwealth Affairs: (2001) 111; (2008) 108, 108n, 110, 111
basic communications model 5–8, 13; and law 6–7; legislative drafting 8–12
Basutoland 125
Bebb v Law Society (1914) 117
Bekink, B.: and Botha, C. 32
Bennion, F. 112
Bentham, J. 19
Bible 59
Bill of Rights 130, 139; Malawi 132, 134, *134*, 135–6, *136*; South Africa 132, 134, *134*, 136–7, *136*
Bills 10, 12, 17, 25, 79, 80, 82, 90, 118; intransitive 30; structure 29–30
Bingham, T. 122
Black Clawson v Papierwerke Waldhof (1975) 121
Botha, C.: and Bekink, B. 32
Bridge of Harwich, Lord N.C.18
British Antarctic Territory 119
British Indian Ocean Territories Order (1965) 110
British Indian Ocean Territory 118–19; legislative accessibility 109; resettlement prevention 110
British Indian Ocean Territory (Constitution) Order (2004) 2, 108–29; ambiguity 114–15; clarity 112–13; gender-neutral language 117–18; inaccessible law 121–6; misleading title 118–21; plain language 115–17; precision 113–14

INDEX

British Indian Ocean Territory Gazette 125, 128, 129
British Indian Ocean Territory (Immigration) Order (2004) 111
British Indian Ocean Territory Orders (1976–94) 113–14
British law libraries 125
Butt, P. 112; and Castle, R. 19–20, 26, 53

Caligula: laws 126
Canada 19; clarity 112; courts 122; gender-neutral language 53; jurilinguists 72
Carr, C. 122
Carswell, Lord R.D. 110
Carter, R. 89
Castle, R.: and Butt, P. 19–20, 26, 53
Central African Federation 1
certainty 19, 20, 22, 26
Chagos Islands 2, 108–29; access to legislation 124–6
Charitable Trusts Act (NZ 1957) 44
Cheng, T.Y.W.: and Moser, M.J. 140
Chief Adjudication Officer and Another v Maguire (1999) 96–7
Chihana v The Republic (1992) 137–8
child maintenance 96
children: rights 134, 135, 136
Children Act (UK 1989) 96
China 2; Constitution 105; legal system 105; legal transplantation 105–6; private contracting 101; private property rights 105–6
Christie, G. 113
citizens: rights 24, 25
civil law countries 132
clarity 2, 11, 14–23, 24–31, 36, 42–5, 46, 50, 51, 52, 84; British Indian Ocean Territory (Constitution) Order (2004) 112–13; Canada 112; definition 16, 42–3, 53, 54; and plain language 28–9, 42–5, 48; purpose 25–6
coconut plantations 109
Cohn, M. 127
Cold War 110
Colonial Government v Vitry (1899) 126
colonialism 101
colonies 109
commercial arbitration: international 103
Commissioners 114, 116, 117
committees 46
common law 79, 133
Commonwealth: constitutions 82
Commonwealth Law Bulletin 1, 3
Commonwealth Relations Office 1
communication 5, 32, 39; formal political 13; intellectual 13; legislative drafting form of 4–13; social 13; theory 4, 5, 12

conciliation 144
consistency 25
constitutional law 72
constitutional transplanting 101, 104–5
constitutions 2, 11, 108, 119–21; Africa 130; Commonwealth 82; making 105; purpose 120
control: loss 66–7
Control of Pollution Act (UK 1974) 95
Convention on the Rights of a Child (CRC) 132, 135, *135*, 139
Cook, R. 110
copy and paste 35
Corbyn, J. 127
Cormacain, R. 2, 108–29
Coroners and Justice Act (UK 2009) 66, 67
Court of Appeal 62, 97, 117, 123
courts 11, 27, 46; Canada 122; decisions 141; Federal 97; High 97; international 104; Supreme (Malawi) 138; Supreme (Malaysia) 97; Supreme (Rwanda) 77; Supreme (South Africa) 138; Supreme (US) 113
Crabbe, V.C.R.A.C. 4, 12, 26
credibility 83
Criminal Justice and Public Order Act (UK 1984) 63
criminal law 83
Criminal Law Act (UK 1967) 68
criminal legislation 58
Crown 118
Crown by Order in Council 108
custody: youth secure 89
customary international law 134
customary law 79

Dale, W.L. 1–2
decree-laws 77
Del Duca, L. 113
delegated legislation 90
developed countries 106
developing countries 87, 103
developing economies 87
Dickerson, R. 16, 24, 78, 112
Dickson, S.: and Hendry, I. 120–1
Diego Garcia 109, 120
diminished responsibility: homicide 68
discrimination: sex-based 60
do-ability 88–90
doctrine of equity 2; West Africa 101
Domer, R. 53
domestic law 131
domestic violence 58, 62–3, 67
Domestic Violence, Crime and Victims Act (UK 2004) 62
Donelan, E. 109
Dorsey, T.A. 4–5

INDEX

drafters 8, 13, 69, 70–6; avoiding ambiguity 17–19; basic legal knowledge 71–2; clarity 26–7, 31; competence 93; critical ability and imagination 74–5; duty 14; English language 72–3; foreign 107; job 51; obligation 15; personal qualities 12; political problems 10–11; practice 75; qualities 71; research skills 75; scarcity 91; technique 11–12; training 75
drafting instructions 10, 24, 25, 78, 81
drafting office 8, 10, 86, 89, 90, 91, 92; Rwanda 77
drafting programme 90–1
drafts 2, 4, 8, 9; and noise 10
Driedger, E. 75
dualism 131, 132–3
Dunne, R. 125
Dushimimana, L. 72–3

Eagleson, R.D. 19, 33–4, 115
effectiveness 50, 51, 54, 57
Elkins, Z.: *et al.* 108, 120
employment 58; harassment 61; law 60; legislation 60–1
enforcement provisions: Malaysia 32, 33, 35, 39, 40
Engle, G. 10
English language 14, 47, 71; drafters 72–3; plain 19, 21, 33–4, 45; Standard 26
Environmental Protection Act (UK 1990) 95
Equal Opportunities Commission (EOC) 60
Equal Pay Act (UK 1970) 60
equality 58, 61, 69; gender 50, 51, 59, 69; legal definition 59–60; legislation 64
equity doctrine 2, 101
Eshelman, M. 120
European Convention on Human Rights (ECHR) 121
European Court of Human Rights (ECtHR) 122
European Union (EU): legislative process 76
Eve 59
existing laws 78–80, 84
extraterritoriality 81

Federal Court 97
feedback 6, 7
Fiji 125
Finer, S. 119
Foreign and Commonwealth Affairs Committee 125–6
Foreign and Commonwealth Office (FCO) 109, 119, 124
foreign drafters 107
forfeiture of things seized 35, *36*, *37*, *38*, 41
formal political communication 13
France: law 102

Freedom of Information Act (UK 2000) 125
Freedom of Information Tribunal 110
freedoms: fundamental 130; violations 79
Friedland, P. 142, 143–4
Fuller, L. 16, 122

Garner, B. 34
gender equality 50, 51, 69; in law 59
gender inequality 2, 58–69
gender stereotypes 69
gender-neutral drafting 2, 14, 21–2, 27–8, 58–69; clarity 55–6; historical background 58–9; precision 55–6; unambiguity 55–6
gender-neutral language 24, 27, 28, 31, 38, 50–7, 108, 127; arguments against 55; arguments for 54; Australia 52; British Indian Ocean Territory (Constitution) Order (2004) 117–18; Canada 53; definition 52–3; New Zealand 53; UK 53
general savings clauses 94–5, 97, 98, 99
Gillard, E.: and Savage, J. 144
Gleeson, M. 122
global economic integration 102
goal fulfilment 88
Gobbi, M. 114
governments 46, 70, 75, 85; changes 11; policies 26
Gowers, E. 17, 21
Graig, L.: *et al.* 146
Greenberg, D. 22, 29, 49, 74, 122, 123, 124
Griffiths, S.: Kelly, L. and Temkin, J. 65
Guardianship of Minors Act (UK 1971) 96

Haji Ismail, N. 2, 70–6
harassment: in employment 61; sexual 61
Hashim, N.A. 2, 32–41
Hayes v Malleable Men's Working Club and Institute (1985) 61
hendaklah (obligation) 39
Hendry, I.: and Dickson, S. 120–1
Her Majesty's Stationery Office (HMSO) 124
hereby 47
High Court 97
Hill, W. 117
Hoffman, Lord L. 110
homicide 58, 66–8; diminished responsibility 68; loss of control 66; loss of self-control 66–7; provocation 66, 67, 68; qualifying trigger 67–8; self-defence 68
Homicide Act (UK 1957) 68
Hoskyn v Commissioner of Police for Metropolis (1975) 62
House of Lords 62, 108, 123
housing: tribunals 98
human rights 105, 121, 122; Africa 136; principles 131, 135–6, 139; violations 132

INDEX

human rights instruments 130–9; impacts 134–8
Hunt, B. 99

ICSID Rules 145
Ikiriza, R. 2, 77–84
immigration 96, 97
Immigration Ordinances: (UK 1971) 110, 111, 126; (UK 2000) 111
imprecision 18
inaccessible law: British Indian Ocean Territory (Constitution) Order (2004) 121–6
industrialisation 88
inequality: gender 2, 58–69
Institute of Advanced Legal Studies 125
institutions 101, 102
intellectual property 105
interdisciplinary research 13
International Accounting Standards Board (IASB) 103
international agreements 131, 133
international conventions 107
International Court of Justice (ICJ) 104
international human rights law 139
international law 82, 132–3; customary 134
international treaties 77
Interpretation Act (UK 1978) 112, 113
Interpretation Acts 27, 28, 94
intransitive bills 30

Japan: penal code 102
jargon 21, 44, 73
jobs: creation 88
Jones, B. 118
Jones, H.W. 90, 91
judgement: moral 81
judges 15, 74; women 68
judicial decisions: Malawi 137–8; South Africa 137–8
jurilinguists: Canada 72
jurisdictions 101, 102
jurisprudence 85
justice 70, 89, 94; natural 94; youth 89
juvenile justice 89

Kabba, K. 50–7
Kahn-Freund, O. 102
Kamugundu, O.B. 2, 85–92
Kelly, L.: Temkin, J. and Griffiths, S. 65
Kendall, J. 144
Kent, B. 110
Keyes, J.M. 122
Kolts, G. 70, 71
Kramer, H.M. 16
Kronke, H. 142–3, 146; *et al.* 144

Lane, Lord G. 63
language 2, 4, 14, 17, 26, 35, 39, 40, 72, 73, 76; archaic 44, 115–16, *116*; complex 11–12; lawyers 19; legal 19; masculine 52, 59; sexist 38, 54, 59, 117, *see also* English language; gender-neutral language; plain language
Latin 44
law 5, 8, 47, 51, 71, 76, 85, 93, 106; access 29; accessibility 44, 46, 48, 121–6; consequences 86; effectiveness 86, 89; efficacy 86, 92; efficiency 85, 86, 92; enforcement 90; existing 78–80, 84; ignorance of 34; implementation 88; international 82, 107, 131, 132–3; interpretation 71; national 107, 132–3; publication 122; reform commissions 15; traditional 107
law libraries: British 125
law-makers 89
law-making: bad 108–29
lawyers 15, 44, 46, 47, 70, 71–2, 74, 76; language 19; writing skills 73
LCIA (London Court of International Arbitration) 145
legal borrowing 101–2
legal certainty 122
legal documents 53
legal drafting 21
legal language 19
legal order 87
legal practice 76
legal standardisation 102
legal terms 47
legal texts 47
legal transplantation 101–7; analysis 102–5; China 105–6; effects 105–6; environmental factors 102; history 101–2; political elements 102; private contracting 2, 101, 102–3, 106; Sierra Leone 106
legal writing 43
legislation 70, 75; accessibility 83; cost 55; cost-benefit analysis 81; delegated 90; enforcement 78, 90; impacts 92; implementation 89; implementation agencies 89; implementation costs 89–90; length 55, 56; multilingual 72; poor quality 111–21; practicability 92; prerogative 126, 127; primary 90; prioritisation 85–92; promulgation 123–4; quality 1–3, 111–12; secondary 90; social change 87–8; social impact 87–8; sound 90; use 31
legislative counsel 74, 75
legislative drafting 61, 71–5; aim 70, 71; analysis stage 77–8, 80, 83–4
legislative norms 73
legislative proposals 81; practicality 82–3, 84

152

INDEX

legislative schemes 12
liabilities 95, 98, 100
libraries: law 125
Libya 1
Lincoln, A. 120
list of things seized 35, 41
litigation 99
Lord Chancellor 123
Ludwikowski, R.R. 105

Mackinlay, J. 116
Mclean, V. 2, 58–69
macro-theory 13
Madonna 138
Majambere, E. 14–23
Malawi 130–9; Bill of Rights 132, 134, *134*, 136–7, *136*; Constitution 131–9; constitutional provisions for human rights instruments *134*; judicial decisions 137–8; Supreme Court 138; treaty norms 134–7
Malay 33, 35
Malaysia: Acts 41; Court of Appeal 97; Courts of Judicature (Amendment) Act (1994) 97; current practice 34–5; enforcement provisions 32, 33, 35, 39, 40; Federal Constitution 94; Interpretation Act (1948 & 1967) 94; legislation 32–41; plain language 32; Supreme Court 97; Wildlife Conservation Act (2011) 35
Mance, Lord J.H. 120
Masculine Rule 59, 61–4, 69
Matemba, R. 130–9
Mauritius 109, 110, 118, 119, 125, 126; Constitution 121
men 59, 60, 64
micro-theoretical tools 13
Microsoft Word 45
monism 131, 132–3
Montesquieu 102
moral judgement 81
Moser, M.J.: and Cheng, T.Y.W. 140
Moules, R. 127
Mowat, C. 115
Muhamad, R. 93–100
multilingual legislation 72
multilingual treaties 101, 103, 104
Munyangabe, F. 2, 140–7
Murphy, W. 120
must 39

national law 132–3
natural justice 94
New York Convention 144
New Zealand 19, 29, 118; gender-neutral language 53; Law Commission 20; Public Access to Legislation project 122–3
noise 7–8, 10

non-governmental organisations (NGOs) 102, 103
normative acts 8, 9
norms: compliance 88–9; legislative 73; treaty 134–7
Northern Ireland: Civil Service 126; Civil Service Commissioners Order (1999) 126; Statutory Publications Office 124; Statutory Rules Order (1979) 124

obligations 97, 98
Odelola v Secretary of State for the Home Department (2009) 96
Offences Against the Persons Act (UK 1861) 62
Official Stamps 114
Olsen, F. 64
organic laws 77
overdrafting 99
Overseas Territories 118–19, 124; human rights 121

Page v Freight Hire (Tank Haulage) Ltd (1981) 60
Paine, T. 120
Palestine 1
panels 46
Parliament 17, 20, 27, 90, 91
party autonomy 140
paternalism 60
patriarchy 58, 59
penal provisions 83
Petersson, S. 117
plain English 21, 33–4, 45; definition 19, 33
plain language 14, 15, 19–22, 24, 31, 32–41, 42–9, 51, 108, 127; arguments against 20–1; benefits 46–7; British Indian Ocean Territory (Constitution) Order (2004) 115–17; and clarity 28–9, 42–5, 48; critics 47–8; definition 33; principles 45–6
plantations 109
Plender, R. 120
policy 51, 80, 82–3; analysis 98; choices 90; formulation 85; ideas 79; implementation 85; proposal impacts 85
policy-makers 30, 69, 81, 83, 89, 91
political disagreements 30
political targets 10
poverty 86, 87
power 5
Power Cobbe, F. 59
practicality: of legislative proposals 82–3, 84
precedents 102
precision 14–23, 25, 31, 35, 39, 45, 50, 51, 52; British Indian Ocean Territory (Constitution) Order (2004) 113–14; definition 16, 53, 54

INDEX

pregnancy 27, 61
prerogative legislation 108–29
prerogative orders 125, 127
primary legislation 90
prioritisation: legislation 85–92
prisoners: mandatory rehabilitation 89
private property rights: China 105–6
Privy Council 108, 124
procedure: changes 94, 95–100
promulgation of legislation 123–4
proposals: legislative 81, 82–3, 84
prosecution 62
provocation: homicide 66, 67, 68
public 27
Public Appointments (Amendment) Order (UK 2009) 116
public bill procedure 82
publicity 122–3, 126

qualifying trigger: homicide 67–8
Quiggin, P. 75, 117

R v Ahluwalia (1992) 67
R v Billam (1986) 64
R v Brown (1999) 65
R v Chamber (2008) 123
R v Goodman (1989) 63
R v Olugboja (1981) 63
Rammell, B. 119
rape 58, 63–6; conviction rates 65; definition 63; immediate reporting 66; ladylike women 64–5; reporting 65; sexual history 65; strangers 64; on the street 64; victims 65, 66; violence 63–4
readers: perspective 29, 30
Rederij Empire CV v Arrocerias Herba SA (2002) 142–3
relocation 119
Renton Report (UK 1975) 113
research skills 72, 75
retroactive law 94
rewriting 33, *36*, *37*, *38*; and analysis 35–9
rights 34, 93, 96, 97, 98; children 134, 135, 136; Chinese private property 105–6; citizens 24, 25; Convention on Rights of a Child (CRC) 132, 135, *135*, 139, *see also* human rights
Rodger, Lord A.F. 110
Ronald, J. 122
Royal instructions 125
Royal Prerogative 108, 109, 111, 121, 124
rule of law 14, 15–16, 25, 34, 80, 112, 122
Russell, A.K.C. 19, 55
Rwanda 77–84, 140–7; arbitration agreements 146–7; arbitration and conciliation in commercial matters 140, 141, 141n, 143, 144, 146–7; arbitration institution 141; Constitution 77, 78, 80–1, 84; drafting office 77; Members of Parliament 79; Supreme Court 77

S v Adams; S v Werner (1981) 138
Salembier, P. 74
sanctions: enforcement 83
Sarawak 1
Savage, J.: and Gillard, E. 144
savings clauses 93–100
Schofield v International Development Group Co (2006) 144–5
sciences 30
Scotland: Standing Orders 118
search with warrant 35, 41
secondary legislation 90
Seidman, A.W.: *et al.* 25
self-defence: homicide 68
semi-democratic regimes 11
Sex Discrimination Act (UK 1975) 60, 61
sex-based discrimination 60
sexist language 38, 54, 59, 117
sexual harassment 61
sexual infidelity 68
Sexual Offences Act (UK 2003) 63
Seychelles 109, 110, 119
shall 35, 36, 39
Shannon-Weaver Mathematical Model (1949) 5–6, 5n, **6**, 7
Siedman, A.: and Siedman, R.B. 86
Sierra Leone 101; Child Rights Act (2007) 106; legal transplantation 106; Road Traffic Act (2007) 103, 106; road traffic issues 103
SIGMA initiative 122
Snoxell, D. 119, 120
social assessments 88
social cohesion 88
social impacts 91
social problems: gravity 86–7
social structures 65n
Society of Legal Scholars (SLS) 46
Songa Gashabizi, A. 2, 24–31
South Africa 130–9; Bill of Rights 132, 134, *134*, 136–7, *136*; Constitution 131–5, 137, 139; constitutional provisions for human rights instruments *134*; judicial decisions 137–8; Supreme Court 138; treaty norms 134–7
special responsibility areas 77, 78, 80–2, 84
specific savings clauses 94–5, 99; changes in procedure 95–8
stakeholders 45, 92
Standard English 26
states 8, 46, 104; legal transplantation 103

INDEX

Statute Book 24
statute law 93
Statute Law Society 46
statutes 18, 47, 48, 94; penal code 56
Statutory Instruments Act (UK 1946) 124
Stefanou, C. 4–13; and Xanthaki, H. 16
stereotypes: gender 69
Straw, J. 126
subject complexity 25
substantive holder of an office 114
Suetonius 126
Supreme Court *see* courts
syntactic discontinuity 116
syntax 29, 43

Tanner, E. 36
tax 30; legislation 25; statutes 56
Temkin, J.: Griffiths, S. and Kelly, L. 65
temporary provisions 117
thereby 47
Third World countries 103
Thornton, G.C. 21, 29, 59, 77, 78, 81, 83, 99, 117
Thring, Lord H. 53, 56, 117
title: misleading 118–21
Tomkins, A. 110, 124
transitional provisions 117
transmission model 6, **7**, **8**, 12, 13; and drafter **9**, **10**, **11**; with noise **10**, **11**
transparency 26, 53, 85, 88
treaties 107, 131, 139; international 77; multilingual 101, 103, 104
treaty norms: Malawi 134–7; South Africa 134–7
tribunals 46; international 104
Turnbull, M. 115, 116, 117

unambiguity 14–23, 31, 50, 51, 52, 75, 114; definition 53, 54
UNCITRAL (United Nations Commission on International Trade Law) 145
United Kingdom (UK): Divisional Court 111; gender-neutral language 53; Government Bills 22; Office of Parliamentary Counsel 22; Parliamentary Counsel 28; Plain Language Commission 45, *see also* individual acts
United Nations (UN): Charter 104, 137, 138; International Covenant on Civil and Political Rights (ICCPR) 121
United States of America (USA): Supreme Court 113
Universal Declaration of Human Rights (UDHR) 132, 135, *135*, 136, *136*, 137, 138, 139

vagueness 24, 25, 84, 113
Vecto Sales Inc v Vinar (2004) 142
Venice Commission (COE 2011) 122
verbosity 36
Vienna Convention on the Law of Treaties (UN 1969) 103–4, 104n
Vine, D. 119
violence: against women 62, 66–7; domestic 58, 62–3, 67; rape 63–4

Waldock, Sir H. 104
Wales: legislation 123
Watson, A. 101, 102, 106, 107
Watson Brown, A. 45, 116
Webb v EMO Air Cargo (1992) 61
West Africa 2; doctrine of equity 101
White, R.M. 83
Wilberforce, Lord R.O. 62
WIPO Rules 145
women 52, 59, 60; autonomy 64; judges 68; sexual history 65; stereotypes 68; violence 66–7; workers 60–1
World Trade Organisation (WTO) 105
writing 4

Xanthaki, H. 1–3, 11, 42–3, 53, 111, 112, 127; and Stefanou, C. 16

youth justice 89
youth secure custody 89

ZL and VL v Secretary of State (2003) 123